Ellen

Ellen
The Real Story of Ellen DeGeneres

Kathleen Tracy

PINNACLE BOOKS
Kensington Publishing Corp.
www.kensingtonbooks.com

Valerie

For always lending a researching hand, or two. Thank God you love your computer as much as you do.

KT

PINNACLE BOOKS are published by

Kensington Publishing Corp.
850 Third Avenue
New York, NY 10022

All Kensington Titles, Imprints, and Distributed Lines are available at special quantity discounts for bulk purchases for sales promotions, premiums, fund-raising, and educational or institutional use. Special book excerpts or customized printings can also be created to fit specific needs. For details, write or phone the office of the Kensington special sales manager: Kensington Publishing Corp., 850 Third Avenue, New York, NY 10022, attn: Special Sales Department; phone: 1-800-221-2647.

Pinnacle and the P logo are Reg. U.S. Pat. & TM Off.

First Pinnacle Books Printing: March 2005

10 9 8 7 6 5 4 3 2 1

Printed in the United States of America

ISBN 0-7860-1750-3

Contents

Acknowledgments

My thanks to Jeff Rovin for his professional generosity and to Bob Diforio for his enduring support.

Introduction

Ellen DeGeneres never set out to be anybody's advocate for social tolerance nor the standard-bearer for gays on television. And she certainly never intended to be the poster child for the lesbian community. Mostly, she just wanted to be funny. "My whole career," she says, "has been based on making people feel happy. That's all I ever wanted to do—was make people laugh and make people happy." She also wanted to live her personal life in relative privacy and have people treat her as kindly as she tried to treat others. She wanted what most people strive for—a fulfilling life and someone special to share it with.

One would have been hard-pressed to think of a less likely personality to be at the center of a media and social maelstrom of controversy than Ellen, who throughout her career projected a girl-next-door mien and an easy-to-get-along-with disposition that by all accounts accurately reflected the person she was offstage as well. But her decision to publicly acknowledge she was gay in 1997 put her squarely in the forefront of an on-going internal struggle within the American psyche as to the acceptance of gays in mainstream society.

Once she was "officially" out, DeGeneres' sexual orientation became the thing that defined her, especially in media reports. Instead of being viewed as a comedian who happened to be gay, she became a gay comedian. Her high profile relationship with Anne Heche, and their frequent public displays of affection, further fueled that perception. Although many in the gay community wanted DeGeneres to take on the role of activist, she stressed her sole intent was to express who she was as an individual and not become the new lesbian standard-bearer. But in doing so she managed to upset both those who disapproved of her lifestyle choice and those who shared it.

The fallout was swift. For almost three years, her career languished, a victim of not just her personal admission but the breathless play it received in the media and the concern by those running networks and studios that Ellen would no longer be accepted into mainstream American homes by viewers. What got lost in all the hoopla is that Ellen was the same funny and gracious woman she always was. But there was a tacit assumption by less forward thinkers that DeGeneres was destined to become a cautionary footnote in Hollywood lore as the gifted performer whose career couldn't survive the queer label.

But a funny thing happened on the way to obscurity—talent won out. Television once again came calling and offered DeGeneres the chance to host her own daytime talk fest. *The Ellen DeGeneres Show* has proven to be the perfect pulpit for Ellen to spread her message of laughter and the ideal format to showcase her unique talents and personality. A bona fide hit, the show has earned the comedian a new legion of fiercely loyal fans who have embraced Ellen as a welcome guest in their homes—and as a comedian who just happens to be gay.

Much of Ellen's appeal is that she really *is* the girl-next-door. It's just that this girl prefers other girls. Even those who disagree with her lifestyle on moral or ethical principles can still identify with her obvious humanity and be seduced by her endearing charm.

The thing about second chances is that by definition they follow on the heels of loss or struggle. To better understand how Ellen was able to turn personal adversity into a professional rebirth it's necessary to look back at her life and put the events that shaped and informed her personality and humor in big-picture perspective. And if there is one lasting legacy to be gleaned from Ellen's life story, it's that we love who we love because we are who we are. And by staying true to who she is, Ellen has prevailed and come out on top.

1
"Were You Funny as a Child?"

"You know how people say it's not the heat, it's the humidity?" asks a longtime New Orleans resident. "Well, it's both the heat and the humidity."

Playwright Tennessee Williams understood better than most how the relentlessly oppressive steamy summer weather of the American South can influence personalities and shape destinies and, for those with restless souls, how the very weight of the air can fuel dreams of escape. This is especially true for someone who knows she is different and who is trying to find a place in the world where she fits in, because the South, which holds tradition in the highest respect, isn't always the easiest place to forge a nontraditional identity.

The Southern states remained insular for much of their history, their residents preferring to conduct their professional and personal dealings with others who shared the same customs and values. Although the Old South may have officially died during Reconstruction after the Civil War, the reality is that the long-held attitudes that originally shaped the Southern personality are still very much alive, which is why the South as a whole has tended to be notoriously politically conservative and socially intolerant.

Paradoxically, though, the culture is also relentlessly polite to the point of being genteel. In many ways, traveling to the South is a trip back in time, so growing up in its confines can create a conflict for the more independent-minded child. The result is likely to be an innately polite and gracious person who develops an often-hidden will of steel.

Other than in New England, there are no older American bloodlines than those that are found in the South. Unlike many Northerners, whose ancestors were among the great flood of immigrants who settled in America in the late 1800s and early 1900s, Southern families can trace their ancestors back dozens of generations to the very beginnings of our country.

The DeGeneres clan is especially well entrenched, and individual family members have a well-researched family tree, tracing their American roots to forefather John Constantine, an adventurous soul who fled from a slave uprising on the French Royal Colony of St. Domaine in 1790 and sought refuge in the newly independent United States. With the help of a black nanny, Constantine sneaked off the Caribbean island under the cover of night and sailed to Alexandria, Virginia. From there he headed for southern Louisiana's thriving French enclave, where he eventually settled and raised a family.

"To be honest, I don't know how much if at all Ellen knows about her family's background," says Kitty O'Neal, née DeGeneres, a cousin of Ellen's father. "Once, my son Peter went to see Ellen in concert, and afterwards he went backstage and introduced himself. They talked for about an hour, and somehow Peter got on about our family tree, with John Constantine and such.

"Well, Ellen was dumbfounded—she didn't have an inkling about any of her DeGeneres family history. She even called her father—who now lives in La Jolla, California—to ask if it were true. When he didn't know, she told him to call his father. She really seemed fascinated."

With its unique traditions, history, and culture, the South can seem positively foreign to the uninitiated. No place reflects that sense more than Louisiana and its signature city, New Orleans, where Ellen grew up. Like most American cities of a certain size, New Orleans can be a study in contrast between the haves and have-nots. Few tourists who spend the night drinking, dancing, and partying in the French Quarter realize that just a few blocks away is one of the city's most deadly tenements, where murder is simply a sad part of daily life.

Louisiana was claimed in 1682 by the French explorer La Salle and, even though ceded to Spain eighty-one years later, was deeply steeped in French heritage by the time the United States acquired the land in the Louisiana Purchase in 1803. In fact, Louisiana's civil law is based on the French Napoleonic Code instead of English common law, like every other state's. The Louisiana curiosity of having parishes instead of counties is also a remnant of the European influence on the area.

The region has an incredibly diverse local population, including the Creoles, who are descended from the original Spanish and French settlers, and the Cajuns, descendants of French-speaking Acadians who came to southern Louisiana over two hundred years ago after being expelled from Nova Scotia by the British. Known for their spicy cuisine, the Cajuns continue to maintain a distinct culture—and language.

It was into this area rich in diversity, yet constrained by tradition, that Ellen DeGeneres was born at Ochsner Hospital in the New Orleans suburb of Metairie on January 26, 1958.

As for many people who find their way into comedy, for Ellen early childhood, although not hell on earth, wasn't exactly the stuff of dreams. Her dad, Elliott DeGeneres, worked as an insurance salesman, while her mom, Elizabeth Jane, whom everyone called Betty, was an administrative assistant in addition to taking care of the house and minding Ellen and her brother, Vance, who was four years older. Being a devout, religious man, Elliott expected his children to behave in a certain way, and for the most part, they did. Both Ellen and Vance were polite and respectful to their elders and stayed out of trouble.

Although it was the first marriage for Elliott, Betty had been married once before, to a young military man named George M. Simon. A slender, vibrant young woman, Betty married George on February 11, 1950, and the newlyweds set up house in Baton Rouge. More accurately, Betty set up house and found herself alone, because Simon was living full time on an out-of-state base. Betty would soon discover that while being married to a soldier was romantic in theory, being an isolated army wife was not always easy. For the young wife—Betty had been only seventeen when they married—it became intolerable.

Being apart more than being together was not the kind of marriage Betty had envisioned, so after only eight months she and George officially separated. Betty returned to her friends and family in New Orleans. Two years later, she filed for divorce in the Parish of Orleans civil district court. George didn't show up for the hearing, although he did file an objection to the divorce petition through his attorney, requesting the court not to grant it. However, because he and Betty had lived apart for two years and had no children and no community property, the dissolution was granted and was finalized in late October 1952.

(Curiously, in a 1997 *People* magazine article on Betty, there is no mention of her marriage to George Simon, the first of three eventual husbands; the magazine incorrectly stated she had only been married twice.)

But Betty hadn't asked to end the marriage just to be

known as a divorcée; she ended the marriage to start another. On November 7, 1952, less than a month after her divorce from George was final, Betty Jane married Elliott, a man five years her senior whom she had met in church. After her experience with George, Betty wanted someone she could count on to come home every night, and Elliott certainly fit that bill. A devout Christian Scientist, Elliott was not flashy or flamboyant, but he was steady and reliable, someone who would be considered a solid family man.

"My father is very religious, very honest," says Ellen. "My entire life, he's never raised his voice, never once."

Both Betty and Elliott came from large families, each of which had lived in either the New Orleans or Baton Rouge area for several generations. While the current crop of Baton Rouge DeGenereses are a close-knit, clannish group, Ellen's branch of the family in New Orleans remained outsiders despite their geographical proximity to literally dozens of relatives.

"Elliott's side of the family sort of drifted apart from the others," Kitty O'Neal says, although she has no idea why. "I don't remember ever seeing Elliott and his family at any family gathering. . . ."

Kitty goes on to say that when told about the extensive DeGeneres genealogy, "Ellen admitted she knew nothing about the rest of the current family and seemed surprised and a bit taken back by it all." At one point, Kitty thought it would be fun to have a big family reunion so Ellen could meet everyone. "We even wrote to her in care of ABC to congratulate her when her show first came on the air," said cousin through marriage, Kathy DeGeneres, in an interview conducted in 1994. "But, we never heard back." Despite the apparent snub, Kathy maintained that there were no hard feelings. "Everybody is thrilled for Ellen. Even if we don't know her personally, she's still family."

During an appearance in 1989 on *The Arsenio Hall Show*, Ellen was asked what it was like having strangers related by blood suddenly popping up now that she had become successful. She deflected the issue with humor. "It's weird. First of all, I have the worst memory anyway. So no matter who comes up to me they're just like, *I can't believe you don't remember me. And I'm, I'm sorry— Oh . . . Dad*. People come up to me, *We were best friends! Don't you remember?* I really don't. And they tell me these wild things we did. I don't even remember *having* a goat, first of all. It happens all the time, so now I'm just, *Oh, sure, sure*."

When contacted shortly after Ellen's show debuted to critical acclaim, another cousin, Buddy DeGeneres, agreed he wished Ellen were closer to the family because he thought it would be fun to spend time with her. And while they were happy for her success, he said, from the beginning they took it in stride; in his opinion, she's just a chip off the DeGeneres entertainer block.

"Talent runs in our family," said Buddy DeGeneres with matter-of-fact pride. "There are a lot of musicians among us. For example my dad was in the group John Fred and the Playboys, and they had a hit record "Judy in Disguise." Also, everyone in the family has a good sense of humor. You should hear the one-liners when we all get together. So it's no real surprise that someone from the family is a famous comedian."

Gene pool aside, though, Ellen *wasn't* particularly funny as a young child, a fact she would later use as comic fodder.

People always ask me, "Were you funny as a child?" Well, no—I was an accountant.

Ellen and her family lived in Metairie until she was in third grade; then Elliott moved them uptown to the Audubon

Park section of New Orleans, a quiet, sleepy area five miles north of the French Quarter. Unlike the striking antebellum-style homes in the Garden District with their sprawling grounds and lush foliage, the DeGenereses' white-collar, middle-class neighborhood offered more modest dwellings built side by side in tight rows, often balanced on foundations of neatly arranged cinder blocks. Because the city is below sea level and gets close to sixty inches of rain annually, flooding is an ever-looming threat, so home owners try to keep their houses as high above the ground as possible.

At the end of the long, dripping summer days, kids in the neighborhood played outside until after dark while their parents sat on the porch stoops hoping to catch a moist breeze, although even at night the air was heavy with dewy heat. Growing up, Ellen's idols were naturalists Jane Goodall and Dian Fossey, and she spent many of those sultry evenings fantasizing about leaving New Orleans to become a devoted naturalist.

"I was obsessed with animals, and I really thought I'd join the Peace Corps or go to Africa and study apes or be a veterinarian." However, Ellen also remembers being fascinated by certain performers she saw on television. "When I was a kid, I would always watch stand-up comics really closely, like on *The Ed Sullivan Show,* no matter who they were. It must have been a subconscious thing because at that time I had no idea that I wanted to be a comic."

According to her parents, Ellen was a tomboy who also loved frilly dresses, dolls, and babies. Sometimes, when she was feeling restless, Ellen would ride her bike to Newcomb College, where her mother worked.

"I rode my bike everywhere. All over the campus. All over uptown. You know, people can grow up in New Orleans without realizing what a unique city it is. I remember thinking then that it was a really neat place. And now, when I say

I'm from New Orleans, people react. It's not like saying you're from Cleveland. When you say you're from New Orleans, people say, 'I love that city.'"

Unlike some comics who are born clowns, Ellen was on the quiet side and didn't make efforts to stand out among any crowd. In fact, a former classmate from La Salle Elementary School remembers Ellen as being rather unremarkable.

"She wasn't a show-off or a class clown or even all that funny—really just sort of average," says Debbie, now a homemaker in the New Orleans area. "La Salle was a small neighborhood school, the kind of place where everybody knew everybody. We'd go over to each other's house for birthday parties or to play, and Ellen's family was no different from the rest. There was nothing that made them stand out in your memory."

Debbie admits that Ellen was the last person she would have guessed would become a famous comic. "That's why I was really surprised the first time I saw Ellen on TV. But the funniest thing is that she looks almost the same now as she did when we were in grade school. I think that's why I recognized her—you look at her face and you still see the same little girl."

Like many babies of two-children families, Ellen had to grow up in the shadow of an older sibling. She has made wry comments about how many pictures her parents took of Vance growing up, while they seemed to take none of her.

"There were statues of my brother around the house, but nothing of me," Ellen says. "My brother was always the star of the family because he was also very good-looking and very smart. Everybody knew who he was." But she's quick to add, "I was in awe of him, not jealous." Betty recalls that Ellen adored Vance who, as typical of older brothers, treated her like a pest.

Part of Ellen's youthful reticence also sprang from having

been constantly uprooted as a child, forced to move several times because of her father's work. Ellen bounced back and forth between New Orleans and Metairie, a mostly middle-class area that is notable for its fascinating array of above-ground cemeteries.

"We just moved around within the city of New Orleans, and I'd have to go to a different school almost every year," Ellen recalls. "I never really kind of adjusted or fit in, so I was just frustrated." Years later, in her early act, Ellen would transmute those feelings of isolation into witty one-liners.

As a kid, I used to wander around the woods . . . be-cause my parents had put me there.

With each move, Ellen was once again the new kid, the odd child out, put in the position of having to make new friends over and over again. She attended a number of public schools, including McMain and Gregory. Ellen remembers the effect it had on her. "When I was a kid, we moved around so much that I always wanted people to like me. It was weird being the new kid in school all the time, so I wanted to feel like I belonged.

"I remember once all these kids were lined up for vacci-nations and I was the only person who didn't have to because we were Christian Scientist. And even though I'm terrified of needles, I remember crying because I wanted to be in that line."

It's not surprising, then, that Ellen, who spent her life try-ing to be accepted by strangers, became an observer of oth-ers at a young age, a trait that would later become an important cornerstone of her comedy. And while none of Ellen's rou-tines ever borrowed openly from her own life, every now and then glimpses could be seen through the layers of humor.

I was coming home from school from kindergarten . . . well, they told me it was kindergarten. I found out

later I had been working in a factory for ten years. It's
good for a kid to know how to make gloves.

Ellen admits that her name didn't make it any easier to be
accepted. "My name is DeGeneres—of course kids made
fun of me. And kids didn't even know what *degenerate*
meant, but their parents taught them. "Go to school and say
degenerate.' I'm sure they did. That's why I'm sensitive, I
guess."

As usual, Ellen uses a shield of humor when talking
about past experiences that are painful. "No, the kids were
pretty nice. I mean, they would poke me with sticks and
throw rocks and stuff, but I think that's normal. My parents
did that, so who didn't do it? Or they'd tease me: 'Look who
has a big head.' But that's just normal—every dad does that."

Her comments bring to mind a bit performed by comic
Rita Rudner. "When I was a little girl I only had two friends,
and they were imaginary. And they would only play with
each other."

The truth is, though, that Ellen has blocked out, inten-
tionally or not, many memories from her early years. "No, I
don't have a full memory of my childhood," she admits.
"That right there says something. I wish I did. And I am concerned about it. Every once in a while, I lie in bed and try to
think of things. I went to therapy to try and find out, but it
was ridiculous. They try to dive into really weird things, so I
blew it off. I have no idea if something really traumatic happened."

And even if it had, Ellen's family wasn't one to confront
traumatic issues head on. "The DeGwatereses just were not
big talkers in the house," Vance recalls. "You didn't talk
about things. Even if it was pleasant."

Betty agrees. "We didn't talk about stuff, no."

"I've struggled with being raised in a family that didn't
talk about anything at all," Ellen told *The Advocate*. "My fa-

ther always said, *Just be nice and make sure everybody likes you*. My father is a very fearful person. He's a wonderful person, a kind person, but he's never been a risk taker at all."

Since neither Betty nor Elliott would have dreamed of talking to the children about their troubled relationship, it was quite a shock to Ellen and Vance when their parents abruptly split up after twenty years of marriage. A childhood that had already been marked by insecurity and vulnerability was about to become even more so.

Although it was Betty who moved out of their house on April 3, 1972, it was Elliott who ultimately filed the Petition for Separation on December 4 of that same year, which was granted by a district court judge.

Of the two DeGeneres children, the separation had a more immediate, direct effect on Ellen. By 1972, Vance was already eighteen and finished with high school, living on his own and working as an announcer at a local radio station, WYES. Ellen, however, was just starting her teen years and suddenly found herself living alone with her now-single parent.

None of the four members of the nuclear family has ever said what caused the breakup, but there are clues. Betty is a very giving woman who likes being with a man, but she's also very independent. Even though she loved being a homemaker, she also had outside aspirations, such as being a violinist and dancer. She didn't know how to satisfy her ambition, but, this being the dawn of the age of women's liberation, she knew she wasn't finding contentment and fulfillment where she was. She also doesn't appear to have been very happy with Elliott in the months leading up to the split, spending much of her time with her own small group of friends.

While there was no longer the same stigma attached to divorce in 1972 as there had been twenty years earlier when she ended her marriage to George Simon, Betty now had her children to consider, and the effect the breakup would have on them caused her a great deal of pain. But in the end, she knew she had to make a change.

After Betty moved out of the house she shared with Elliott, taking Ellen with her, she rented a modest apartment at 4045 Division Street in Metairie, a neighborhood not unlike the one she had just left. Even though Betty had been the one to leave, she still went through some dark moments in the months following the split. Out of her anguish came an epiphany for Ellen.

"The divorce helped me realize how important humor was," Ellen says now. "My mother was going through some really hard times. It's a hard adjustment to be a single mom and to go through everything she was. She was depressed— I don't even know why—but I could see when she was really getting down, so I would start to make fun of her dancing. Then she'd start to laugh and I'd make fun of her laughing. And she'd laugh so hard she'd start to cry and then I'd make fun of that. So I would totally bring her from where I'd seen her start going into depression to all the way out of it.

"To be able, as a child, make your mother who you look up to change her mood from depression to one of so much happiness is a very powerful thing. As a thirteen-year-old kid, to realize that you can manipulate somebody and make them happy is a really powerful thing. And my mother was someone I idolized. She's my mother, yet I'm changing her. To know that I could make my mom feel good started pushing me toward comedy; that's when I started working on it."

Ellen also discovered that humor could make not only people happy but agreeable, as Betty vividly remembers. "The few times I had to fuss at her, she'd break me up, and I'd laugh so hard it was the end of the fussing."

Humor could also make other people more apt to like you. Ellen notes, "If you're pretty and you need something, you play on your looks. I was funny, and I used that to fit in when we moved."

Although Ellen may not have realized it, humor was also a wonderful way of hiding pain and unhappiness. And it helped to deflect questions and distracted people from probing too deeply into her psyche.

Ellen quickly applied her newfound skills at school, entertaining her classmates with impressions of teachers and other students, and coming up with outrageous excuses for kids who didn't do their homework. One student recalls Ellen suggesting that she sprinkle milk on old homework and leave it in the sun for a few hours. She figured that the stench would be so bad that the teacher would quickly push the offending paper aside and wouldn't notice the assignment had been recycled.

Elliott and Betty remained separated for a year; then, in December 1973, Elliott filed for divorce. He did not argue custody and amicably left Ellen, then fifteen, in Betty's care and contributed to Ellen's support in exchange for liberal visitation rights.

By the time the divorce was finalized in January 1974, Ellen and her mom had moved again to a new apartment. This time, her new home was only a block away, at 4151 Division Street, meaning she was still enrolled in Grace King High School.

An average, although not a particularly avid, student, Ellen meandered her way through classes in high school. However, once again her family's religion set her apart from some of the more universal experiences most teenagers have in school.

"Because I was raised Christian Scientist, I was excused from all my high school science classes; I wasn't supposed to learn about the human body," she explained in her book, *My Point . . . and I Do Have One.* "The plus side was I never had to dissect a frog. The negative side was that for the longest time, I didn't know anything about the human body at all. When my stomach hurt, I said I had a stomachcake—

I didn't know it was a stomachache. While that sort of mistake is cute in a four-year-old, in a teenager it raises a few eyebrows."

Ellen also began standing out in the crowd for a different reason around this time. While other girls her age were into fashion and makeup, Ellen shunned lipstick and mascara. But it wasn't the first inkling for Ellen that maybe she really wasn't like other girls her age. "If you look at pictures of me when I'm 11 years old, wearing a tie when I'm playing," she observed to writer Judy Wieder. "I wasn't raised to think about makeup. No one taught me. I was raised by the wolves. All male wolves. They didn't wear makeup, although one did wear deodorant, so I learned about that."

As soon as the divorce from Elliott was final, Betty jumped into another marriage. Enjoying freedom is one thing; being alone is quite another. Betty's third husband was salesman Roy Gruessendorf, who bought rights-of-way for the electric company. While Betty might have considered it a marriage made in heaven, for Ellen it came as a shock.

By the time she was sixteen, Ellen had grown into an attractive young woman who tended to hang out with older friends of both sexes. But Roy was a strong-willed stepfather who was a stickler for responsibility and who made it clear he didn't approve of Ellen's crowd. Because of the disapproval she felt from Roy, Ellen tended to stay out even more than she otherwise might have, preferring to be anywhere but home.

Although life at Grace King High School wasn't as painful as some of her elementary school experiences had been, Ellen still felt like an outsider. "Back then in New Orleans I didn't have any hangouts; I moved around too much for that. I had a lot of different friends, but all the time I was trying to find myself. I didn't know who I really wanted to be—or what I wanted to be."

She began taking tentative baby steps to find out. One of

the biggest changes was that after her parents' divorce, Ellen ceased being a practicing Christian Scientist. "And if you want me to prove it, I'll take an aspirin right now," she once quipped to an interviewer.

But Ellen's forays into independence would be quickly truncated. Betty was worried about her daughter's hours, the company she was keeping, and her overall rebelliousness. She talked the situation over with her new husband and came to an abrupt decision, which hit Ellen like a bombshell. They were moving to Texas. Immediately. She wouldn't even be allowed to finish out her junior year. Once again, Ellen was being uprooted from everyone she knew.

"I had been hanging out with people who were older, staying out late, and I think that was one of the reasons my mother thought it would be good to move to Atlanta, Texas— five thousand people and a downtown a block long," Ellen recalls.

Even more traumatic than leaving the sophisticated, cultured New Orleans area she considered home was the harsh fact that she would now live in a small rural town located in the middle of nowhere. She was also leaving her brother, Vance, behind. Ellen was so upset at the thought of having to move again that for a while she seriously contemplated moving in with her maternal grandmother, who lived in New Orleans.

Betty was desperate not to alienate Ellen completely, so she took a more gentle approach. She took Ellen on a trip to Atlanta to show her around the town, and she encouraged her daughter to concentrate on the positives. They would be moving into a beautiful home. The high school was small and modern, and—most important to Ellen—it had a tennis team. The young people of Atlanta seemed genuinely personable, and Betty promised that Ellen would be able to visit her friends in New Orleans during vacations.

In the end, Ellen finally let herself be convinced, primarily because she wasn't ready to make the break from her mother. For all the rebellion she exhibited, Ellen adored her mother, and the thought of being separated from Betty made her feel worse than leaving her friends and stomping grounds.

Although she still wasn't happy, Ellen was determined to get through it. The move also provided her with one advantage: She would be able, in a way, to reinvent herself in this new town where nobody knew her. She could become whoever she wanted to be, and she was going to make sure not to slip back into her former wallflower mode.

Besides, it was only a year and a half until her high school graduation. She was counting the days.

2
First Love

Atlanta, Texas, is situated approximately twenty-five miles south of Texarkana on U.S. Highway 59, a short car trip northwest of the point where Texas, Arkansas, and Louisiana meet. Up until the time Ellen became a celebrity, the most famous residents of the area had been the four Shields brothers from Greenville, known as the Texas Giants around the turn of the century. These four Paul Bunyanesque boys were each a quarter inch shy of eight feet tall and toured with the Ringling Brothers Circus.

Pine trees flourish in and around Atlanta, a quiet town untroubled by dirty air or polluted water. Nestled squarely in the Sun Belt, the area enjoys moderate weather year round, with temperatures in the winter rarely dropping below fifty degrees.

As in New Orleans, the summers were hot, but the Texas air was sandpaper dry.

The majority of people who lived in Atlanta when Ellen moved there worked for the local timber industry or one of the community's eleven manufacturing plants. Those who didn't were probably employed by the Texas Highway Department, whose district office headquarters is in Atlanta.

Roy moved his new family into a charming old house on Taylor Street in one of the oldest residential areas in Atlanta, located just off Main Street in the southwestern corner of the town. Although the neighborhood has since become run-down, at the time, it was one of the loveliest.

In 1975, the population of Atlanta was a mere five thousand people, and the town's small size was a bit intimidating to Ellen at first. She recalls, "It was real hard because everyone knew everybody and now there's this new person in town."

She's not exaggerating. Even if everyone didn't specifically know everyone else in Atlanta, it was a matter of one or two degrees of separation at the most.

Nor was there the energy that a bustling, twenty-four-hour-a-day city like New Orleans projected. Ellen could look forward to one movie theater, the State, which has since been closed down. Before the advent of cable TV just a few years ago, there were only three channels, and those had spotty reception.

"No building was taller than one story, and you hung out at the loop—which was the Dairy Queen," Ellen remembers. "And at the time, the height of aspirations was to get your name in iridescent letters on the back of your boyfriend's pickup truck."

Because of the region's strong work ethic, many of the young people in Atlanta held part-time jobs after school. Others spent time participating in activities organized by the local churches, which ranged from Bible study classes to field trips to the very popular youth choruses, which performed in concerts as far away as New York and Hawaii.

One of Roy's main pastimes was fishing. On a couple of occasions Ellen tried it, but she was never able to fully appreciate a sport that involved killing animals. So, like many of the other kids in town, Ellen hung around City Park, which offered shade from the hot summer sun during the blistering days, and at night would pass the hours at the Dairy Queen listening to music on eight-track tape players.

Even that was a culture shock to Ellen. Back home, she and her friends had rocked out to bands like Queen and the Tubes. In Atlanta, teens were into Willie Nelson, Waylon Jennings, and other singers who were part of what became known as the outlaw movement in country music.

Not only was the area a cultural desert for Ellen, the county was dry—drinking was frowned on for adults, let alone kids. But having little else to do, the local teenagers would drive forty-five miles whenever the urge for a beer struck them. "And when you got there you didn't want to get just a six-pack since you'd driven all that far," Ellen explains. "So you got a case."

Case firmly in hand, Ellen and her new Texas buddies would find a big, empty field, build a bonfire, and drink beer. In addition to the pleasures of getting intoxicated under the stars in the barren Texas countryside, some of her peers would lick frogs to get high from a chemical produced by the amphibian's skin. "Thank God this didn't catch on," she laughs. "Can you picture going to a trendy bar, people standing around with a frog in their hand?"

Beyond drinking and frog-licking, though, the kids of Atlanta were mindful of their ways and never caused any trouble, nor would the townsfolk of Atlanta have tolerated it.

Ellen admits she was as much a shock to Atlanta as it was to her and jokes that it was she who introduced Hot Sox— those knee-high stockings made in Day-Glo colors—to the small Texas town, changing everyone's idea of fashion. She also spoke out for women's lib, a daring thing to do in such a conservative environment. "She was the original Footloose" is how one of her former neighbors describes her, referring to the movie starring Kevin Bacon as a city boy thrust into the milieu of a repressive small town.

Unlike the character in the movie, however, Ellen wasn't a social outcast, in part because she made it a point to ingratiate herself with the other students, largely through her humor. "Instead of being the pretty girl people flocked to, I was the one who said something to make them pay attention," she commented in later years.

Despite her determination to reinvent herself, it was still an effort for Ellen to be Ms. Outgoing. For one thing, she arrived in Atlanta on the chubby side, having been consoling herself with food ever since learning about the pending move to Texas. And at five feet, eight inches, she stood out. She felt awkward and was still suffering bouts of depression and homesickness. But even when she didn't feel like it, Ellen would beam that big smile and flash her blue eyes. She willed herself to be outgoing and cheerful—and funny. Even so, she wasn't flashy with it.

"No, I was not the class cutup," Ellen says. "I really am uncomfortable with being the focus. So it was more a way of me just dealing with life. Humor was part of my personality. I was funny around my friends, but I was never confident enough to stand up and be loud and obnoxious. I wouldn't have called that kind of attention to myself, to try to be funny and try to get that approval. It was only with my friends."

"What a gift from God that was," comments Jimmy Wade, a close friend of Betty's. "Her mother loved her humor, and so did Ellen's friends. Humor was always in the air around her, like a refreshing breeze."

Atlanta High School is a single-story building that was only three years old when Ellen transferred there. Situated in the northeastern section of town, the school had six hundred students, with an integrated population that was three quarters white and one quarter African American.

Sidney Harrist, a teacher at the time, says the word gregarious springs to mind whenever he thinks about Ellen, though "not in a negative sense. Ellen was impulsive in a very warm and charming way. She had no trouble making friends quickly, and she had no trouble keeping them. Nor can I recall her ever saying a cross word about anyone." Harrist recalls Ellen always having a smile on her face and a twinkle in her eyes. "She had a propensity for finding the comical in everything."

By this time, Ellen had begun to evolve into a performer, although she never did anything to hurt or insult anyone. Nor was she rude or impolite, which reflects her Southern heritage. While the rules of etiquette are much the same across the country, Southerners tend to take them more to heart. Ellen's clowning was more fanciful with friends, and teachers remember her doing things like playing with a sandwich at lunch while doing voices as though it were a Muppet, or pretending to be a pine tree begging for mercy.

Ellen's senior high school English teacher, Ruth Trumble, agrees that Ellen was blessed with endearing qualities as a teenager. Trumble enjoyed having Ellen in her class because she was a good student and because she had a good sense of humor without being a disruptive class clown.

"She was really rather quiet in class, but she had a shy, sly grin," recalls Trumble, comparing her grin to that of the Cheshire Cat in *Alice in Wonderland*. "Even though Ellen didn't say much, I could tell her mind was always working."

Kim Miller, who was two grades below Ellen, recalls that "Ellen always had an upbeat attitude and a smile on her face. She also had a great sense of humor, even back then. She was always the center of attention." Watching Ellen in her sitcom, Miller says "it's just the same character she was in high school. The very same character." In a comment that echoes Ellen's friend Debbie from La Salle Elementary School, Miller adds, with just a trace of detectable jealousy, "She hasn't aged a bit. I don't know what her secret is."

Although nearly half the students rode the bus to school, Ellen was driven by Roy on his way to work, a subtle but pointed way to keep tabs on the formerly rebellious teenager. But Betty and Roy had little to fear, even though Ellen had by now mostly rejected her Christian Scientist upbringing.

"I took my first aspirin when I was sixteen. I remember the night well," she says, only half-facetiously.

While on occasion she and one of her best friends, Julie Battenfield, would buy funny sunglasses and cigars and go hang out for the day at a nearby lake, Ellen would spend most of her free time involved in school activities. She particularly liked singing in the chorus and was also a varsity tennis star for the school team, the Rabbits; her first year there, she won the team's Outstanding Player Award. In her senior year, however, she lost out to her rival and friend Gladys Johnson.

In fact, Johnson, who later moved to the Dallas suburb of Richardson and became a teacher and coach, continued to remain a good friend, even after Ellen's show went on the air. She recalls that Ellen never entertained the idea of being a professional comic, even though she had obviously honed her humor to a razor-sharp edge. "If anyone was ever meant to be a comedian, she was," Johnson asserts, going on to say that, thanks to her quick wit, "Ellen was able to establish an almost instant rapport with almost anyone."

By far, Ellen's greatest rapport, and most serious high school relationship, was with Atlanta High football star and top student Ben Heath. Ellen first became friends with the blond, tall, and handsome Ben late in their junior year. They shared an interest in athletics, and Ben was smitten with Ellen's sense of humor, even if on occasion he was the gentle butt of her teasing. Classmates recall Ellen sometimes putting Ben on, saying things like "What?! You didn't study for the big test?" when there wasn't one. Ben would just laugh with everyone else when he realized she had gotten him again.

One of their first official dates—in 1975, when they were seventeen—was to see the movie *Return of the Pink Panther*. According to Heath, Ellen "laughed all the way through it." He remembers that when they were able to get good enough reception, they watched the then-new *Saturday Night Live*; both became huge fans of the show and especially of Chevy Chase. He also recalls her being partial to Warren Beatty.

Their relationship went from the tentative flirtations of first crush to the emotional abandon of first love. By the time their senior year was drawing to a close, Ellen fantasized about becoming Ben's wife, and he was just as eager to settle down with her. To that end, he gave her what was then called a promise ring, with a small diamond in it.

"We were serious about each other," Heath recalls. But Ben was preparing to go away to college, and after a lot of soul-searching, he knew in his heart they shouldn't rush into marriage.

"I wanted to marry Ben desperately," Ellen admits. "But he told me he thought we should wait."

According to the woman who eventually did marry Heath, "It broke Ellen's heart"—but maybe not as much as everyone, including Ellen at the time, actually believed.

Not long after she and Ben had agreed to put their future together on hold, Ellen was forced to come face to face with a hitherto unacknowledged attraction to women. Some gay women know from childhood that they have absolutely no sexual or emotional attraction to men, but Ellen's journey to self-realization wasn't so definitive.

"I do like men. There are certain people who know early on and that's who they are. But I didn't know at all," explains Ellen, who doesn't necessarily believe she had to follow through with her attraction to women. "People make choices all the time. Ben's now the mayor of some small town in Texas. I could be the mayor's wife. You know, I'm sure I'd have a nice place with Ben somewhere and we'd have kids and I wouldn't have known. I could have chosen to live my life in a way just to fit into society. But," she adds quietly, "I would not be happy."

That realization would be vividly brought home when she was eighteen and became physically intimate with her best girlfriend. As opposed to being a sexual epiphany, the affair mostly confused Ellen at first. She resisted contemplating the implications of the relationship.

"The first time it happened, it was not my idea," Ellen recalls. "She told me she loved me. And I just said, 'I live you, too.' And she said, 'No, no, I love you.' I just thought, you know, 'What is this? Where is this coming from? What are you talking about?' I was freaked out even by the thought of it. I was scared."

But not too scared. She and her friend, whom Ellen refuses to identify other than to say the woman is married, continued their sexual relationship for many months under the noses of friends, family—and boyfriends.

"We both had boyfriends and were double-dating, and yet we were together. But nobody knew. We didn't know what we were doing. It was this fun little experience that I guess some people have. I didn't think about being gay. I just thought it was just her, it was just because we really were best friends and liked each other a lot, and then I went on dating men. And then I met someone else later and that came up again and that freaked me out again. So for a while, I just tried to ignore it. Clearly, it was just me still fighting it."

Perhaps one of the reasons Ellen had been so desperate to marry Ben was that she was trying to keep her attraction to women buried deep inside her psyche. Considering her family background and religion and the conservative environment of Atlanta, Texas, it would have been so much simpler to conform. Marrying Ben, or any other man, would have guaranteed Ellen acceptance. But it would have also entrapped her in a life that would have ultimately stifled her.

Now when he talks about Ellen, Heath sounds oddly detached, as if he's speaking about an acquaintance as opposed to someone he once contemplated marrying. He says he remembers her as "really just a nice, outgoing person. She was real entertaining and lots of fun to talk to." Whatever romance had once blossomed between Ellen and Ben had slipped away, like the vivid dream that you can't quite remember when you wake up.

In the spring of 1975, while Ellen adjusted to the prospect of a Ben-less life, her mother was still adjusting to life in Atlanta. Betty had been so worried about Ellen being accepted that she hadn't considered the possibility that she herself would have trouble blending into the new surroundings. The truth was, Betty Gruessendorf was seen as something of an oddity by the residents of that small Texas town.

Employed as a secretary at Guardline Industries, a manufacturer of safety apparel, Betty drove herself to work every day on a motor scooter. She also rode her scooter all the way to Texarkana to take her beloved violin lessons. Years before jogging and fitness became national fads, Betty took a four-mile walk every day during her lunch break.

While some may have admired her tendency to march to a different drummer, there were many local women who found it unseemly and off-putting. Though they all agreed Betty was genuinely charming and undeniably kind, they still kept their distance. They didn't want to be considered odd by association. Others were intimidated by her sharp intelligence and worldly-wise aura. It was a case where they felt she was better than they were, which was off-putting in a different way.

This is not to say she was without friends. One of her coworkers at Guardline, Jimmy Wade, believes that some people in town were simply jealous of how confident and self-motivated Betty was. But he, for one, sings her praises. "She was the most caring person I ever met," he declares. "She and Ellen used to have an open house at Christmas and would set out food and treats for anyone who cared to come by."

It wasn't Betty's style to spend too much time worrying about what other people might think. Her energies were focused elsewhere, specifically on Ellen's future. Betty would have loved nothing more than to see her daughter marry Ben, be taken care of, and live happily with him ever after—all the things Betty would have wished for herself.

But now that Ellen's romance with Ben was over, the future was a question mark. She had absolutely no idea what she wanted to do with her life. She would have loved to become a professional tennis player but knew she wasn't good enough. She also liked golf but didn't think she could make a living at it. Singing was something else Ellen enjoyed immensely, but she seriously doubted that anyone was going to pay to hear her do that. And although she had once fancied becoming a naturalist, reality had curbed that dream.

"I'm not book smart," Ellen acknowledges. "So when I started getting older, I had no idea what I wanted to do. I was funny, but I never thought it was a career option. That just fell into my lap."

But not until years later. So, as her high school graduation approached, Ellen felt rudderless. She had no desire to go to college, had no career she yearned to pursue; nor, quite frankly, did she have any goals. For his part, Roy tried to help out by suggesting schools she might attend or jobs she might go after. He also tried to encourage her to date other boys.

The fact was, Ellen didn't want another boyfriend. Nor did she want to spend more years going to school at some university. "I hated school," Ellen readily admits. "I have a very short attention span if something isn't really interesting to me. And I think I was taught in ways that were sort of boring."

By the same token, the idea of being a secretary or an assembly-line worker certainly didn't hold much appeal for her. It wasn't a case of Ellen feeling she was above such jobs; she just knew they didn't match her personality, because she had already tried.

"I worked in a glove factory for about a day and a half. My mother worked there, too, and I remember midday the second day I said, 'I'm not feeling well. I'm going to go home.' She said, 'You're not coming back, are you?' I said, 'No.' And so I never came back. I worked jobs like that—for just a day or two. I think my parents were very worried about me," DeGeneres says in an understated way.

Even though Ellen knew she didn't want a traditional future, she didn't know *what* she wanted. What Ellen was going through is not uncommon for teenagers who do not have a clear vision of a career or vocation, but as one friend noted, "Ellen seemed to be running from the idea of conformity. She wanted to do something that people either didn't expect from her or from a woman, or else after hearing it would say, 'Hey, that's neat.'"

Neither Ellen's malaise nor her apparent refusal to develop any goals sat well with Roy. No matter what her stepfather offered, Ellen was having none of it. People who knew them say that Ellen never really truly accepted Roy as a father figure. And although he was courteous and had taken her in as family, Roy never really understood his stepdaughter or her restless spirit. As a result, he and Betty argued frequently, and knowing that she was the cause of tension made Ellen even more unhappy. She hated it when butting heads with Roy put her mom in the middle, but she also couldn't abide being talked to as if she were still a mindless kid.

Later, Ellen would say of her life at this time, "There's

nothing wrong with taking life seriously, of course, but sometimes you feel, 'Is it just me who wants to have fun and not take this life so seriously?' I think New Orleans definitely had that influence on me."

Or, as Katharine Hepburn once noted, "If you obey all the rules, you miss all the fun."

Well, it certainly wasn't Roy's way of thinking, but the more he kept after Ellen to buckle down and get a job, the more he depressed she became about her future—and the more she tuned him out. She felt she was being emotionally and spiritually beat up, so she would stay out at night as much as possible to avoid Roy. They couldn't argue if they weren't in the same room.

When they were together, Betty tried without success to make things right between Roy and Ellen and smooth over the hard feelings. But the two were so at odds that even the ever-patient Betty would get exasperated and feel like throwing her hands up in defeat. Many times these "discussions" would end with Ellen furiously storming out of the house with Betty running after her. When she caught up to her daughter, the two of them would end up going for long walks and talking things out between themselves.

What Betty didn't know was that Ellen was harboring a dark secret—in 1975 Roy had sexually molested her. "He did horrible things to me and was a bad man," she'd later tell *The Advocate*. But because her mom was recuperating from a mastectomy at the time, Ellen didn't tell her, thinking, *"She doesn't need to hear that her husband tried to rape her daughter.* I didn't want to hit her with this news too so I just didn't tell her. But I should have—right away."

Years later Betty would discuss the abuse in her book *Love, Ellen*. Looking back now, DeGeneres says she gave her mom permission to disclose the incident because "we thought it was important to show her journey and what women go through and how they'll justify anything to stay married, to have a husband—even go so far as to not believe their own child—as if your child would make something like that up. The statistics are that one in three women have been molested in some way and there should be more people talking about it; it shouldn't be a shameful thing. It never is your fault. So I don't mind talking about it. And that's the lesson, hopefully, someone gets from the book: Don't ever stay silent when something like this happens. You should always—always—tell somebody. That's the important message."

Betty feels deep regret that even after Ellen told her, she stayed in the marriage for several more years before finally divorcing Roy, who is now deceased, in 1990. "I rationalized. I don't know what I did. Thinking back, it is my greatest regret that I didn't act immediately and leave once and for all. I'm so blessed that our relationship not only survived it, we're closer and stronger."

As much turmoil as Ellen was experiencing, Betty was going through her own kind of hell, aching for the daughter she adored but feeling impotent to help her. In her heart, Betty knew Ellen would never be happy or find her destiny in Atlanta, but she was frightened by the alternatives—or lack of them. Without a college education or any obvious marketable skills, whatever road Ellen chose would be a hard one.

Betty's concern over Ellen's future obsessed her. At work, she would find herself staring out the window, lost in thought, for hours every day. Ironically, though, part of her had absolute faith that her daughter had the potential not only to make something of herself but to be really special in an enormous way. According to Jimmy Wade, who worked with Betty, more than once Betty used the words star and Ellen in the same sentence. "She believed Ellen possessed the keys to success—a very positive attitude and a joyous spirit."

The problem was Ellen's lack of motivation and focus. According to Wade, Betty believed that Ellen could be a professional athlete if she would just try, or that she could be a politician or even an entertainer because she was so easy with people. Betty even imagined Ellen becoming a musician or singer—but considering these were Vance's interests, it's easy to see why Ellen rejected those areas. She had already grown up in his formidable shadow; she didn't want to walk in his adult footsteps, too.

Betty believed that all Ellen needed was someone to help guide and encourage her and often told Wade, "I think I could help her develop her skills, but I can't be with her to do that if she leaves. And she is going to leave, I'm sure."

If nothing else, Betty knew her daughter. And the only thing Ellen knew for sure was that she would never find the life she wanted in Atlanta, Texas. She was not a convert to a slower way of living, nor of conforming to small-town expectations. Knowing she had to decide something, Ellen made a few long-distance phone calls and made up her mind about at least one thing. She was going back to New Orleans and would live with her grandmother until she was able to afford a place of her own.

Betty was heartsick at the thought of her daughter leaving the nest but relieved that at least she would be living with family and near her brother. Nor did Betty have much time to adjust to the thought of an empty house. Ellen planned to leave the day after her graduation. So it was especially bittersweet for Betty as she watched Ellen take her diploma and move the tassel from one side of her cap to the other before tossing it into the air.

That night, Ellen came home from a party and immediately finished packing her things and loading them into her yellow Volkswagen. Even though four people could barely fit inside the car, it held all of her earthly possessions comfortably—clothes, records, stereo, boxes of books, and a few mementos of her brief life in Texas.

The next morning, Ellen got up early and had breakfast with her mother, who walked her out to the car. Betty managed to hold back the tears until she went to hug Ellen goodbye. "Try whatever you want to try until you find what makes you happy," Betty told her. "And don't ever be afraid of failing."

Ellen hugged her mother back and assured her she would be fine. She also said she hoped her mother would find ways to make herself happier.

Before Ellen drove away, Betty resisted the urge to tell her daughter she would always be welcome back; Betty knew that would never happen. But she did tell her to write or call if she needed anything, even though she knew Ellen never would. She was far too independent, proud, and defiant to ever come home with her hat in her hand. She would rather do without.

Shortly after Ellen left, Betty and Roy moved to a new house just off Williams Street, on the corner of Live Oak and White Oak Streets, next door to a nursing home. It was a smaller home. It was also a place without "Ellen memories" for Betty. But despite the new surroundings and daughter-free environment, Betty was suffering from acute separation anxiety and missed Ellen intensely.

Jimmy Wade recalls that after Ellen left, the normally vibrant Betty became uncharacteristically moody. She would be very "up" when Ellen called or wrote, but then went right back down again. There weren't a lot of people with whom Betty could share her feelings. Roy was nursing issues of his own concerning Ellen, and Betty hadn't made many close friends in Atlanta. But she did have Wade, and they spent a lot of time together, going to movies or doing volunteer typing at Betty's church. A couple of times they even drove to Shreveport, Louisiana, to hear Vance play guitar with his band. Ironically, Shreveport also happened to be the home of

Paula Records, for which Thomas DeGeneres, Buddy's dad, recorded with John Fred and His Playboy Band.

As much as Betty worried about Ellen, she felt secure that Vance would find his way without too much trouble. For a long time, it certainly seemed as if Ellen would forever struggle to live up to her brother's achievements, a perception of which she was very much aware. It was Vance, for example, who first became a national celebrity, although nobody ever saw more than his hands.

One night in 1977, Vance and two buddies, Walter Williams and David Derickson—who were at the time living at the Butterfly Terrace Apartments—came up with an idea for a short movie, which they then shot and submitted to *Saturday Night Live*. The show's producers loved its sadistic humor and decided to air it. Vance and his friends titled their effort "Home Movie," with the subtitle "The Mr. Bill Show."

"Hoo-hoo, kiddies," the red, white, and blue clay figure cheers when he appears on-screen. "It's so good to see all your bright faces out in front of the TV set."

After introducing his helper, Mr. Hands—played by Vance—Mr. Bill watches in horror as his soiled dog, Spot, is cleaned by being dropped in boiling water. Then the sadistic Mr. Sluggo visits, running over Mr. Bill with his convertible. ("Oh, nooooo.")

The short was a huge hit with the audience, and the response convinced the *Saturday Night Live* producers to commission more films starring the forever-being-brutalized clay figure. What started out as an unbelievable opportunity for three unknowns later degenerated into a bitter and nasty legal battle over profit participation when Williams sued Vance over their collaboration and creation. In order to afford legal counsel, Vance gave away a third of his interest in Mr. Bill as payment to his attorney; in the end, the case was settled out of court, and Vance parted ways with his former partners and

Mr. Bill. The lawsuit not only drained Vance financially, it left him an emotional wreck.

By the time Williams filed the lawsuit, Vance was busy pursuing a music career. From 1979 through the mid-1980s, he was the bassist and songwriter for a New Orleans band, the Cold. For a while, it looked as if the Cold might become a breakout band capable of making national noise.

In 1980, the Cold was written up in the Times-Picayune. Vance said, "The thing about the band is that not everybody is a great musician. Everybody's come a long way and we all have the same thing in mind. We're just trying to get a record contract and put out a decent first album. But that really doesn't guarantee us anything."

Their single "You" made a major New Orleans radio station's playlist, and their live performances were drawing crowds of nearly a thousand people. Unfortunately, the Cold simply didn't have enough heat to make the leap from being merely a popular local club band to a band with national potential.

It was a bitter disappointment, but Vance would keep trying, later performing with several other bands, including Apt. B, the Backbeats, and the Petries. Even though he might not have been a household name, Vance was still a New Orleans celebrity. "I was known as Vance's sister for a very long time," Ellen admits.

In 1985, after working as a deejay at a French Quarter bar named Melite's, he moved to Los Angeles and formed another band, House of Shock, with the former drummer of the Go-Gos. When his music career failed to catch fire, he moved to television, writing several episodes of *Erie, Indiana* and working as a staff writer for Dick Van Dyke's *Diagnosis Murder*. He also worked as a segment producer on *Mike & Maty*.

During all this time, while she was very proud of her

brother's accomplishments, Ellen was also understandably envious—not necessarily over what he had done, but over the fact that he'd had the motivation and passion to do anything at all. As Ellen reacquainted herself with her hometown, she hoped New Orleans would help her find a Mr. Bill opportunity of her own.

3
"Is That All There Is, My Dear?"

After she had unloaded her reliable Volkswagen and settled in with her grandmother, Ellen searched through the want ads to see if anything interested her and looked up old friends to find out what they were doing, perhaps hoping to get a clue about what she wanted to do from them. Comic Paula Poundstone notes in her act that "adults are always asking little kids what they want to be when they grow up because they're looking for ideas."

Ellen spent one semester as a communications student at the University of New Orleans. "I hated school, but I started college because everyone else was going. I majored in communications. I think. Or communications and drama. I just remember sitting in there and they were talking about the history of the Greek theater or something and thinking, 'This is not what I want to know.'"

So during the day she looked for work; at night she hung out with friends at bars, including gay bars. Increasingly, Ellen found the company of women stimulating, deep, and honest. She began to spend more and more time in gay bars as her comfort level increased. She would dance and flirt and talk and laugh and feel as if she belonged.

Recalls club owner Rosemary Pino, "She was a clown, always kidding around."

Even though Ellen was the life of the gay bar party, she still struggled with her sexual identity. Initially, she had looked on her lesbian affair in Texas as a one-shot experimentation, "thinking, *it's just her,*" Ellen recalled later to Judy Wieder. Then once back in New Orleans, "I met a group of girls. One girl was bisexual, and I had an experience with her. I was still dating guys and I remember thinking *Okay, this was just her again.* And then I got into a relationship with this girl, and we went into a gay bar. It was my first experience. I was 18 years old, and it was the weirdest thing in the world to walk in and see a whole bunch of girls all dancing together. And I was uncomfortable. But it didn't take long for that to wear off. Then I lived in gay bars. Not the healthiest experience, which is what's really sad. It's the only place where we could go then."

But finding love isn't easy regardless of the gender you are attracted to. "I kept having bad experiences with girls, so I tried dating guys again. Then I thought, *I'm running out of genders. Where am I going to go next?* I was with a really sweet guy. I tried to have sex with him and just didn't enjoy it. I mean, just kissing a girl was so exciting to me, and kissing a guy was just so blah." After years of resisting the label, "I realized I was definitely gay."

Looking back, Ellen was now able to recognize that the signs had been there all along. "I was the only virgin in high school. I didn't have the desire to be with a man sexually." But DeGeneres chose to view her lack of desire as moral rectitude. "I just thought I was a good girl. I was proud of myself that I was a virgin and then when I finally did sleep with a guy, I just had that Peggy Lee song in my head, 'Is That All There Is?' I just kept singing, *Is that all there is, my dear? Then let's keep dancing.* I thought, *Am I crazy?*" But she had still resisted the implications, thinking "Well, I just need to meet the right one. Never could, though." Ellen was evolving personally, but her future was still vague. She took a succession of jobs in what she calls "an odd-job binge," holding each one for months, weeks, or hours, depending on how quickly she became bored, restless, and self-conscious. She was an employment counselor under the name of Kathy Cole ("You had to have a fake name so people wouldn't call you at home"), baby-sat, worked at a car wash, wrapped packages in a department store (which would be the inspiration for the wrapper's rap she used in her early act), did accounting for a man who owned a wig store, and took a job as a clothing salesperson at the Merry-Go-Round, a local chain store.

She had a longer, more varied career at Willie G's, where she started as a hostess. "I was a little smart-alecky with the customers, and they thought I'd be better behind the bar." While working behind the bar, Ellen also had to shuck oysters using very sharp knives; she says she still has the scars on her hands to prove it. After Willie G's, she moved on to paint houses, then became a waitress at Ground Pat'i.

"That's how I gained all the weight," Ellen says of her zaftig late teens. "I found the food I loved—cheeseburgers and peanuts." Although that was a diet familiar to most teenagers, it was new to Ellen, who had grown up eating traditional New Orleans fare. "I had red beans and rice and crawfish, that's all I ate as a child. 'Here, you're good—have a crawfish.' That was my treat."

She also worked as a landscaper. That job, however, lasted a total of four hours. "I thought it meant watering the lawn. It turns out I had to mow the neutral ground on a busy street where my friends might see me. I was afraid I'd cut off a toe."

She didn't fare much better as a vacuum-cleaner sales-

person for Hoover. "I'd go to different stores and demon-
strate when people were shopping. I'd throw mud in front of
them. That's what I did. Boy, did that job suck. That was one
of my first jokes when I started doing comedy. I would use
humor to sell. I was so good with just coming up with something. The most expensive vacuum cleaner had a light on the
front of it. I was trying to make that sale, and when the
woman said, 'Why do I need a light on the front of my vacuum cleaner?' I said, 'That's so you can vacuum at night and
not wake people up by turning on the lights.' She bought it."

Ellen liked outdoor work better than indoor work, preferring physical labor to sales. But none of these jobs struck her
as anything she would like to do the rest of her life.

Ellen's grandmother gave her the love and support she
needed, but she wasn't able to provide Ellen with motivation.
At that time in her life, there was only one person with the
power to spur Ellen on. Whether it was the self-imposed pressure of trying to be the best she could be at tennis, or getting
through her breakup with Ben Heath, Ellen had always found
encouragement and inner strength in the long talks she would
have with her mother. Though Betty came to visit now and
then, and Ellen went to Atlanta for holidays, it wasn't the
same as having her mom around full time.

But Ellen also needed her mother now for another reason.
Since returning to New Orleans, Ellen had come to realize
that the affair she'd had with her best friend in high school
hadn't been a fluke and finally acknowledged to herself that
being intimate with a man "was not a natural thing for me;
when I was with a woman, it was. But it took me a long time"
to accept that truth.

Once Ellen had been honest with herself, she felt compelled to be honest with the person most important to her—
her mother. Ellen didn't want to deceive Betty, nor did she
want to have to live a lie around her. She wanted her mother
to know the truth. The right time presented itself when Ellen

was nineteen. She and her mother were taking one of their regular constitutionals in Pass Christian, Mississippi, where Betty's sister lived and where the entire family had congregated for a gathering.

"We were walking along the beach with our pants rolled up and barefoot, and the water was coming in," Ellen recalls. "I said, 'I'm in love.' And she said, 'That's great.' Then I said, 'It's with a woman.'"

Ellen started to cry, both out of relief and because she knew this wasn't what her mother had dreamed for her. She was desperate for her mother's approval, or at least her acceptance.

Betty wept, too, out of confusion and deep worry. "I was shocked. I had no inkling that she might be gay. I guess I said, 'Are you sure? How do you know?' All those things. I came from a time where you grew up, you got married, you had a husband and he took care of things. Period." Betty later admitted to Diane Sawyer, "One of my frivolous thoughts when she told me was, *Oh, her engagement picture will never be in the paper. I'll never be the mother of the bride.*"

Concern over her daughter's material security and social inclusion seemed to consume Betty more than any thoughts of recrimination or concerns of Morality.

"The most ironic thing about this was that her whole fear was, 'You're not going to meet a man? Who's going to take care of you?'" Ellen says wryly.

Betty had always been supportive of Ellen and wasn't about to change now, even though Ellen's announcement shook her world. Later she would go to the library and pore over books dealing with homosexuality. She was trying to find answers to unanswerable questions, looking for some hope that this was just a passing phase Ellen would grow out of.

They stayed on the beach for quite a while, then went back and rejoined the rest of the family, who couldn't have suspected the emotional scene that had just transpired. In fact, the family wouldn't know Ellen's secret for many years to come.

"Her parents knew, but there was no hint to anyone else," says cousin Lan DeGeneres. "It never came up."

Unfortunately, Ellen's decision to be honest with her father as well resulted in a painful rejection. Although Ellen assumed all along that "because he's very religious, I thought he would have a hard time with it," she had no idea it would be as traumatic for them both as it turned out to be. "He's the kind of guy that says, 'I love you for whoever you are, but I don't understand it. And let's never talk about it again.'"

She was still nineteen when she decided to tell her father and his new wife, with whom she was living at the time, that she thought she was gay. "Actually, he figured it out," Ellen recalls. "I was upset about something, and he kept saying, 'Did you rob a bank? Did you kill somebody?' And I kept saying, 'No, I just don't want to tell you.' And finally I told him.

"Then after I told them," Ellen says, "they asked me to move out of the house. I mean, they just thought it would be better for me to live somewhere else because the woman he married had two daughters. Even though I didn't acknowledge it for years, that was bad, because they loved me and I loved them, and yet they didn't want me in the house. They didn't want that to be around her little girls."

Not intending for his daughter to be on the street, Elliott cosigned a loan so Ellen could get her own apartment. Despite the intense hurt and sense of betrayal Ellen felt, she still found it in her heart to accept her father's position without rejecting him in return. Miraculously, she refused to let his rejection keep her from loving him and including him in her life whenever possible.

"Everything was still fine. It was just they didn't want me

living in the house with two little girls. That was just their ignorance, you know? They just didn't know," she says.

Today, Elliott DeGeneres admits it wasn't right to turn his daughter out. "I was wrong, just that simple. Was it ignorance? I don't know. I never really studied it or read about it and thought about it. I guess when you don't have all the facts in anything, that's a factor of some ignorance."

Ellen knows that while she could have chosen not to live her life honestly—she could have kept dating men she was not sexually attracted to and chosen to ignore her emotional and sexual feelings for women—she could not choose not to be attracted to women. That was part of her. That was who she was, for better or worse. It was, quite simply, how she was born.

"Nobody in their right mind would choose something that's so hard. You're not only a minority in society, you're a minority in your own family. At least when you're black, your parents say, 'Hey, we're all black and this is hard sometimes but be proud of who you are.' But when you're gay, your parents are not saying 'Good for you!' They're like, 'Oh, how did this happen?'"

While Ellen was coming to terms with who she was, she still had no clue what she wanted to do with her life. The months turned into years, and one day Ellen realized she'd been in New Orleans for three years and had yet to find something that moved her. At twenty-one she was still in the same directionless rut she'd been in the day she graduated from high school. She needed to put her life in perspective. It wasn't that she needed to get away from New Orleans, it was more that she needed to go to the person who'd always been her source for inspiration. So she packed up her Volkswagen again and went back to Texas.

Betty had no idea she was coming until her daughter pulled up in front of Guardline Industries, slid out of the parked car (of which one Guardline employee recalls, "You couldn't have fit a piece of straw in there"), and shuffled in. Ellen quietly walked over to Betty, who literally gasped when she saw Ellen. The two then hugged and proceeded to cry themselves out.

When she was finally able to let her daughter go, Betty left the office and went home with Ellen. They talked through the night, with Ellen pouring out her heart. After all this time, she still knew only what she didn't want, not what she did. Ellen needed time to think things through, and Betty was more than willing to give it to her.

Ellen approached her temporary stay in Atlanta with a positive attitude, including attempts to find work. She knew she didn't want to be cooped up in an office or a restaurant, so she applied for a job with the state highway department; there was a lot of construction going on at the time, and she hoped she could get a job holding up stop signs at construction sites. She was turned down.

Downhearted and more than a little annoyed, Ellen put job-hunting on a back burner and instead looked up old friends and hung out with them. Roy was upset over her continued lack of ambition. He didn't care what job she got, as long as she found one. To Roy's way of thinking, an honest day's work, a restful night at home, and a weekend of golf or fishing or some other form of recreation was the way life should be lived. In fact, that was the way most of the residents in Atlanta thought. The town was already convinced Betty was an eccentric; now that Ellen was back, aimlessly going day to day, it merely added to the family "oddball" reputation.

The fact that Betty was so patient with Ellen and so willing to leave her to her own devices really stuck in Roy's craw. He couldn't fathom why Betty didn't pressure Ellen to buck up and do something. It was the cause of more than a few heated discussions, with Roy wanting to know just how long Betty was going to let Ellen sit around the house doing nothing.

The answer was seven months.

Although Ellen didn't work much during her stay in Atlanta, she wasn't completely idle, either. Toward the end of her extended visit, Ellen began to write humor features, which she thought magazines such as Ms. or National Lampoon might buy. She might have stayed longer in Texas and continued working on the articles, but when she became aware that her presence was forcing her mother to take sides against Roy, Ellen realized it was time to leave.

In what was becoming an all-too-familiar ritual, Ellen packed her Volkswagen one more time—but on this trip, she made room for her mother. Betty had decided to take a three-month leave from her job and stay with Ellen in New Orleans. As they headed east for Louisiana, Ellen felt more positive about her future than she had for a long time, just knowing her mom would be there to lean on.

They stayed with Ellen's grandmother until Betty helped Ellen find a furnished apartment, which she rented with a slightly older woman. During the days, Ellen would go job-hunting while Betty would come over and clean the apartment until it literally shone. Betty also seemed to accept Ellen's new friends. In the liberal environment of New Orleans, Ellen found herself very much at ease in her new lifestyle—especially because of her relationship with her roommate, Kathy "Kat" Perkoff. According to friends, Ellen's feelings for Kat went from "like" to "trust" to "love."

According to the owner of Charlene's, a popular New Orleans lesbian bar, Ellen and Kat met in the late 1970s and were friends before they became lovers. By 1980, they were madly in love. Perkoff, blonde and pretty, was a poet, and Ellen thought she had found her life mate.

Spurred by her relationship with Kat, Ellen continued writing in her free time, though she still hadn't come up with anything she liked enough to send out to editors. The pages sat in her drawer, or she would send copies back to Atlanta, where her mother would read the pieces and then proudly show them off to her few friends.

On the job—whatever job that happened to be in a given week—Ellen kept her spirits up by slipping easily into her old joking ways. She always enjoyed coming up with a quick quip or observation that made someone laugh. More than one of her coworkers encouraged Ellen to try her hand at stand-up. Eventually, the opportunity presented itself.

Through some acquaintances, Ellen was asked to participate in a luncheon benefit. She recalls, "Somebody needed to raise money for something, and no one had access to Eddie Murphy or Aerosmith, so they put a band together and asked me to go onstage and be funny. This was probably 1980, and I think it was someplace in the French Quarter. I don't even remember if there was a stage. In fact, I don't think anyone there had ever worked a mike before, or a sound system. It was one of those let's-put-on-a-show-in-the-barn things. I had no material; I had nothing to talk about. I couldn't think of anything funny. So I ate the whole time I was up there.

"I always thought it was funny when people have something to tell you and they take a huge bite of something, and then they make you wait, to finish that bite. And then when they're halfway through the sentence, they take another bite.

"So I got onstage and said, 'I gotta tell you about the funniest thing that happened to me the other day. But I'm sorry, this is the only chance I'm going to get to sit down and eat today, so if you don't mind, I'm going to eat my lunch.'"

On her way to the show, Ellen had bought a Burger King Whopper, french fries, and a milk shake. She started to tell her story, then took a big bite of Whopper.

"I'd finish that, then start a new sentence, take another huge bite—that was back in the days I didn't mind eating tortured animals—and by the time I finished everything, I looked at my watch and said, 'Oh, my time is up. Gotta go.' Then I left. I'd gotten maybe ten words out. It was a huge chance."

It worked, and although Ellen admits the material she used that night wouldn't be funny today, she says the experience was incredible. "I loved it. It was the greatest feeling."

The thunderous applause took her completely by surprise, as did some people in the audience who came up to her after the show. "Someone saw me and asked me to work at a little coffeehouse, which I think was at the University of New Orleans."

Caught off guard, Ellen said sure, she would love to. They said great, and gave her a date that was just a few days away. The panic didn't hit her until she was driving home. When she walked into her apartment, she and Kat looked over the stack of things she'd been writing, and suddenly Ellen's confidence soared. All those days of writing were about to pay off. The stories and observations that never quite worked as humor pieces for a magazine were perfectly suited to be delivered from a stage behind a microphone. She quickly wrote some additional material to round out her routine.

"I just wrote really outrageous stuff. I was very confused, because half of it was Gallagher and half of it was Newhart."

Here it was. She had the material. She had a venue. She finally had the motivation. There was only one question left: Did she have the nerve to get up there and follow through?

The first time she went onstage at the coffeehouse, Ellen admits, she was afraid, mostly because she didn't have that many minutes of prepared material. She did her food bit again, which worked well with the Animal House crowd that came to the coffeehouse; she also talked about the value of higher education, without which, she said, they would end up eating Whoppers on coffeehouse stages.

She took a deep breath and tried some of her writings on the audience.

*Friends will write me letters. They run out of room on
the front of the letter. They write "over" on the bottom
of the letter. Like I'm that much of a moron. Like I
need that there. Because if it wasn't there, I'd get to the
bottom of the page . . . "And so Kathy and I went shopping and we . . ." That's the craziest thing! I don't
know why she would just end it that way.*

For Ellen, the night was an unqualified success: The audience loved her, and she got paid fifteen dollars.

After that, she was asked to appear at small venues at
other colleges, such as Loyola or Tulane. "I had nothing else
to do, and I was making good money, and I just kind of stuck
to it," Ellen recalls. "But I would get nervous every single
time I went onstage."

After a few more gigs, Betty believed her daughter had finally found a calling. "This is what you're meant to do," she
told Ellen. "I'll support you in any way I can."

Inspired by her mother's encouragement, Ellen busied
herself perfecting the material she already had and writing
new routines. But her life was about to come to a screeching,
emotional halt when Kat was unexpectedly killed.

What made her grief worse was that she and Kat had been
on the emotional outs after DeGeneres discovered Perkoff
had cheated on her. "We were living together and I moved
out to teach her a lesson so I was staying with someone else
at the time, but always thinking that I'd go back. My brother's
band was performing that night, and I saw her at the club. It
was really loud, and she kept saying, *When are you going to
come home?* And I kept acting like I couldn't hear her, like
the music was too loud. She left first, and then I left."

On the way home, Ellen passed a horrifying accident on
the Interstate. "It had just happened, and the car was split in
two. The sirens were behind us. We slowed down and said,

Jesus! Look at that! And we kept going." At 6:00 a.m. the next morning, Kat's sister showed up where Ellen was staying. "She said, *Kat died last night.* When she told me where, I realized that I was there." But Ellen hadn't recognized the car because Kat's friend had been driving. In a split second, her life had turned upside down.

Ellen recalled to *The Advocate* that Kat had lived for several hours. "But she didn't have ID on her so they couldn't call. And I was like, *She was alive. I could've been there.* My mind was so full of so many things: If I had just gone home with her that night, if I wouldn't have been such an asshole . . .

"It was a pretty devastating event in my life because I felt tremendously guilty. I really thought I could've done something. But it was a horrible accident, and there was no way she was going to make it. I don't know what she would have looked like, and it would have stayed with me forever. So I wasn't supposed to see her. And she was supposed to go. It was her time to go.

"I was 20 years old, and it was my first taste of knowing that somebody could be gone like that—you could be talking to them and then by the next day you will never see them again. And I started thinking how she was a cute girl. She was a bartender at a gay bar. She was very popular. She used to look at herself and check out her ass in the mirror and fix her hair. She was very vain and very confident and I thought, *None of that matters anymore.* It doesn't matter about her hair. It doesn't matter about how great her ass was. It doesn't matter about how many girls flirted with her. It doesn't matter. And it made me start living a different way and realize what's important."

But in the immediate aftermath of Kat's death, "Ellen was devastated," Kat's sister, Rachel Perkoff, told an interviewer. "They were two very creative people, crazy and young and very much in love. My sister was a passionate, charismatic person. Ellen was a good influence on her. She was stabilizing and helped her focus on her art. It would have been a long relationship."

"Ellen was just grief-stricken," says another acquaintance. "She couldn't believe someone could be ripped out of your life without any warning; was gone never to be seen or talked to again. It really almost destroyed her. Not only had Kat been the love of Ellen's life up to that point, she had also been her best friend. So it was a double trauma to lose both a friend and someone she was in love with."

Numb with grief and unable to pay the rent by herself, Ellen moved into a place where the surroundings reflected her mental state—a squalid, flea-ridden two-room hellhole with only a mattress to sleep on. But like so many artists, Ellen somehow used her gift to rise above her depression. More to the point, her pain became material.

"I'm laying there on the floor, wide awake, depressed and mourning, thinking, *Why are fleas here and this beautiful girl is gone? I don't understand this. What do fleas do?* My mind just kicked into what all of a sudden would happen if you actually picked up the phone and called God—how it would take forever, how it would ring for a long time because it's a big place. And it was like something came through me. I remember writing it non-stop, not thinking what would happen next."

No, I didn't realize how many people were employed by the flea-collar industry. Not to mention sprays. Well, I guess you're right, being who you are.

Ellen wrote furiously, nonstop until she had it all down on paper. "I wrote it in like ten minutes. When I finished it I read it, and even though I had just started doing comedy, I said, 'I'm going to do that on Johnny Carson one day. And he's going to love it. And he's going to invite me over to sit on the couch.' I just saw that over and over in my head. I knew it was more than funny. I knew it was classic. My way of coping at the time was comedy. And it saved me."

It allowed Ellen to get on with her life and pursue her desire to make a name for herself—even if comedy still wasn't paying the rent. At least one friend believes Ellen had suddenly been given a new sense of purpose. "Anyone who is close to Ellen knows what an important part of her life that relationship and friendship was—and to an extent still is. To this day she's very protective of Kat's memory. She wouldn't want any negative things said about her or for people to think badly of her. It took Ellen a long time to get over her death, and after she did, it's almost as if Ellen dedicated her success to the woman."

Ellen doggedly held down odd jobs during the day and sometimes at night, when she wasn't performing at a college venue or some other place that wanted to enliven the establishment with humor. She remembers that once she was "doing stand-up at a restaurant and there was a chalkboard on the street out front. It said SOUP OF THE DAY: CREAM OF ASPARAGUS. ELLEN DEGENERES." She sat at home and wrote late into the night. She didn't know how or why she would use this material, she only knew she would.

"Then out of nowhere," she recalls, "the comedy club opened up."

4
A Bourbon Street
Stand-up

Although Ellen grieved deeply over Kat's death, she didn't want to spend the rest of her life as a hermit. Slowly but steadily Ellen fell back into her old life, hanging out with friends, patronizing the local gay women's bars, and getting by, earning just enough money to pay her rent, buy a few drinks after work, and support her comedy "hobby."

Ellen has often said that her brother, Vance, was one of her biggest inspirations and influences. "Obviously, I got a lot of my humor from him. I remember as a kid watching him through the bushes and listening to him with his friends and thinking he was a funny guy, although he wouldn't let me hang out with him."

When they were adults, Vance and Ellen became closer, even if, to her recollection, there was some strain because of her preference for women. Ellen remembers Vance being a little ashamed, although neither he nor her mother recalls him having a problem with it at all.

"I think we dated a couple of the same girls," Ellen says. "That was a weird thing. He didn't like that."

Interestingly, Vance doesn't deny this. "I think we did actually date a couple of the same people, as odd as that sounds. And it sounds odd, I agree. But you know, New Orleans is a small town. What is it, nine-hundred thousand people or something? So you're bound to date the same people anyway."

Ellen was still working at various jobs during the day while doing comedy "as a joke" at night. Her old high school friend Gladys Johnson came to visit Ellen and watched one of her earliest performances. She remembers being thoroughly impressed by the material, Ellen's confidence, and the audience reaction. "People laughed at her, and she was encouraged to come back, again and again."

Ellen was having fun, and she had finally found a place where she felt she belonged—up on stage, making people laugh. She was both comfortable and challenged. Ellen had started performing in public and getting paid for it, albeit little more than cab fare, but comedy still wasn't something she could realistically view in career terms, even if she did spend most of her time writing material and dreaming of somehow making people laugh on a grander scale. The opportunity to stretch her comic wings came at a most unexpected time from a most unexpected source.

Clyde's Comedy Corner in the French Quarter wasn't just *the* humor showcase in New Orleans. It was literally the *only* showcase where local comic talents such as Donna Thompson and Renee Dodge could try out their routines and hone their skills.

When the comedy club opened in December 1980, Ellen was one of the first stand-ups hired by owner Clyde Abercrombie, who envisioned his club becoming a nationally known spot for headlining comics on weeknights and Saturdays. Clyde's establishment usually featured professional comics, but on Sundays amateurs ruled the roost. Auditions were held on Sundays and Mondays for local comedians, and those who did well enough were presented on the club's Amateur Night.

"It was like a lot of places in the Quarter," says attorney Daniel J. Markey, who prepared the incorporation papers for the club. "It was small, smoky, and dark. But it was quite popular for a while and made a local name for itself as a place to go if you wanted to hear known stand-ups or were brave enough to get up and perform as an unknown."

By the way, there's always been some confusion among laypeople about whether the term within the laugh industry is comedienne or comic. In general, among those who do this for a living, comedienne refers to those who act, whether it be in plays, television, or films, such as Julia Louis-Dreyfus. A comic does stand-up. "I've never wanted to be considered a comedienne," Ellen says now. "It's kind of like saying you're a clown."

The Comedy Corner was located first at 400 Dauphine Street but soon moved to 300 Bourbon Street. Bourbon Street, which lies deep in the heart of the French Quarter, attracts tourists and locals alike with the music clubs and restaurants that populate the upper part of the streets, as well as the X-rated sex clubs that can be found further down.

Ellen agreed to do one show a night during the week and two a night on Fridays and Saturdays. She was so astounded that Clyde even knew of her, much less wanted to hire her, that she would have probably worked for free. But she didn't. "I was getting paid like three hundred dollars a week, enough so that I didn't have to work a regular job."

Although Clyde's attracted a rather broad cross-section of patrons, it was also a haven for on-the-edge types—a priceless pool of potential comedy routines for Ellen, who was already entrenched as an observational comic, one whose humor comes from observing others around them, even if she didn't know the terminology. Ellen didn't know whether Clyde's was a typical comedy club; all she knew was that now she had a place to do work that meant something to her.

"I had nothing to compare it to," she admits. "I learned what it was all about by on-the-job training. I was so excited to be working at all that I don't think I noticed that some nights there were only forty people out there. To me, it was a packed house."

When she had been playing the college venues, her audiences had been pretty much the same from night to night, but during the first few weeks at Clyde's, Ellen had to learn the basics of playing to a different type of audience each night. The seats at the Comedy Corner were filled with people of different ages, different races, and different financial and social backgrounds. She learned by trial and error and by watching others.

She mastered the art of keeping her delivery slow, which suggests confidence and also allows the performer to gauge, and adjust to, audience reaction. She learned how to draw the audience in by talking to individual members, loosening them up and making them part of the act. The most important thing she learned was to be true to herself.

"Somewhere along the line I realized that people laughed at me because of the way I was naturally. I figured that if I could, onstage, be the same person I am offstage, then it would work. So it is basically me up there, with a tiny bit of something—a sneeze-guard, if you will—to protect me from the audience."

Before going onstage, Ellen would practice in front of a mirror; once performing, she would find a pleasant face in the crowd to use as her center point. "One night," Ellen said, "there was a woman in there just looking at me like I could be the most funny person in the world. That's when I realized maybe I could be."

For Ellen, the rule of thumb was to "keep it clean, get rid of the filth, and just be yourself."

At first Ellen simply transferred the act she'd been doing at the college sites virtually intact to Clyde's. But it didn't take her very long to discover what worked and what didn't with the widely diverse crowd who patronized the comedy club.

"I knew instinctively I couldn't just keep eating onstage," Ellen says. " 'Oh, hey, it's that girl who eats onstage. Gee, she's huge. . . .' " So then I started getting away from prop stuff and weird stuff and started getting into more story-telling and just kind of esoteric things."

She wrote new material, some of it based on exaggerations about her family.

My grandmother started walking five miles a day when she was sixty. She's ninety-seven today. We don't know where the hell she is.

Much more of it was based on the behavior of the more eccentric people she came across in her daily life.

When you're in the grocery store, do you ever try to figure out what the person next to you in the checkout line had to come for and what they were just picking up when it's just a few items? Hmm, whipped cream, douche, and a lawn chair. (Slow reaction of looking the person up and down.) Well, you think it's a lawn chair.

Buddy Morra, one of the top managers of stand-ups in the business, says that every successful comic learns what Ellen learned early on. "You shouldn't give an audience what they want. Give them what you want."

"I try to appeal to all ages, and for that reason I stayed

away from youth-oriented routines that older people might not relate to," Ellen recalls. "I don't insult people, either; I'm not a Don Rickles type. No one's going to be offended by my humor, and I won't be embarrassed if my parents happen to be there."

Ellen began developing what would later become her trademark—quirky observations she'd twist into "DeGenerese." For instance, her dad asked her what she wanted for Christmas.

"Gosh, Dad, what I'd really like is a dolly." So on Christmas day, he wheels in this tremendous metal thing. You ever try to dress one of those things? They're impossible.

She went on to say that they had fire drills in her house. Everyone was assigned objects to save. Her father grabbed the pets, her mother the jewelry; her brother was supposed to run and get help . . .

. . . and I was supposed to try and save the washer and dryer. Good thing I had that dolly.

"What works for me, and what I hope works for my audience, is a different type of humor that I happen to think is funny," Ellen said years later, when asked about the evolution of her comedy style. "Some of that humor is more physical than others, some more subtle. Some of it depends on the line, rather than the image I project.

"I don't have the luxury of being able to draw, but the humor I'm talking about is almost like inside-out thinking. When I provide the line, the idea, I can only hope the audience has enough creativity and imagination to draw and complete the comic picture."

When Ellen started her tenure at Clyde's, she began as the opener, the one responsible for getting the audience in a fun, laughing mood. She started with less than ten minutes of material and eventually worked her way up to twenty. In 1981, Clyde's hosted an amateur competition "laugh-off," and a Metairie comic named Lance Montalto won. Ellen came in second.

Once she had proven herself to Clyde and the other comics, she was moved up to the middle spot and given thirty minutes. Finally, she was promoted to the closing act. By late 1981, she was onstage for forty-five to sixty minutes in addition to emceeing the other acts.

She was making a name for herself as a local talent with tons of potential and a potential national career. This didn't always sit well with some of the other comics, who had spent years trying to break through only to see this newcomer waltz in.

"I basically had no experience, and all of a sudden I was working with all these national headliners, who would tell me, 'You're very good—but you have to get out of town, because other than Clyde's, there wasn't a lot of support for comedy in New Orleans then.' "

Not only was her material funny, she had a knack for being able to establish an almost instant rapport with even tough audiences and win them over. Ellen was aware that some of the other comics had her in their sights. "All the people working in the club would get onstage and try to blow me away because they were angry and bitter that I didn't have the experience, and yet here I was surpassing them."

Although she worked alongside other comics who were well known locally, the Comedy Corner had in truth become Ellen's personal showcase. As a result, she was able to butt heads with Clyde and win.

Ellen credits Clyde's with giving her the opportunity she needed to learn her craft, but they didn't always get along personally. He was a freewheeling promoter type who struck Ellen as someone who cared more about profits than about comedy. That wasn't entirely true; still, he was not above doing whatever it took to increase the number of patrons coming through his front door.

Sensing he could make some extra money, Abercrombie decided to add a third, X-rated show on Saturday nights, hoping to appeal to the bawdier among the French Quarter crowd who flocked to the numerous Bourbon Street clubs boasting XXX-rated nude dancing-girl shows. He wanted Ellen to be his X-rated girlie emcee.

"I explained to him that I wasn't dirty," Ellen says. Like Jerry Seinfeld, she is considered a "clean" comic: no crass sex jokes, and no four-letter words for mere shock value. "He explained to me that I had to be dirty if I wanted to work there. And I explained to him that I would quit before I would be dirty."

Not wanting to lose his top draw, Clyde capitulated and found someone else to host his dirty comedy show. Ellen's refusal to participate in Clyde's raunchy shows was a glimpse of the spine she usually kept well hidden. It was mettle she would need if she were truly serious about making comedy a career.

However, her reluctance to work dirty is not to say Ellen completely shied away from references to sex, especially in her earlier days. In some of those routines, she alluded to her boyfriends. Other times, she talked about her lack of a social life.

> *It's been a while since I've been with anybody, and I'm sort of afraid I forgot how to do it. A friend said, "Ellen, sex is like riding a bike." I know it's been a while, but I don't remember pedaling ... okay, once, but I was really, really drunk.*

Looking back at some of Ellen's earliest performances now, it seems obvious that she's least comfortable during

routines in which she talks about her alleged romantic dealings with men. It also seems obvious that Ellen felt obliged
to at least try to project that image. Unlike her later stage
persona, early in her career Ellen wore much more makeup
and dressed in what many would consider a more "feminine" manner. Her voice even seems slightly higher pitched,
although her observations show the same unique view, just
in a rawer form.

> *Did you ever break up with someone and tell your
> friends all the horrible habits that person used to do,
> then you get back together with them the next day?
> Now your friends think you're crazy and you're stuck
> with him for the rest of your life because your friends
> have all left you.*

By the summer of 1981, Ellen was beginning to consider
the stage her domain. She would break the ice with the audience by pretending she was filming a video for her mom
back in Texas. "So act hysterical," she tells them. Surprisingly,
many do, bending over in faux laughter. She goes on to win
the crowd over completely with comic bits about a mother
who responds in baby talk when speaking to adults, giving
instructions in the garbled tones of a cab radio, and imitating
people appearing on a nightly news segment.

In a 1981 article in the *Times-Picayune* about Clyde's
comedy regulars, Ellen said she got her ideas from watching
people shopping at Walgreen's and Woolworth's, riding city
buses, or walking down Canal Street. "You can," she said,
"find humor in anything." There were exceptions to that rule,
though, at least for Ellen: sex, politics, and religion. "My father is a very religious Christian Scientist, and he used to
come see me all the time, so I'd clean up my act in case he
came in." Then she added, "But I don't think I patterned my
act around what my dad's wishes were."

She told the interviewer that before she got into comedy a year earlier, she was a singer and songwriter. That must have come as quite a surprise to those who knew her, but Ellen was already learning the art of not revealing too much personal information. She said that her ultimate goals were to move to California and have a backup career selling shoes but that comedy was still her obsession for the moment. "After a good night, I'm on top of the world. But sometimes, after a bad night, I go home and talk to my cat."

DeGeneres called the Comedy Corner home for over a year. During that time she developed an act, honed her skills, and slowly built confidence in her material.

What are perfect strangers? Do they have perfect hair? Do they dress perfectly?

"What I didn't realize in the beginning, but what I realized later, is that it's honesty that people pick up on. All I can do is present it, and people will get whatever they want to get. I don't always know what that will be, but I do know that people appreciate honesty."

Despite her growing skills, DeGeneres says she still suffered from chronic stage fright. "I was raised with a lot of fear and I witnessed people who never did anything out of the what-ifs and the fears. I didn't want to end up that way." But her drive to be a successful comic always overcame her innate trepidation. "I wanted to be famous; I wanted the attention, and I wanted to feel that people thought I was special."

And they did. For the first time in her life, Ellen had a real sense of accomplishment. She finally had a direction and, most important, a goal. She truly believed that with a little more experience and a few more solid routines, she would never have to hold another day job; she felt she could really make it as a stand-up. What she didn't know is just how hard that road would be—and how long.

"I was at Clyde's for a little more than a year, and all the headliners who came in kept telling me that I was good enough to move to New York or Los Angeles or wherever. I didn't really know those people, however, so it wasn't until a friend of mine moved from New Orleans to San Francisco and called up saying the same thing that I paid any attention. 'You won't believe this place. It's beautiful. There are comedy clubs—you'd do very well here.'"

Ellen says the call convinced her. She sold her car and shipped most of her belongings west and arranged to stay with her friend and two other girls. Even though she hates flying, "probably because I'm not in control," Ellen boarded the plane for California glowing with optimism. Indeed, her first impression of San Francisco was everything she had hoped for, and more.

"It was beautiful. When I got off the plane there I had no idea that air could be like that. I thought everyone lived the way we did in New Orleans—sweating while they blow-dried their hair."

Ellen was also introduced to a thriving gay community that was even more open and embracing than the one in New Orleans. While her hometown only had a small handful of clubs for women, San Francisco had many, and it wasn't uncommon to see two women walking hand in hand down the street or kissing freely and comfortably in public.

Equally as intoxicating were the dozens of comedy clubs dotting the city. Although Ellen was able to get some spots at a number of them, she was suddenly a small fish in a very big pond; an outsider who had no reputation, no local buzz, no heat, and not enough bookings to make ends meet.

"I loved San Francisco, but I didn't have any money," Ellen recalls. "I was having to work at a regular job. After a few months, I got homesick and came back to New Orleans.

But when I got there, Clyde's had closed down and suddenly I'm out of comedy." And back working a nine-to-five job at a New Orleans law firm.

Ellen didn't know it when she left for San Francisco, but she had gotten out of town just before the ax fell on Clyde's Comedy Corner and his dreams of national prominence. The club closed abruptly in 1990 after Abercrombie left New Orleans for a hurriedly planned indefinite vacation.

"You could say he left very quickly," laughs attorney Markey. "Clyde apparently ended up owing a lot of people money—literally all over the South. I guess you could say he was an equal opportunity borrower. It seems he got so far over his head he thought it was time to leave New Orleans. Needless to say, he didn't leave a forwarding address, and nobody seems to know where he is even today."

Today when Ellen thinks back to her days at Clyde's, she's not exactly sentimental about the club. It seems to be a faded memory. "I know it was somewhere in the French Quarter," Ellen offers. "I have no idea where, though. I'll find out eventually—it will all come back in therapy."

Since she had to make money quickly, Ellen took the first job she could get—working as an office assistant for a law firm. She made coffee and photocopies and very little money. Suddenly, her life as a self-supporting comic seemed as if it had happened a long time before, to someone else.

"When I was working at the law firm, I really tried to tell those people that I was really a comic," Ellen remembers. "They'd say, 'Sure you are . . . now go make the coffee.' And I would have to make the coffee and do the Xeroxing and fit into that little world that I have never felt I was a part of." Even the dress code made her feel like an outsider, so she eventually started "wearing what I felt like wearing . . . and it wasn't dresses."

One of Ellen's coworkers, Pat Barnhill, who worked the switchboard, remembers DeGeneres vividly—as the one who was always putting callers through to the wrong extension or hitting the wrong button. "When I was at lunch and heard a ruckus, I said, 'Ooh, Ellen's out on the board. I have to smooth some feathers.'"

"I could never understand anybody's name," Ellen complains.

"I was hoping that she was prepared to do something else later in life," Barnhill smiles, then adds warmly, "But she was a doll."

Despite the goodwill she always seemed to leave in her wake, Ellen felt herself sinking into despair over her circumstances. She had no comedy prospects on the horizon, and she was back living hand to mouth.

"I lived in another flea-infested apartment in a basement, and I took the bus to work. I was totally lost. I've had lots of experience. Then one day the phone rang, and it was Showtime calling from New York. You can't even imagine—here I am in this horrible apartment, the phone rings and it's Showtime."

Beginning in the late 1970s, cable had become the premiere medium for showcasing comics. They had the freedom to air language and content that broadcast television networks couldn't dream of, so comics like Richard Pryor, Steve Martin, George Carlin, and Robin Williams were given chunks of time to perform. It was good for the performers, who were able to reach millions of viewers, and good for cable networks like Showtime and HBO because these acts pulled in big ratings and increased their subscriber base.

Thus a new synergy was born—as was a new option on nights out. Instead of going to movies, people whose appetites had been whetted by cable shows, would seek out local comedy clubs. Soon such places were a fixture in towns literally all across America, from Alaska's Pierce Street Annex in Anchorage to Sir Laughs a Lot Comedy Castle in Wisconsin, where the young Tim Allen started making a name for himself.

It was a natural progression for cable networks to try to nurture comedy talent. Showtime, in the forefront of that movement, had decided to sponsor a contest to find the Funniest Person in America. All anyone had to do to enter was send in a videotaped performance. Ellen did, but she would have preferred to audition in person. "It's real hard for me to look at a tape of myself, because I hate most of what I do, you know, in terms of how I look."

To her utter amazement, she was named Funniest Person in Louisiana. She was sick with the flu and running a fever the night of the competition and now considers that performance "a complete embarrassment."

Years later, when Oprah Winfrey aired a clip from Ellen's audition tape, DeGeneres visibly winced at seeing her 1982 self. "It's so scary. It's one thing when people see your photo albums when they come to your house, but to show that on national television. . . . Remember the eighties? Everyone looked like that. It wasn't just me."

Her fashion sense aside, soon after she won the Louisiana title, Showtime notified her that she was a finalist for the national competition. She and the other finalists performed their routines on a Showtime special. They were reviewed by a panel of judges that included Soupy Sales, Harvey Korman, and Pee-Wee Herman.

Ellen won. She was floored. "But I think it probably surprised Steve Martin and Woody Allen more than it surprised me," she wryly notes. Although it was yet another career achievement, DeGeneres says it was an awkward title to be saddled with. "Showtime was not that big at the time and it was a ridiculous contest to try to get attention. I competed against other secretaries and gardeners. And I won. In one year, I went from making coffee for lawyers to being 1982's Funniest Person in America. Imagine having to wear a title like that around your neck for a year. It was a lot to live up to when you had five minutes of material."

One of Ellen's better memories of that time was when "Phyllis Diller came to see me because she was curious about the funniest person in America. She was in the front row. And everybody was excited that Phyllis Diller was there. But she couldn't quite hear. So the person she was with would have to repeat what I just said. So everybody would laugh. And as the laugh would die down, you would hear *hah, hah, hah* (laughs like Phyllis Diller). So that was a fun thing."

But mostly, it was a discomfort. "I'd be appearing somewhere and instead of saying 'Seen on *The Tonight Show!*' or '*Letterman,*' they'd say, 'Funniest Person in America.' I figured I'm just going to end up in the circus next to the fattest man and the skinniest woman or something."

Fortunately, there was more to her win than a mere title. "I won like five hundred dollars and a little special. They flew me to New York, which was my first time there. And I taped a special, and Showtime showed it as two-minute spots between movies. And I got to travel around in a van and have the title of the Funniest Person in America. It was so ridiculous, though. It was such a publicity ploy for Showtime."

(Ironically, Showtime dropped New Orleans from its list of audition cities just two years later, apparently finding the talent pool too small.)

With the snippet of national exposure the contest gave her, both as a door-opener and an albatross, she knew it was time to take her act on the road. She understood that at some point, comics have to go on the road in order to become known, seasoned performers. The general rule of thumb these days is that it takes from four to seven years of near-constant traveling before those who prove themselves good enough reach the top of the profession. At that point, comics can expect to earn $100,000 or more on the circuit of comedy clubs, cruise ships, and awards and industrial shows.

So, in 1983, she bought a van, attached a large nose above the front bumper, and once again headed to San Francisco to make the city by the bay her new home base. This time she would strike out on her own, intending to hit the road to Anycomedyclub, USA. It was now or never to see if she really had what it took to make it as a big-time stand-up.

5
Johnny Carson:
The Big Leap to Fame

Without question, winning the title kick-started Ellen's career and quickly led to other engagements, some of which worked—and some of which didn't. "For instance," Ellen recalls, "once I performed for three hundred marines. I thought that was a good idea, and it wasn't a good idea at all because they didn't agree with my title" of Funniest Person in America.

The experience with the few and proud almost ended her career before it had a chance to begin. At that gig, "an Andrew Dice Clay–type comic" was whipping the audience into a misogynistic frenzy. It was the first time Ellen had experienced rejection simply because she was a female comic. This audience wanted blood and was not the type of crowd that would appreciate her "Phone Call to God" monologue, but it was a little late to write a new routine now.

One of the other entertainers on the bill that night remembers thinking that he wished he had brought a cartload of pies to give Ellen as she walked out onstage. There were scattered catcalls when Ellen stood behind the microphone, but that was easy enough to absorb. She had faced tough audiences before and knew she just had to get through it. But she wasn't ready for the depth of the rudeness that was about to be hurled in her direction as she began her "Phone Call to God."

"The front row was a bunch of guys who actually turned their chairs around and faced the other way. They didn't even give me a minute. I was onstage and they were screaming out they wanted to see body parts, and I couldn't quiet them down. There was so much testosterone raging in that room, I had no control, and I didn't have the experience to handle it. So I just dropped the mike and ran offstage and was crying. I was so upset."

When it was finally, mercifully over, the emcee came back onstage and gave the knife one final twist. "The emcee felt it necessary to keep emphasizing, 'One more time for the Funniest . . . Person . . . in . . . America!' The audience was laughing at him saying it over and over, and I was crying. I wanted to go home and get out of the business. I thought, 'This is the worst business; it's so cruel.' That was the only time I ever walked off a stage. To this day, I just break out in tears whenever I see a marine."

As for the emcee, Ellen says, "That was very mean, and I still know who he is. And he's a real jerk."

But even when the audiences were receptive, being on the road was difficult because "I was sandwiched in between comedians who were doing the exact kind of humor that I am totally against," DeGeneres recalls. "Everything's negative and everything's mean-spirited, and I just didn't fit in." In a *Parade* interview, Ellen would later admit, "I'm sure that somewhere inside of me, my subconscious was saying the obvious—that I was not being true to myself in many ways." The conflict was rooted in her childhood. She was taught it was important "that everyone has to like me" even if it meant being unhappy. "Of course I end up in a business where everyone has to like me." DeGeneres was so afraid of being rejected she chose to keep her sexuality closeted from her public.

Even though her first attempt to live in San Francisco had been a dismal disappointment, Ellen was determined to try again. "There wasn't much support for comedy in New Orleans. Just as one example, New Orleans is a city where they canceled *The David Letterman Show*. And as far as working locally, opportunities were very limited."

As it turned out, her second time around in San Francisco was a vastly different experience from her first visit. "It was the hottest city there was for comedy, and it was amazing how well things worked there. I really didn't struggle at all. Things just clicked and people started paying attention to me."

Ellen quickly won over club owners and audiences alike with her increased confidence and improved material.

In the beginning there was nothing. God said, "Let there be light!" And there was light. There was still nothing, but you could see it a whole lot better.

Although Betty was prouder than she had ever been, Ellen's new success brought with it a whole new set of concerns. First, she worried about Ellen touring the country on her own, fearful she might attract weirdos. Because Ellen didn't have an agent who knew the club scene, Betty fretted that her daughter might find herself in some unruly bar with drunk or rowdy patrons in an unsafe part of a strange town. If Betty could have figured out a way to do it, she would have gone on the road with Ellen, offering her services as a quasi-manager and -bookkeeper.

Ironically, Betty was just as concerned for Ellen's well-being when she was home, which was now San Francisco.

For someone of Betty's age and background, the idea of her daughter living with other young women in a big city seemed entirely too risky. Even worse, she knew that Ellen enjoyed going to bars and clubs, which meant she would be coming home late at night.

As it so happened, Ellen was experiencing just as many worries about her mom's well-being. Just as Ellen's career started taking off after the Showtime title, Betty began going through a series of misfortunes. First, shortly after Ellen had moved to San Francisco and started going on road trips, her mom went into the hospital.

Although it was just for minor surgery, it still sent a shiver of fear and panic through Ellen. She was also guilt-stricken because she couldn't rearrange her performance dates, which meant she wouldn't be able to be with her mother. Fortunately, Betty's mom was able to come up to San Francisco. That made Ellen feel better, but she was still wracked with guilt and felt miserable not being able to be with her mom. She phoned several times a day and sent flowers every time she passed a florist.

To Ellen's great relief, Betty recovered quickly and was soon back on her feet. But she was now facing a more un-treatable, and more upsetting, problem: Her marriage to Roy was coming to an end.

Around the time Ellen moved to San Francisco, Betty and Roy had moved one hundred miles southwest of Atlanta to Tyler, Texas. The change of scenery was emotionally devas-tating to Betty. Not only was her daughter now living thou-sands of miles away, she had been forced to leave her adored best friend, Jimmy Wade. Betty felt more alone than ever. The sad truth was, Betty never grew as close to Roy as she had hoped she would, and now that sense of isolation was even worse. Their emotional estrangement from each other only served to heighten the realization that she simply had to make something of the second half of her life; she had to do something that would benefit her daughter or others, not to mention herself.

Her mind made up, Betty filed for a separation from Roy and moved back to New Orleans, where she enrolled in a program to become a speech therapist. Although she wasn't completely sure that this was the profession to which she wanted to devote the rest of her life, at least for now she was doing something she knew she would enjoy and could be proud of.

While Betty was setting up her new life, Ellen was doing the same in California. As it turned out, Betty had little reason to worry about Ellen's safety in the big city; she was rarely there for very long at a stretch. Even though San Francisco was where she lived, and she played all the Bay Area comedy clubs whenever she was in town, it wasn't really home. It was more a home base.

Ellen was concentrating more on her career than on creature comforts. A mutual friend had offered to introduce her to comedy guru Budd Friedman, the monocled, Los Angeles–based humor impresario who had funded the famed Improv clubs. Fans of A&E's Evening at the Improv know him as the show's host.

Ellen went to Los Angeles to meet Budd and recalls, "I auditioned and he gave me some great spots. Instead of having to wait around for hours like the rest of the beginning comics, he had me booked into the good time slots."

Don't you hate it when somebody says they're gonna call you about seven and it's seven and they haven't called? So you say, "I'll fix a drink." So you have a drink, then you have another, then you have another, then you have another. Now you're drunk. Now it's five after seven and they still haven't called. You can't trust people, you just can't.

The importance to a young performer of appearing at the Improv cannot be overstated. Like its primary competitor, the Comedy Store, the Improv attracted scores of agents, talent scouts, directors, and producers from both film and television in their constant search for new comedy talent with a fresh, unique voice. But possibly the most important relationship to come out of performing at the Improv was the opportunity to work on the same bill one night with Jay Leno, who was already an established headliner. Leno would later play a vital role in her career, having been impressed with Ellen's comic vision and voice.

Not everybody was equally enamored. "Many comics reveal something about themselves," Tom Sawyer, a San Francisco club owner, told *People*. "Ellen's humor was impersonal—there was no connection between her act and her life. She was going through the motions."

In the months that followed, Ellen began spending less and less time in San Francisco. If she wasn't sleeping on the couch of her friend in Los Angeles when performing at the Improv, she was constantly on the road, traveling an average of three hundred days a year. It was an exhausting, draining schedule, and at times it would take its toll on her. She usually opened her act by greeting the audience by its town's name. "How are you doing, South Bend?" There were nights when the name of the town or city she was in completely escaped her, but she would manage to turn even that into a joke. "Hey, there, East Berlin!"

She found the constant traveling and endless series of interchangeable clubs numbing. "This is such a weird line of work. You sit alone all day in a hotel in a strange city. But as soon as I walk onstage and hear and feel people responding to me, there's no profession like it." Still, it was a good life, better than anything she had known in all her then twenty-five years.

As difficult the travel was physically, it was the mental

wear and tear that was the hardest to cope with. Ellen explains, "I can't just go to work and sit behind a desk and type. You have to self-start. It's my job. I've got all those people out there looking at me. But there is no greater feeling than to see a thought, a tiny idea, transform into a story onstage in Minneapolis and two thousand people laughing."

However, like most comics, Ellen knew she would never be completely satisfied with her routine; she would always be looking to improve her act. "If you work in an office, it's all based on performance. You have to do your job well and be nice to your coworkers and boss. But with this profession, you want to perform well enough to please millions of people, which is, of course, impossible. You can only be true to yourself and hope there are people who like what you do. After all, it's only entertainment. My job is pretty low on a scale of what's important in life."

The constant travel did offer Ellen a whole new world of comic possibilities. A couple of her best-known routines from the mid-1980s deal with air travel. Because of her delivery style, none of Ellen's bits stayed the same from telling to telling, but the main routine went like this:

> *Did you ever notice that whatever you ask the stewardess, whatever the problem, the answer is going to be club soda?*
>   *"Excuse me, I have the hiccups. Could you . . ."*
>   *"Club soda will get that. Be right back."*
>   *"I spilled a little red sauce on my pants . . ."*
>   *"Club soda will get that. Be right back."*
>   *"The wing is on fire . . ."*
>   *"Club soda will get that. Be right back."*

Ellen also honed in on airline snacks.

The stewardess's job is to bring us the food—six peanuts in this little tiny package. Anywhere else, anyone offers that to us, it's "Get that away from me, six peanuts!" But on the plane, we need that.

She also targeted flying in general.

First of all, I don't think they have to go that high in the air. I think they're showing off, those pilots. I think we could just go really fast just a few feet off the ground. Just high enough to miss the animals.

As her national exposure increased, so did the critical attention paid her, and it was uniformly positive. *Esquire* praised her "sweetly expressed mistrust of everything" and her "penchant for anxious free association," referring specifically to her observation that Californians believed that going around naked in front of total strangers for mud baths was somehow relaxing.

The New York Times applauded Ellen for her "offbeat storytelling, strategic pauses, and dramatic facial expressions that remind some people of Bob Newhart."

In her book *Stand-Up Comedy,* comic Judy Carter called Ellen a master of "the callback," which means where reference is made to something the stand-up said previously.

Dogs hate it when you blow in their face. I'll tell you who really hates that—my grandmother. Which is odd, because when we're driving she really loves to hang her head out the window.

Later in her act, Ellen talks about her grandmother's philosophy of life.

She said to me, "Life is like a blender. You have so many different speeds, you have mix, blend, stir, and you never use them all. In life you have so many different abilities, and you never use them all." I said, "Grandma," and then I just blew in her face.

Although Ellen became known primarily for her stories, several critics were especially partial to her ability to create funny one-liners out of the otherwise ordinary and familiar, such as a joke about her family running a petting zoo.

And then a heavy petting zoo for people who really liked the animals just a whole lot.

Animals were a big part of her act, and it was one area where she let her true feelings seep into the routines. An avid animal lover who was dead-set against killing for sport, Ellen often put hunters in her comic sights.

I ask people why they have deer heads on their walls and they always say because it's such a beautiful animal. There you go. (pause) I think my mother's attractive, but I have photographs of her.

When asked to describe her brand of comedy, Ellen said she really couldn't, nor did she want to define it in terms of other comedy types. "I don't want to be able to be compared to anyone else, because I want to be me, not a version of someone else."

However, she was quick to point out her comic preferences. "To me, David Letterman is the funniest man on earth. He's brilliant—always quick, always clever. He makes me laugh."

With each passing year, Ellen's comfort level onstage visibly increased. So did her comfort level with herself. Instead of the tailored pants with feminine shirts tucked in and sensible shoes she had worn early in her career, Ellen began wearing man-tailored shirts and jackets and alternated between tennis shoes and Hush Puppies. She toned her makeup way down, to just the bare minimum needed. But her comedy remained essentially the same—wry observations that were funny without being vulgar.

Ellen explains that she didn't censor herself out of a sense of moral obligation or as a result of her upbringing. "I mean, if I slam my hand in a car door, I'm certainly going to curse. It's not like I don't curse and I don't have other sides to me. But you know, this is just who I am. This is how I talk. So I never thought it was necessary to add words to make something funnier by cursing."

Although she appealed to a broad cross-section of people, she was especially popular among women, who were tired of seeing the stereotypical female stand-up act, which usually consisted of humor so self-deprecating as to be self-abusive. Ellen resolutely refused to dip into that comedy well.

"It's a shame that so many female comics are self-destructive, like the way Phyllis Diller makes herself look terrible, then jokes about her appearance," Ellen has said. "I don't think that audiences have accepted good-looking female comics—the women feel threatened, and the men just want to stare instead of listening. I don't consider myself a feminist, but I don't do that kind of material. We're all human, and we all have the same basic experiences and situations in life, so I'd rather work from that approach."

In an interview conducted while she was living in San Francisco, Ellen said: "I like to be off-the-wall and unpredictable. These days I usually come on after one or two opening acts, so my approach really has to be fresh. I also play on the contrast between acting off-the-wall and my wholesome girl-next-door appearance."

Because of her girl-next-door looks, few among the straight crowd would have suspected her true sexual preference.

"When I started headlining, it was always guys on before me. I would always follow somebody doing either dyke jokes or fag jokes and doing the lisp thing, and the audience is going crazy and laughing. I just thought, 'Oh, God. What if they pick up I'm gay?' It was that fear and shame."

Ellen certainly made no references to her sexuality in her act, but among the lesbian community it was no secret that she was gay; as a result, when she performed in major cities, a large portion of her audience was gay women. As her star rose in the national comedy circuit, she was also becoming more embraced by the lesbian community as one of their own who made good.

In 1984, Ellen hired a manager, Bob Fisher, who worked with other comics, including Paula Poundstone and Dana Carvey. Not wanting to mislead Bob in any way, Ellen drummed up the courage to confide in him. She told him, "I want you to know something. I'm gay."

Fisher says he looked at her and said, "Yeah? And?" She was very relieved it wasn't an issue. "I already knew Ellen was gay. It was sort of taken for granted. It didn't play a part in her act, and she would neither confirm or deny it to the press."

Eventually, among other comics, it would become understood and mostly accepted that Ellen was gay. Few said anything, although there might have been an occasional testosterone-heavy stand-up who made occasional snide remarks, primarily, according to Fisher, because "several guys had crushes on her." But for the most part Ellen, now twenty-six, was left alone, largely because she was genuinely nice. Besides, as she has frequently pointed out, Ellen liked men as people so she didn't exude any hostility. And even though she was now exclusively dating women, she still held out the possibility that she might one day find a man she wanted to marry.

In any event, that day was a long way off. Right now, her career was her spouse and child wrapped into one. It was also her main identity. Because of her reluctance to express her sexuality openly, she found herself in the netherworld that most people who live double lives experience. "I never felt like I belonged anywhere," she would say years later. "I never felt like I belonged to the gay community. I never felt like I belonged to the straight community. I felt like this in-between."

Like many other comics before her, Ellen discovered one of the great ironies in the life of a stand-up: The more time she spent working on her comedy, the more serious she became in her day-to-day life, whereas in the days when she floated from job to job, quips would fly fast and furious among her coworkers and friends.

"Just because I'm a comic doesn't mean that I'm always cracking jokes, that I'm always funny," Ellen comments. "If anything, I'm too serious, I think. Sometimes I can't watch the news because I get too depressed, thinking, 'What are we doing to our planet and what are we doing to each other?' There is so much hate in this world. I cry at least three times a week from stuff that's going on in the world. Hell, I cry at those sweepstakes commercials when they go to someone's house and tell them they're millionaires. I cry all the time in L.A. Driving around, seeing women on corners with signs and babies. I give them money but it's like putting a Band-Aid on cancer. So I'm only funny when I have to be or when I feel like it. Or if someone is crying, like if someone falls down . . . or if some authority figure is telling me what to do."

Like any beloved hobby that becomes a vocation, being funny had become no laughing matter to Ellen. From the lost high school student with no drive or ambition, she had matured into a savvy performer, carefully nurturing her career. Consequently, she made sure to keep a window in her road schedule so she would be in San Francisco for the city's prestigious Comedy Festival. As usual, Ellen came across polished, approachable, and very funny.

> *Penguins are monogamous for life. Penguins mate for life. Which doesn't exactly surprise me that much 'cause they all look alike. It's not like they're gonna meet a better-looking penguin someday.*

When the votes were tallied, Ellen was the festival's runner-up. The winner? Sinbad, who would go on to a big-time career of his own. But as far as Sinbad was concerned, the distinction between first and second place was negligible to the point of being nonexistent.

"I think it's crazy that people feel this need to pick a best at these things," Sinbad once commented. "'Cause I mean, I'm not better than Ellen DeGeneres and she's not better than Richard Jeni or anything like that. We're different, that's all. I remember one of these things where Eddie Murphy finished second or third behind I don't even remember who. It's nuts. And you can see that coming in second didn't hurt Ellen."

Even though she was runner-up, it still afforded Ellen the chance to be seen by "some of the big people from L.A." Perhaps the most important development that came out of the San Francisco Comedy Festival was that it brought her to the attention of manager Buddy Morra, whose longevity and client list have earned him a great deal of respect within the comedy world. He filed her name away in his mental Rolodex and began following her career from afar. Although Ellen couldn't know it, he would later play a pivotal part in helping her fulfill one of her most cherished dreams.

Suddenly, Ellen started meeting with managers and was

headlining at some of the country's more prestigious clubs. Her ultimate goal, though, remained the same—to earn an appearance on Johnny Carson's *Tonight Show*. So even though she loved San Francisco—the culture, the nightlife, the air— in 1985 Ellen, then twenty-seven, moved to Los Angeles, in part because of her *Tonight Show* dream but also because she wanted to enter into a new phase of her career. Weary of constant travel, Ellen was ready to start the transition to tele- vision, specifically some of the popular cable comedy shows. She had also started getting the first itch to try her hand at acting.

In a February 1985 interview, she noted with some amazement, "I've talked to two of the major networks and read scripts, and there is a chance of a role in a sitcom. Eventually, I would like to get into serious acting and out of comedy. That's a recent discovery for me. But a sitcom would be good now. Hopefully, it would be a good one like *Cheers* or *Night Court*."

Series television was still several years off for Ellen, but her dream of appearing on *The Tonight Show* was about to become a reality. In the end, her cause was championed by an unlikely combination of supporters who weren't friends, just fans of her talent.

"This was back in 1985," Ellen remembers. "What really happened was that I was pretty well known in San Francisco, and when I got to L.A. Buddy Morra had heard about me. I had been in L.A. about a year, and Buddy saw something in me and thought he could help me. So he got the talent coor- dinator of *The Tonight Show,* Jim McCauley, to come see me. 'You gotta pay attention, you gotta watch.'"

Her other cheerleader was Jay Leno. "I had opened for Jay Leno at the Improv, so Jay sat Jim McCauley down, and Jim was between Jay and Buddy and he never had a chance."

After her set was over, McCauley came up to Ellen and bathed her in compliments, then gave her his verdict. "He said, 'You're on next week.' It was amazing. It was this huge validation and stamp of approval." Ellen has said that if she could have bottled and sold what she felt at that moment, she would have been the wealthiest person on earth.

Her date with Johnny sent Ellen's head into another zone. "The next morning I drove to Quinn's, which was this little health store on Melrose, and there were three minutes left on the meter. So I ran in real fast, but when I came out my car was gone, and I'm thinking, 'Oh, man, my car couldn't have gotten towed that fast.' Then I hear cars honking—I had forgotten to put my car in Park, and it had rolled three blocks into a major intersection. And the doors were locked, so nobody could get in to stop this car slowly rolling down the street causing all this havoc. Needless to say, I stayed excited for a long time."

Then came the night she was supposed to tape. After waiting for so many years, Ellen got bumped. "Jack Paar was on and talked too long, so I didn't get on."

The disappointment was crushing, but McCauley rescheduled Ellen, and the next time she would make it on the air. "I was as nervous as you can possibly ever be in your lifetime. I could hear my heart. I thought that everyone would hear my heart in my chest."

At that time, *The Tonight Show* was the mecca for any stand-up because an appearance virtually guaranteed invitations to other shows and big bookings nationwide. However, that wasn't uppermost in Ellen's mind. She already had most of those things; what she was really after was what she had promised herself five years earlier—even though she knew that not once in Johnny Carson's twenty-four-year reign had a female comic ever been asked to come sit on the couch by Johnny.

Being invited to join Johnny was something that was never rehearsed, and nobody, not even Carson, knew what he would do until the routine was over. "That was totally his decision, and he doesn't decide until he sees you," Ellen explains, adding, "He had never seen me."

If Johnny was impressed enough, he motioned the guest over. If he wasn't, the camera made a quick cut to Johnny clapping, then the show went to a commercial. "They say, 'You just stand there. He'll say thank you and you walk back off through the curtain,' Ellen remembers. "That's what I thought was going to happen. But in my head I had known for five or six years that he was going to call me over."

As Ellen waited to go on, her heart was racing and she fought to keep her composure. "To grow up watching *The Tonight Show* and hearing that music, when I walked through the curtain to see Ed McMahon and Johnny Carson, it was the most surreal thing I've ever experienced."

Ellen opened with material that had been finely honed and perfected, drawing the audience in. It was obvious she was giving the performance of her life, and the audience, and Carson, were with her. She closed with "Phone Call to God," which she had written so many years before just for this moment.

Ellen phones God to find out why there are fleas. She gets Him on the phone, but He puts her on hold, "Somebody's at the gate," so she sings along with "Onward, Christian Soldiers." "It's not a tape? They're good!"

When God comes back, in answer to her question, God tells Ellen that he created fleas so that people could be gainfully employed. She has to admit that he's right. "Of course you're right, being who you are." After God sneezes ("Bless yourself," Ellen says), He tells her some really bad jokes that Ellen feels she has to laugh at. "Okay, who's there? God. God who? Godzilla." Ellen finally finds the nerve to tell God she has to run.

The audience roared with approval, and Ellen paused a moment before glancing to her right. When she did, she saw a smiling and clapping Carson. She started to look away, and then she saw him crook his index finger at her, indicating he wanted her to walk over and join him. Ellen DeGeneres was about to become the first and only female comic ever to be invited to sit on the couch after her first appearance on *The Tonight Show*.

As she walked toward the couch, she experienced a rush of emotion. The memory of the years of stops and starts, the pain of writing the piece, the long and lonely nights on the road all washed over her. She had emerged on the other side and reached the spot she had promised herself, and Kat, she'd get to one day.

Johnny said, "That's really good."

Ellen replied, "Thank you. Thank you."

"Everything after that was a blur," Ellen admits. She felt as if she were having an out-of-body experience. "That was amazing to hear that from him, who'd seen it all." She knew that somewhere in heaven both Kat and God were smiling down on her. It was as wonderful as she'd thought it would be "to get that affirmation, to have him tell you you're fresh and clever and original, which is all I ever wanted to be. I don't want to just be good. I want to be original. I want to be myself."

It was a wish that would be fulfilled in ways Ellen couldn't even begin to imagine.

6
Her Toe in the Tube

Ellen did five more *Tonight Show* appearances before Johnny Carson retired, and she continued to appear after her good friend Jay Leno took over. But it was her first spot that she will always credit for launching her career to the next level, which was the jump to television, even if it did take longer than she would have liked.

Although Ellen had made *Tonight Show* history, it didn't change her life. "Everybody acted like it was such a big deal," but she wasn't in a position to take full advantage of the appearance. "There was a little bit of heat, and then it just went away, so it didn't mean anything as far as the average person coming to see my show. But for the industry to see Johnny Carson call me over to sit down on my first appearance, that was a big deal. I got respect, and people started paying a little bit more attention to me."

Already in constant demand for club appearances, Ellen was now just as sought-after for cable shows and comedy specials. The most notable of these appearances were the 1986 HBO special *The Young Comedians All-Star Reunion* and another HBO show, *Women of the Night,* on which she appeared with Judy Tenuta, Paula Poundstone, and Rita Rudner and performed her "wrapper rap":

So you bought a little gift
And you need to get it wrapped
Well I came here to tell you 'bout that
We got red ribbon, blue, green, and white
Everybody gonna have a package tonight

Ellen also appeared on *The Comedy Club Special,* which aired in September 1988 on ABC in prime time. Her increased exposure as a high-profile comic made her a highly paid performer, earning well into six figures annually. However, she still wasn't exactly a household name to most television viewers.

Once, while at an ABC radio station to promote a show, Ellen walked up to the receptionist to announce her arrival. The receptionist was brusque. "You're not on the list." When Ellen insisted, gently, that she should be, the receptionist called the person Ellen had been scheduled to meet.

"Your guest is here for three-thirty. Miss Generis."

Ellen politely corrected her. "It's Miss De*Gen*eres."

The woman talked into the phone again. "Miss *Dee*-gen*aires.*"

Those small humiliations were just part of the price Ellen was willing to pay to pursue her goal of moving into acting, which was the primary reason she had relocated to Los Angeles. Although she already had friends in L.A., Ellen soon found herself surrounded by family as well. Her brother moved there within a month of her arrival. Soon after that, both her mother and father relocated to the West Coast— Elliott to the San Diego area, which is approximately two hours south of L.A., and Betty to near where Ellen was living. Their rapid trek West prompted Ellen to joke later, "Yes, the family's all out here. They smelled the money and moved right out."

As usual, Ellen was covering another of life's painful truths with humor. Money was the last thing her mom was after; Betty, too, was looking for a new start. After separating from Roy and enrolling in her speech therapy classes, Betty had briefly returned to Texas and tried to make her marriage go one more time. It didn't work. She and Roy divorced, and Betty finally did what she'd been wanting to do all along—be with Ellen on a more full-time basis and help her daughter manage her flourishing career.

The 1980s and 1990s will probably be remembered as a Golden Age for comics. The biggest stand-up-to-television success story of the 1980s was Roseanne, which debuted in October 1988 and starred Roseanne Barr (as she was then known), the self-proclaimed "domestic goddess." She seemed to come out of nowhere, with only a couple of cable specials under her belt and a unique, if grating, voice that couldn't be ignored. She was unpolished and unsophisticated, but she struck a chord in many women who felt underappreciated and overworked. "The way I look at it, if the kids are alive when my husband comes home from work, then I've done my job," she would say in her act.

The downside is that precisely because comics have usually spent years honing their routines and stage personas, they are resistant to any tampering, which can, and usually does, lead to what Hollywood likes to euphemistically call "creative differences." The rest of the world would call them knock-down, drag-out arguments, and they usually result in a revolving-door series of frustrated producers; it's easier to replace a producer than the star of a series. However tense it becomes, though, the synergy between television and stand-up comics will remain.

"Of course it will," says writer and producer Linda Bloodworth-Thomason, creator of *Designing Women*. "What stand-up or actor wouldn't want forty million pairs of eyes on them in a single night? And what writer wouldn't want the advantage of knowing ahead of time the strengths and weaknesses of their comic performer?"

Ellen was well aware of this appeal. "I'm getting the feeling that studios and networks are sending people into malls and just walking up to people saying, 'Have you ever done stand-up? Are you thinking about doing it? Yeah? We've got a development deal for you then. Here's a hundred dollars, don't go to anyone else.'

"It's really true. They're just taking anybody who they see, putting them on hold, and developing shows. It's just like anything else—the good things will last, and the things that they made mistakes on will go away. So you just have to ride it out."

Unlike many other stand-ups, Ellen never thought she would be a TV star. She thought she would end up the "best friend," Ethel or Rhoda instead of Lucy or Mary. She was self-critical enough that she didn't see how her laid-back style, low-key personality, and offbeat storytelling would translate to a weekly sitcom. And in movies, she hoped for supporting character roles.

"When I'm onstage and things have gone well, everybody is cheering, that's an ego stroke. But I don't need to be the center of things."

She used to joke that she was so not a leading actress type that casting directors never knew what to make of her when she came in. When she went on auditions, she commented, it was "usually more like me and Gary Coleman."

But behind the joking was the truth that Ellen did want to act and was willing to work her way up, knowing she was the antithesis of the traditional leading lady and certainly no sex symbol. "I've always been a person where there's some beautiful woman and all these guys hold the door open for her and I'm right behind her and they just keep walking and they just let the door close right on my face, I swear."

What Ellen did have going for her was the self-assurance that had come from appearing in front of hundreds of audiences. "The roles of stand-up comic and actress are alike in a lot of ways, but they're different in a lot of ways, too. To me, when I'm onstage, I'm acting. For me, it's not like someone like Steven Wright, who has that one note he plays the whole time, or a lot of other comics who have one personality that they display while onstage. I may do a lot of different attitudes in a performance, a lot of different portrayals. I may be the eye of the storm, or I may be looking into it from everybody else's perspective. They're different roles."

The sixties were when hallucinogenic drugs were really, really big. And I don't think it's a coincidence that we had the type of shows we had then, like The Flying Nun.

Ellen loves television and couldn't wait to be a part of it. "I watch probably too much TV. I'm fascinated by talk shows because I am just fascinated that there are people who will get on a panel like this and just share their sex lives and tortured lives with everybody. But I watch real things more than anything. I mean, it sounds stupid, but I really do try to watch PBS and the Discovery Channel and things like that."

Even so, Ellen refuses to jump on the television-bashing bandwagon. "I don't think sitcoms have an effect on society. I think films, maybe, because it's bigger than life, have more of an effect on society than a situation comedy."

However, sitcoms do have a monumental effect on television programmers, who seem to be unable to get enough of them on the air. Ellen knew that if she waited long enough, she would get her chance. It finally came in 1987, although the experience would sorely test her faith that she could find the appropriate vehicle for her brand of comedy on network television.

Her first regular series was *Open House,* a spin-off from the moderately successful series *Duet.* More accurately, it was a revamped version of *Duet,* which debuted April 19, 1987, and was on the air for two and a half years, until August 20, 1989. During that time, the series underwent a dramatic change of focus, and as a result was never able to find a voice.

In the beginning, *Duet* was intended to be a romantic comedy about two thirtysomething singles, Ben and Laura, played by Matthew Laurence and Mary Page Keller, who meet and fall in love. Ben, a mystery writer, and Laura, a caterer, have their relationship complicated by Ben's sister, Jane (Jodi Thelen), his best friend, Richard (Chris Lemmon), and Richard's wife, Linda (Alison LaPlaca). Eventually, Richard quits his job as a patio furniture salesman to be a cocktail pianist; Ben has his first novel published, and he and Laura get married.

When the series returned in 1988, time had been pushed ahead two years. Ben and Laura had just returned from a two-year honeymoon, and Richard and Linda suddenly had a toddler. However, Ben and Laura were now only secondary characters; the primary focus was on Richard and Linda. This was largely because of fan reaction to LaPlaca's edgy characterization of Linda, who was now a realtor. By *Duet*'s final episode of its summer run, Ben and his sister had been written out.

One week later, on August 27, 1989, *Open House* made its debut. This incarnation was set at the Juan Verde Real Estate company, and Mary Page Keller's character, Laura, was also now a realtor. By midseason, Richard had divorced Linda, diminishing Chris Lemmon's role to the point of nonexistence. The series was now a basic workplace comedy, with Linda trying to outsell and outmaneuver the equally pushy Ted Nichols (Philip Charles MacKenzie).

It was in this mix that Ellen got her first opportunity to act. She played Margo van Meter, the receptionist variously referred to as dotty, scatterbrained, fey, and wisecracking. Margo was a barely competent, man-hungry young woman who spent most of her time lusting after her boss, Roger McSwain, played by Jon Cypher in the first episode but replaced thereafter by Nick Tate.

"It was a tiny part, and I was just happy to get it," Ellen recalls. "I thought, 'Okay, I'll just learn. I'll get on the show and try to figure this whole thing out.' It was kind of a cult hit; it wasn't a big ratings success, but a lot of people watched it and the character I played was popular."

Whenever actors work on a series, they have to consider the possibility that they will be tied to the show for a minimum of five years if the show is a success. Some performers get hives at the thought of that kind of commitment, but Ellen didn't dwell on it.

"I probably would have enjoyed it," she said in retrospect. "It was my first experience; I enjoyed it and I had nothing to compare it to. It was just . . . I was playing this really ditzy, ridiculous character who had no grasp of reality, which is close to me, but there's still some intelligence that I would like to show."

To some critics, with the new premise and change of locale, *Open House* was an improvement over its predecessor. Richard Hack observed, "Director Dwayne Hickman uses his own background in comedy to blend physical humor with funny punch lines, making *Open House* another in Fox Broadcasting's collection of laugh-packed half-hours."

Variety was more muted in its assessment. "It's always tricky business to wrap a show around a character originally conceived for a supporting role. As much as LaPlaca's witch-princess dominated *Duet,* there seems to be a structural flaw to a show if it promotes such an antagonist to star status."

But the venerable trade publication singled out Ellen's contribution. "Helping to overcome that possible flaw is a solid supporting cast. . . . Ellen DeGeneres is a scatter-brained receptionist with a routine that may eventually catch on like Maxwell Smart's 'Would you believe . . . ?' bits."

New York Daily News critic Kay Gardella positively gushed: "For those who like the Fox style of comedy—out-spoken, direct and . . . abrasive—this series should be to your liking. It doesn't pretend to do much more than enter-tain, and that it does. The laughs come fast and furious. It should do better than *Duet.*"

So much for the prescience of critics. The series was can-celed before the first season played out, with the final episode airing in July 1990.

Ellen herself had been confident enough that while wait-ing for the pickup on *Open House* she bought her first home, a comfortable house located on Jewett Drive. Fortunately, though, she had a night job to fall back on once *Open House* was taken off the air.

Although the cancellation was a setback for her acting career, her stand-up career was as strong as ever, and soon HBO approached Ellen about doing her own special. This was further acknowledgment that she was now in the upper echelon of stand-up comics, a fact not lost on her.

"HBO has a half hour of me," she noted. "I can look at it and say, 'That's mine.' It's the same format as *One Night Stand* [another HBO comedy showcase], only that one was shot in Chicago in the snow and this was shot in Miami, where it was hot and humid. I guess that makes it a new ex-perience. It's new material, and I have new clothes."

And it won her new critical praise. Said one review: "For this forty-five minute performance, she seems to be working more with acting than joke telling. She explains what it means to recline in an airline seat by adjusting her posture a fraction of an inch. She performs most of a joke about singing along with the radio without making a sound."

At this stage of her career, Ellen began to be asked to lend her name to various causes. One that she agreed to participate in was a benefit for battered women that was aired as a Lifetime cable network special.

"It was a good cause," Ellen said afterward while describing the experience. "It was taped in an old theater. It was so hot, it looked like a Baptist church, with everyone fanning themselves. I chose to be the first one on, which is always rough. There are clips from different celebrities, like Delta Burke, saying, "I was raped . . . I was abused, and here's a number you can call instead of being so scared." It's a way to get people's attention."

One thing that caught Ellen's attention was her increasing awareness of how certain celebrities seemed to be special targets of the tabloid press. "Delta Burke was the sweetest person. I don't see them, but I hear she's in the tabloids all the time," she observed in the early 1990s. "You wonder what people need to do that for."

Talk about foreshadowing. But at the time, Ellen was pleased that she was forging a successful career without having to sacrifice all of her privacy. "It's a real good time for me," she told one interviewer. "I'm happy."

In 1991, DeGeneres, thirty-three, appeared in a Canadian-produced documentary called *Wisecracks,* which aimed its camera at the world of female stand-up comics. In what was beginning to be a trend, even though the movie was held up to some pointed criticism, Ellen was uniformly singled out as being one of the bright spots.

In a lengthy critique, the *Washington Post* noted: "*Wisecracks,* Gail Singer's stunning documentary about women stand-up comics, may be the funniest film you see all year. It's chock-full of jokes on subjects that male comics are less likely to address—abortion, periods, that single stubborn hair growing out of your breast—but which take on an almost revolutionary aura, a feel of personal revelation, when talked about by women."

The film struck a sour note for some critics, though, with its contention that stand-up comedy is an abyss of sexism, a world where females are held in check by both their male counterparts and the audience.

"Comedy is angry and aggressive and profane and, well, unladylike," the *Post* review noted. "As a result, audiences still have to get over their discomfort at having a woman make them laugh at themselves. 'The comment I hear all the time,' says Ellen DeGeneres, who does a hilarious bit about waiting for an elevator, 'is *I don't usually like female comics, but I like you.*'"

DeGeneres says she "never, ever" gave gender "a thought. I never thought about the fact that I'm a woman. I think I'm somewhat of a feminist in the sense that I believe women should be equal to men, and it's a ridiculous notion that somebody would think that we're not. But to me that's not being a feminist; it's being a humanist.

"I wanted to be a person who said funny things that everybody could relate to, and I didn't want to target a certain audience and say, 'Am I right, ladies? Back me up on this, ladies.' I don't even think of myself as a woman. I think of myself as a funny person who's onstage saying funny things. But I think there are men who are going to focus on male humor and there are going to be women who focus on things women relate to, and I never like to go to either side. I don't like extremes. I just like to talk about human nature."

Ellen points out that when she plays in theaters, "I have ten- and twelve-year-old kids who come see me that are fans, and I have grandmothers who are sixty and seventy in the audience, too. So I would like to think that I can appeal to everybody. What I'm doing is not like rocket science where some people are gonna go, 'I don't understand.' I really want everybody to get it. I would like to think that what I do is not typical stand-up comedy. I try to put something more into it."

That is how Charlene, who runs a popular lesbian bar in New Orleans, remembers Ellen's humor. "All of Ellen's comedy is from life experience. It's not gay or straight. It relates to everybody."

The *Post* reviewer felt *Wisecracks* failed at exactly that. "The movie's only problem is that, at times, the feminist militancy becomes whiny and strident. It's not exactly a life for the faint-hearted, and, occasionally, Singer and her stars appear to be lobbying for special treatment."

Newsweek deemed the documentary indulgent and misguided. "What the filmmaker and some of the female comics seem to miss is that funniness cures all social ills. The women who've developed good material and know how to deliver it don't seem to have the weight of the Western World on their shoulders. . . . Perhaps the sharpest comic of all, though, was Elaine Boosler, who declined to be in the film, saying that she didn't believe in labeling someone a woman comic. She's right. Funny and not funny: in comedy, those are the opposite sexes."

Ellen came away unscathed precisely because her comedy is rooted in observations that cross gender lines, so in her routines men are not the enemy. She doesn't use any particular group as the butt of jokes; the humor comes from just noticing the details of people and the world at large.

If imitation is truly the most sincere form of flattery, Ellen should have been delirious over discovering that her material was being "borrowed." Unwittingly, card-giant Hallmark had bought an idea from a writer that was an obvious rip-off of Ellen's joke about her grandmother walking five miles a day. "The guy changed it to his aunt walking, real subtle," she would later comment. Although Ellen says she never sued Hallmark, which she considers a duped victim, she does acknowledge that the company "started sending me money."

Although most documentaries are seen by relatively few people, Ellen was given a boost when her appearance in the film was given two thumbs-up. "It's a movie I'm hardly in, but after Siskel and Ebert talked about me, the phone started ringing," Ellen recalls.

But she wasn't willing to jump at the first offer that came in. She was earning plenty from stand-up and didn't want to appear in just anything for the sake of being on television. "I'm pretty picky," she said later, explaining that quality was more important to her than appealing to what she called "the lowest common denominator. I like taking you on the whole ride. There was a two-year break when I didn't work in television at all. Then I got a little tiny part on *Laurie Hill*."

Ellen was convinced that *Laurie Hill* was the vehicle that would put her in that driver's seat. (Ironically, after seeing the pilot, she went out and splurged on a Mercedes for herself.) The project was the brainchild of Carol Black and Neal Marlens, the married producing-writing team that had created the immensely successful *The Wonder Years* and the long-running *Growing Pains*. *Laurie Hill* was a mostly serious look at the life of working mother Dr. Laurie Hill, played by DeLane Matthews. In the series, Hill must juggle her career with her five-year-old son, Leo (Eric Lloyd), and her husband, Jeff (Robert Clohessy), a writer.

The series had been conceived out of Black and Marlens's personal tragedy of suffering the death of a child in the late 1980s. "When we lost a child," explained Marlens, "we tried to imagine what the lives of doctors who deal with this are like, how you face this all day and then go home and deal with your own child."

After several years of trying to get a green light for the show, Marlens and Black got a go-ahead from ABC. The show, produced by Disney Television, taped in Santa Monica, meaning Ellen had to commute an hour to work. "Now I know why people look forward to the weekends," she said dryly.

Once again Ellen found herself playing a supporting character, and once again it was a position she was comfortable assuming. "If it's your show, it's not just 'the show failed,' it's 'Ellen failed.'"

Even though she wasn't the lead, the hours were long—especially when compared to stand-up. While working clubs, Ellen could lounge all day, show up to the gig at night, go out for drinks at a local gay bar, then go home and sleep until noon. The schedule of a sitcom meant she had to be up early and was gone the bigger part of the day. "There's not even a spare minute to do anything."

On top of that, she was still performing stand-up. "I can work as much or as little as I want, and I try to jam everything in, but I still don't want to overbook myself," she said at the time.

When she joined the cast, Ellen assumed that her character would be at least as involved as Margo had been on *Open House,* but she kept waiting for that to happen. "Basically, I have the same amount of work as in the pilot—about two minutes. But if the show establishes itself, like what happened with *Open House,* they say they'll put the character in more. I've heard they're writing an entire episode about my character," she said in an interview.

The series debuted September 29, following *Roseanne,* then moved to its regular Wednesday 9:30 p.m. time slot, after *Home Improvement,* the following night. Because of Black and Marlens's pedigree as producers, much was expected of the series, so when it failed to live up to expectations, the critical response was harsh.

TV Guide dubbed the series "The Blunder Years," opining that nobody was going to want to watch a show about people who were as unhappy as the Hills. However, they also went on to say that Ellen, who played nurse Nancy MacIntyre, "provided desperately needed comic relief—and not enough of it."

Critic Benjamin Morrison had this to say: "*Laurie Hill* is a warm and fuzzy dramatic comedy series coming to ABC in a month. We can wait. There's nothing wrong with *Laurie Hill* so much as there isn't a whole lot there. It has a promising leading lady, a less promising leading man, and a good supporting cast that includes Ellen DeGeneres."

Variety failed to mention Ellen, too intent on dissecting the show. "Cloddish, cloying writing and the series' personality crisis take the joy out of Delane Matthews's smart performance as a working mother in this comedy-cum-drama, which winds up doing neither well. . . . There's little to laugh or cry at in *Laurie Hill,* despite its heavy-handed attempts to elicit both reactions."

Despite the critical skewering, the series actually was ranked twenty-second out of 102 shows, but after just five weeks it was canceled. Neal Marlens sounded bitter in an interview with *The New York Times*. "It came down to a network that didn't have a time slot. What we think of the show as a success or failure really has very little to do with why the show was canceled."

One factor that can lead to yanking a fairly high-rated show is the shows that surround it. Following *Home Improvement,* which would end up ranked number three for the year, ABC executives needed a show that would keep a high percentage of *Home Improvement*'s lead-in audience. *Laurie Hill* was losing too many people—to NBC's then-new *Mad About You*—and as a result, it was pulled off the schedule. However, Marlens and Black believed that ABC simply needed to squeeze in the Roseanne-produced Tom Arnold vehicle

The Jackie Thomas Show somewhere and that *Laurie Hill* was sacrificed.

TV Guide's Jeff Jarvis, who, it should be noted, was a huge fan of *The Wonder Years,* begged to differ. "Primarily, it was a show I didn't want to watch. It's whiny. The people are uncomfortable and unhappy with their lives."

So unhappy were Carol Black and Neal Marlens over *Laurie Hill* that they let it be known that once their contract with ABC for two more shows was fulfilled, they would reassess their involvement with television.

So unhappy was Ellen that she let her true feelings about the experience be known. "It was a show I took because it was Marlens and Black. I thought maybe they would see something in me and start writing for me, but the show was just about *Laurie Hill.* My friends were going, 'What are you doing, doing like two lines on a show? You should have your own show.' And I'm, 'Yeah, I should but I don't.' "

"I had so little to do it was ridiculous. I think in the pilot I had maybe two lines. I carried a folder. It was very frustrating to have a line like 'Bye-bye' for the entire show. Literally, that was one of my shows—I had 'Bye-bye' as a line. I was praying for it to get canceled. So I was kind of relieved that it didn't go."

The show's cancellation left Ellen 0 for 2. Despite her bitter disappointment, she chose to let go of the sour feelings and instead concentrate on what she did have. "I've got my own career to keep me going. Acting is just icing on the cake. I'm happy with the way my life and my career have progressed," she said at the time. "I'm definitely not sitting home crying. I have a home, I have dogs—the neighbors are already complaining. One old man is a grouch."

Even that wasn't enough to make her complain. "I like to be home. I've slowed down to a couple of club dates a week. I'd like to have a huge farm and rescue every dog I see, but that's down the line."

While having been on two failed series did nothing to raise Ellen's stock in the eyes of the networks, neither did it particularly hurt her, since she hadn't been the lead in either show. A few offers came in after *Laurie Hill*; some of the scripts simply weren't very good. Others offered roles that were obviously wrong for her.

For instance, in 1993, Ellen was under consideration for a lead role in a highly touted NBC series about a young divorcée from Minnesota who goes to Paris and gets a job at a popular bistro. Despite the buzz surrounding the project, called Café Americain, Ellen was less than enthused and was actually relieved when the role went to Valerie Bertinelli—especially after the show proved to be a major bomb.

Her early television experience had taught Ellen that she needed to find a project that let her shine, not another one that kept her in the comic shadows.

7
These Friends of Mine

Comedian Sinbad was a very successful stand-up and had started getting decent movie roles when he agreed to star in his own sitcom, *The Sinbad Show,* which premiered in the fall of 1993. When asked why he had taken the risk, Sinbad denied it had anything to do with greed or ego.

"We crave entertainment in America because man, when you got a bad job, you're living a bad life, and you're just bored, when you watch a show, well, it takes you to another place. I love TV," he said.

So do most people who make it their life's work. Thus, after licking their wounds and regrouping following the painful demise of *Laurie Hill,* Marlens and Black assessed their options and began to think of a new project. Despite the fact that Ellen had been associated with what turned out to be a very bleak experience for them, Carol and Neal were quite high on her. They felt she had an appealing personality and a persona that played well on television and with audiences. They were also keenly aware that the networks couldn't get enough stand-ups on the air fast enough. Many of these comics turned actors, such as Brett Butler, Roseanne, Paul Reiser, and Tim Allen, were becoming powerful TV stars.

"Stand-ups are taking over everything, aren't they?" Ellen asked. "If there were this many dry-cleaners, they'd be having shows, too."

Equally as important, Marlens and Black had a commitment from Disney's Touchstone television division to create a new series so the couple approached Ellen and asked what she thought about working with them again and about letting them develop a sitcom around her.

Ellen wasn't as excited and thrilled as some might have expected her to be, in part because she was worried about trying to fit herself into someone else's half-hour sitcom concept. She had a very clear vision of what she as a performer and her comedy were about and the kinds of situations that inspired it. Unlike many other stand-ups, Ellen never relied on other people to write jokes for her, and she wasn't sure how comfortable she would feel starring in a show with others writing her material.

Still, it was a chance to have a sitcom of her own, something she had always dreamed about but never thought would actually happen. And it wasn't as if other people were knocking her door down with acting offers. Her film work consisted of a thirty-second appearance in *Coneheads,* playing Connie Conehead's diving instructor.

The film's cowriter and coproducer, Bonnie Turner, who would later develop *3rd Rock from the Sun,* remembers Ellen as being very "patient and professional and that her job in the film was more actress than comedian. She was generous in that she knew the laugh was on Connie's splashless dive and that she was setting up the joke. This is a quality that is hard to come by in many comics."

The truth was, as able as Ellen was to set up others, the idea of having her own series was much more appealing. "I think acting is a natural progression from stand-up comedy, at least the kind of stand-up comedy that I do. But to be believable it's got to be a smooth transition."

Although she was still hesitant, Marlens and Black presented her with what sounded like a doable process. They agreed to let Ellen look over their shoulders as they worked and to allow her to contribute as much or as little as she wanted or was comfortable with as the project developed. While it was understood that the producers weren't obliged to incorporate her ideas, they both assured Ellen that if the finished script was not to her liking, she didn't have to shoot it. She wasn't driving the car, but she could apply the brakes if she wanted.

What Ellen was about to learn is that often in television collaboration, there tends to be much more compromising necessary than anyone ever imagines when they start out. The Standards and Practices people must approve every line of every script, and network executives add their input and request changes. Broadcast networks, as Ellen would later find out firsthand, are generally reluctant to address controversial issues. It took someone with Roseanne's formidable clout, which comes from having a top ten show for seven years running, including one year as television's number one comedy, to address birth control or have the "lesbian kiss" with Mariel Hemingway on her show. The very successful but occasionally risqué *NYPD Blue* was yanked by several affiliates because of content.

But the stars do get seduced by the excitement and ego boost of being the center of attention and at the thought of becoming a household name and face. Even well-intentioned comics like Ellen can and do get waylaid—in part by the money, which is considerable. A relatively unknown star of a new sitcom can make $35,000 an episode for the first season, which escalates quickly if the show is a hit, and add to that a share of the tens of millions of dollars a successful show can demand for syndication. For a stand-up, there's the additional bonus of going back on the road playing to sold-out houses, signing the inevitable movie deal, and setting up a production company to produce shows for other actors. A lot was at stake for Ellen.

Perhaps the most important element for any stand-up when they go into a sitcom is hooking up with the right producer. Drew Carey, who had experience in a failed series before hitting the big time with his own, says he saw that a big part of the problem with many troubled series was that the producer and comic were on two different planets, with no single vision. If the star doesn't click with his or her producer, the show is bound to have trouble.

Before any network buys a show, it will spend close to a million dollars to commission a single episode, called a pilot. This is how executives judge whether the idea for the show is viable and whether the necessary chemistry and potential are there. If a pilot starring Ellen turned out to be a bust, she would find it that much more difficult to get another pilot commissioned. So in the end, she had to decide whether or not Marlens and Black were the right producers for her. She also had to consider whether the *Laurie Hill* fiasco had tarnished the producers in the eyes of the networks, which might color their perception of her show.

In the end, Ellen told herself to just do it. She believed that if she worked closely with Carol and Neal and monitored every step of the process, there was no reason anything should go seriously wrong. And the same audience who embraced Candice Bergen as the vibrant and feisty Murphy Brown, Brett Butler's mellow mom in *Grace Under Fire,* and Roseanne's refreshing bluntness might also take a liking to sunshiny, well-meaning, and slightly off-center Ellen Morgan.

Ellen wanted to be on TV, so she told Marlens and Black she had decided to go forward. She told herself that if it were a total, embarrassing disaster, she could go back to stand-up, regroup, and try movies again or even write books like Rita Rudner and Woody Allen and the host of other comics turned writers.

Early in the spring of 1993, Ellen signed a deal with Black/Marlens Productions. She put all her reservations aside and looked forward with excitement to the prospect of brainstorming with Neal and Carol and developing a new show. Her show.

In September 1993, *TV Guide* referred to *These Friends of Mine* in its "Series in the Wings" column as "Seinfeld in skirts." The magazine described the show as "three female yuppies who complain about things like dates and driver's license photos. Oh, yes—to add the Elaine factor, there's also a guy on hand."

The comments were neither fair nor accurate. As Ellen later said, "On his show, Jerry is the more or less normal one and there are all these colorful characters around him. On my show, I'm the one who always trips."

The fact is, long before there even was a Seinfeld, and before they had Ellen under contract, Black and Marlens had had various ideas that would eventually comprise *These Friends of Mine.* Like all producers, Carol and Neal had files filled with notes and concepts. Among these were ideas about a single woman living with a platonic male friend, two young girlfriends with radically different personalities, and an eager-to-please noncareer woman who goes from job to job. However, they had put all those ideas back into the file in order to devote their energies to *Laurie Hill.*

As soon as they struck the deal with Ellen, Black and Marlens added David Rosenthal, who had also worked with them on *Laurie Hill,* to their creative team to help brainstorm and develop a series concept that would accommodate Ellen's talents. According to Rosenthal, there was a *Seinfeld* factor to Ellen's fledgling show. "*Seinfeld* enabled us to go to

ABC and say, 'We have a really talented comedian,' and we really didn't need any high-concept premise to make it work. She didn't need to run a corporation or host a talk show."

The process of coming up with a television show isn't as simple as fitting a comic into a concept. This is especially true where women are concerned. Pat Richardson, who co-starred in *Home Improvement,* says there's a problem all women face when they go into television: breaking free of stereotypes.

"I and so many actresses feel so angry in so many ways about the way things have been going down on TV. I think that television is incredibly powerful and influential, and drama and comedy can both offer a potent examination of masculinism and feminism. But it can't be one running roughshod over the other or crashing into it and getting no-where the way it was on *Married . . . With Children,* where she's a total bitch and he's a complete idiot. Both people have to have a valid point of view.

"The problem is, when women try to be serious on TV comedy, like *Murphy Brown* and *Roseanne* did, women tend to love it while men, including critics, just say they're being crabby, not serious."

Her costar, Tim Allen, agrees. "Of course men and women relate differently to TV. They watch differently. Women are looking to connect, for relationships and stories. Men are just looking for explosions, car chases, fire, and breasts. Instant thrills. I'm not a sociologist, and I don't know when and if that'll ever change."

It was within this environment that Black, Marlens, and Rosenthal were working when trying to devise the perfect vehicle for Ellen. The creative trio had no intention of breaking new ground, which is why they decided against one of the first ideas that came up in their brainstorming—to have Ellen Morgan be a lesbian. The idea was quickly dismissed, reveals an ex-staffer.

"We thought (a) we wanted to make this show about a very funny woman. We didn't want to make her sexuality an issue. And (b) we thought it would be an impossible row to hoe with the network."

What they wanted most of all was to have a hit series after the debacle of *Laurie Hill.* They wanted to go for laughs the same way Ellen did onstage—with wry observations rather than deep social commentary.

They knew they had to start with the typical sitcom "home base"—that is, they needed to give Ellen someone to continually talk to and play off of. At the same time, they had to keep up a steady flow of new characters to trigger what they described, in one early summary of the show, as Ellen's "humorous musings that celebrate the mundane moments of life—with a twist." Hopefully, what they'd come up with would be a lot funnier than it read on paper.

One of the first ideas they considered was something along the lines of *The Mary Tyler Moore Show,* with Ellen living alone and hanging out with a sympathetic but quirky Rhoda-esque girlfriend. The neighbor evolved into the character of Holly, who they decided would be a friend of Ellen's from high school. That would give the writers someone who could remind Ellen of some bonehead things she'd done in the past.

The concept of living alone didn't seem quite cutting-edge enough, though. Nor did they like the idea of Holly moving in with Ellen. That was too much like *Laverne and Shirley,* and besides, it just wasn't Ellen. The idea of having a male best friend as a roommate was fresher and much more appealing, especially if the two were completely platonic. Without sexual tension and flirtation, the differences between men and women could be explored in a more honest and, they hoped, funnier way. The roommate, named Adam, would end up taking more ribbing from Ellen than he doled out.

The reason they named her TV character Ellen was simple, explains DeGeneres. "The first week they called me Cindy and I wouldn't turn around."

Even though they had their quirks, as conceived, Adam, Holly, and Ellen were all relatively sane, so the creative brain trust added the loose cannon, a wild friend dubbed Anita who was meant to supply occasionally outrageous behavior. Once the main characters were set, next came trying to figure out what kind of job Ellen should have. After rejecting several, including a complaint department clerk and a travel agent, the idea of a coffee shop setting was floated. Not a diner, as in *Seinfeld,* but something more upscale, like an espresso bar.

The creators felt that such a setting was conducive to a strong ensemble show, like *Cheers*—only with caffeine instead of alcohol. (Ironically, as so often happens in that weird Hollywood zeitgeist, producers David Crane and Marta Kaufman would use that exact setting in another series that also debuted in 1994—*Friends,* a series that Ellen had passed on.) The "friends" would hang out there, and Ellen could play a role like either Ted Danson or Kirstie Alley had on *Cheers.*

That was the problem. The whole idea sounded too much like *Cheers,* so the creators altered the setting to be a combination bookstore and coffee bar where Ellen would work. That would not only give her the steady stream of new faces to use as a comedy source, but she could comment on trendy new book titles, work on creating unusual displays, and play off her boss, Susan, and a coworker—named, of course, Joe—who manned the coffee bar. Susan would be endlessly cranky, Joe a bit of an airhead.

Now came an extremely important but often overlooked part of the process: naming the show. The first two titles that came to mind were "The Ellen DeGeneres Show" and "Ellen." However, the producers wanted to emphasize the ensemble nature of the series, so they went with *These Friends of Mine.*

At first, it wasn't a decision with which Ellen agreed. She believed that the audience would relate to a person—as in *Roseanne* and *Seinfeld*—better than they would to a concept. " 'Ellen's World' is good," she quipped helpfully. "I've asked people all over the place if they liked the title *These Friends of Mine,* and a lot of people don't like it," herself included. "I'd like to think of something other than that, because it is kind of long."

After *Laurie Hill,* though, Black and Marlens were gun-shy about using names as titles and wanted to be as clear as possible about what the show was about. Besides, *The Wonder Years* had been an enduring hit for them, and at the time *Home Improvement* was the biggest comedy on television. So over Ellen's objections *These Friends of Mine* stayed, although she made it a point to say, "There's a possibility that it will change."

Once everyone had more or less agreed on the title, key character elements and setup, Black, Marlens, and Rosenthal wrote a script, with Ellen's direct input. When it was finished, Ellen read it. Her initial response was positive, so she read through it again. One of the keys to judging comedy is if you start to laugh anticipating a joke you've already heard.

Ellen laughed. And once she had a chance to absorb the material, she began to have strong, positive feelings about the show. "I was laughing out loud when I read the script. I knew what I could do with it."

Ellen was struck right away with how the three writers had captured perfectly what it was like "being single and trying to figure out things in life the hard way." She also liked that Ellen Morgan was at the stage "in between. You've just finished with the cinder-block and plank bookshelves but you're not married yet."

And she told the *New York Post,* "Ellen is this person

who's desperate to make everyone happy. Unfortunately, when she does that, she ends up putting her foot in her mouth."

In that, Ellen saw tons of comic potential, so she called the producers and told them she would be thrilled to do the show. Once she was aboard, the script was sent to Disney and ABC, and in short order both the studio and the network had given the project a green light. By late winter of 1993, the creative team was deep into preparations for filming the half hour pilot.

At that stage, Ellen was comfortable about the series being written by others because the basis for the show was going to be "how I look at life. So it's my take at the super-market behind someone with way too many items to be in the express lane. It's just about life, stuff we can all relate to but with my spin on it, which usually means it spins way out of control."

One thing Ellen wanted everyone to understand was that what she was going to do on the show was indeed acting. She wasn't just going to get in front of the camera and be Ellen DeGeneres.

"I think the character I play is a lot more naive and a little more gullible than I am. I put my foot in my mouth some-times and realize, 'Oh, man, that was the wrong thing to say' and try to backpedal out of it. But the character I play is con-stantly doing that. She's self-conscious, but at the same time she'll do anything. She's a goon, but yet, there's an intelli-gence behind this gooniness. She tries so hard, but she's al-ways getting into trouble. And I would like to think my life's not like that. But this is something that's going to be a weekly thing, so I wanted to play someone who was close to what I created for all those years as a stand-up."

She was also pleasantly surprised to discover that being a series lead instead of a supporting player was easier than she had thought it would be. "It's actually a lot easier because it was created for me, so it's me playing things that are closer to me. The first show I did, *Open House,* I was playing a character that was so far from me that I felt like it was cartoonish, it was such a character. And then the next show I did, *Laurie Hill,* I carried a folder, so. . . .

"But they write so well for me that it's not scary at all. I think it'd be scary if I had people who were handing me scripts that I was just going, 'Oh, my God, this is not me. This is Nell Carter.' Not that there's anything that's wrong with Nell, I love Nell, but. . . ."

As for *These Friends of Mine* itself, Ellen said, "It's a little like *I Love Lucy.* A smarter, hipper version of *I Love Lucy.* But it won't go so far that I'm in a man's suit with a mustache trying to fool Ricky that I'm not his wife."

Ellen wasn't comparing herself to the legendary Lucille Ball or saying that her show would be the next *I Love Lucy.* Her point was, she wanted to do a show that was funny but at the same time stayed true to the kinds of things viewers might be thinking, facing, and feeling, just as her stand-up routine had done. She wanted a show that, as she put it, "everybody talks about the next day."

One of the biggest unanswered questions was whether Ellen could make the transition from brilliant stand-up to sitcom lead. Comics who do characters, like Richard Pryor, Billy Crystal, or Robin Williams, usually have an easier time making the switch. Stand-ups who are, for all intents and purposes, themselves onstage, as could be said of Roseanne or Richard Lewis, find it harder to portray anyone else.

Series veteran Annie Potts notes, "Playing someone that is too close to themselves, or only playing one kind of role, is risky. Anytime someone imagines that an actor and the role are the same, the actor has been issued a death sentence. Because then people want to see you like that all the time, and who wants to be anything all the time?"

If her pilot was going to succeed, Ellen had to overcome

that hurdle—and others, such as working with a studio audience. Unlike a club audience, people watching a taping are in a grandstand far removed from the set, behind the cameras and hanging television monitors, which cuts them off from the actors on the set. This makes what Ellen refers to as the "immediate gratification" of the audience difficult, and when a scene has to be redone several times, the audience may stop laughing at jokes that might not have been all that funny to begin with.

Also, comics who perform their acts on television occasionally look directly at the camera as if it's part of the audience, usually when delivering a punch line. But in story-based television, the camera is behind what is called "the fourth wall" of the set and is supposed to be ignored.

Then there's the adjustment of having to work with other people after spending years commanding sole attention on a stage. Sharing the spotlight with an ensemble is always a challenge, even for trained actors, and it would prove difficult for Ellen as well.

Perhaps the hardest part of moving from the club stage to the sound stage, though, is having to say words written by others. As Ellen notes, "There are many voices involved—from the producers to the studio to the network. With my stand-up, it's me onstage, saying things that I wrote. It's exactly what I want to say." In truth, there were a couple of things in the pilot that Ellen would have never written and that made her slightly uncomfortable. But she trusted that Marlens and Black knew what they were doing.

Despite all the challenges facing Ellen, shooting the pilot went as smoothly as anyone could have hoped for. Neal Marlens was going to direct the show himself, which helped alleviate some of Ellen's jitters. On the first day of the shooting week, the cast met for a read-through of the script, going over lines on the set with the writers, who were there to make whatever changes were necessary. Over the next few days, in what are called blocking rehearsals, the actors' and cameras' movements were worked out; white tape x's were placed on the floor so the actors could "hit their marks." During those days, the actors started working without scripts as they memorized their dialogue. Unlike talk shows, where the monologues are put on cue cards, in sitcoms the actors have to memorize—and then forget—over twenty scripts every season.

Everyone except Ellen had plenty of experience doing that. Holly Fulger, who was cast as Holly, came to the pilot fresh off her stint as Hollis Amato on *thirtysomething*. She had also appeared as Jamie Lee Curtis's ditzy friend Robin Dulitski on *Anything but Love,* Myke Blackman on Sable, Carol Greene on *Jack and Mike,* and Carolyn on the now-you-see-it, now-you-don't series *Doctor, Doctor,* which was aired in four different installments between June 1989 and July 1991.

Arye (pronounced "Ari") Gross had made his film screen debut in the little-remembered action flick *Exterminator II.* From that inauspicious beginning, he went on to appear in a number of films, including *Just One of the Guys, Soul Man, House II: The Second Story, The Couch Trip, A Matter of Degrees, Coupe De Ville, For the Boys, Boris and Natasha,* and *Tequila Sunrise.* Despite all of his movie experience, *These Friends of Mine* was Gross's first series.

Although Ellen had no hand in the casting, she says she was pleased with the actors chosen. "We had great chemistry and just clicked. As soon as they were cast I called up and asked them to go to lunch, and we just really liked each other. . . . We became friends pretty fast, and I think that's evident in the pilot."

While the camaraderie was comforting, it couldn't alleviate Ellen's anxiety. And not only was Ellen nervous, her mom was just as anxious that everything go well for her daughter. Betty visited the set now and then to provide whatever moral support she could. Thanks to that, plus her very giving costars, who offered professional support, and the producers, who were making it a point to do a lot of "hand-holding," Ellen felt comfortable and positive.

The pilot taped over two days, April 15–16, 1993. It delivered exactly what the producers wanted it to, which was to introduce the core characters, the "friends," and show off Ellen's style of humor and her appealing persona. Marlens directed a show that was intended to be entertaining and endearing, with just enough daring so that viewers, and the network, would want to come back a second time.

Left out of the pilot were the bookstore, Susan, and Joe. Subsequently, Susan would be played by Christine Rose; David Higgins, previously a member of the comedy troupe Higgins Boys and Gruber, had been cast as her coworker Joe Farrell. The pilot instead concentrated on Ellen and her platonic roommate, Adam—who tells a Spanish-speaking date in one episode, "We just live together. No está intercourse"—and their friends Anita (Maggie Wheeler) and Holly.

The pilot opens with Ellen and Holly in line at the Department of Motor Vehicles. Ellen is debating whether to smile or look serious for her driver's license photo; neither facial expression seems very appealing. Holly realizes she knows the man behind them, having met him at the Lost and Found at the bank. Holly, always looking for a date, and the man, Roger, arrange to meet. Meanwhile, Ellen tries to pose nicely, until the photographer makes her angry.

As soon as she starts to yell, he snaps the picture. Ellen looks like the Wicked Witch of the West.

Later, back at Ellen's apartment, Anita gives Ellen the lowdown on Roger, which she got from a mutual friend named Steve. The good news is, Roger is an attorney; the bad news is, he "barks like Arsenio Hall during intercourse."

Ellen sags upon hearing this choice tidbit. "It's good that I know this because now, if she marries him and spends the rest of her life with him, I'm going to have to think about this every time they come over for a barbecue."

In the following scene, Holly announces that her date—or, as Ellen labeled it, her "major intergender ordeal"—was a success. But Ellen is busy dealing with her own trauma. After seeing her driver's license picture, she calls and makes another appointment so she can have a new one taken. This time she shows up in full makeup, hair coiffed, dressed to the nines. She steps in front of the camera and smiles—and smiles and smiles.

The photographer is busy talking on the phone to his wife about potty-training their toddler. Just as Ellen loses her patience and starts to complain, the photographer snaps the picture. This one is worse than the last.

Later, at home, she rips both licenses up, telling Adam, "I'm into this for seventy bucks, I might as well go till I get it right."

Suddenly a more pressing matter comes up. Anita has learned through Steve that Roger is planning to sleep with Holly, then dump her after the deed is done.

"Men!" Ellen says to Adam. "Men are scum."

Hoping to spare Holly this humiliation, the three friends jump into the car. First, though, Ellen leaves a message on Holly's answering machine about Roger's plans, calling him a "lying, sneaky, slimy, son of a slug."

As Ellen's luck would have it, on the way to Holly's, she's pulled over for speeding. Because she doesn't have a license, having torn two of them up, she also gets a ticket for driving without one.

When they finally arrive, they hear a "wuf, wuf, wuf" sound coming from Holly's house and realize they are too late. "Maybe they're just watching Arsenio," offers Adam, who, along with the other two, is hiding outside the front-room window.

They are still there when Holly and Roger come out of

the bedroom, so they hear Roger admit that although he was going to dump her after tonight, he now realizes he's in love with her and never wants to leave her. Just then, Holly sees the light on her message machine blinking.

Realizing what's on it, Ellen springs into action. She frantically rings the doorbell, desperate to prevent Holly from listening to the message, especially with Roger standing right there. When a surprised Holly answers the door, Ellen says they all came to borrow . . . the answering machine. When she tries to get it, Holly stops her, and as they struggle over it, the message plays.

"This is certainly awkward," Ellen says sheepishly.

Holly throws Roger out for having blabbed to Steve about everything. After he's gone, she admits to the others that she's not upset, because she had intended to dump him that night anyway. She just wanted to sleep with him first.

"Women!" says Adam with disgust. "Women are scum!"

After the pilot was edited, everyone at Touchstone believed it was a keeper. *These Friends of Mine* suddenly had that all-important commodity, a positive "buzz." ABC's executives were even more enthused and kept the buzz alive by giving the producers the go-ahead to shoot six more episodes, (a typical order for a series planned for use as a midseason replacement). The network also gave them a green light to write six additional scripts, for a total of thirteen episodes counting the pilot.

When ABC's order was received, there were hugs and backslapping all around the Black/Marlens office. While Ellen was also happy, her elation was tempered by her awareness that there was an awful lot of work to do. And while she was glad to hear that the studio and the network liked the pilot, she was more concerned with how the television public would receive her show. From the start, Ellen insisted that it was the audience—not her, not the producers, and not the network—who would control the series.

"We're always thinking of our viewers," Ellen would say. "Whatever they want to see, we'll give it to them. If they want to see Arye in a monkey suit, so it shall be. If they want to see Holly naked so we can compete with *NYPD Blue*—whatever."

That, of course, was Ellen's tongue-in-cheek official party line for the press. The reality, although she didn't know it at the time, was that once the show took off, there was going to be only one person calling the shots—especially after she learned that the pilot episode wasn't going to air quite the way it had been filmed. Ellen was annoyed with some of the changes, but not enough to make a stink. Yet.

After the episode was in the can, the theme music underwent a change. The visuals for the opening sequence—the four friends strolling in the wide open spaces, playing footsie in a kiddie pool, and then sitting on a sofa to watch TV (still in some remote wilderness)—were New Age enough without the vocals on the soundtrack. Those were replaced with good old safe instrumentals.

There were trims here and there, most notably a reduction of the number of wufs guest star William Bumiller barks during the sex scene. It's inconceivable that edits like these still go on in these cable-wired, post–*NYPD Blue* days, but they do; as *TV Guide* correctly observed, "Apparently, they—the censors—know just how many barks it takes to offend America."

Actually, Ellen herself wasn't too happy with the barking aspect of the show. "In my stand-up," she said, "I do an hour and a half or two of clean comedy. Because the show was created around me and because in essence I'm playing myself, I'm really sensitive to things like that. I don't do anything that offends anyone, and I certainly don't want to do a show that offends anyone, either.

"It's not that I'm offended by the guy barking, but it certainly isn't something I would have written. It's just not me.

I know my dad was uncomfortable with it. My dad is very religious, and I think he kind of represents the TV viewers. And I think he was uncomfortable with it, and I'm sure that there are some people who will be uncomfortable with it."

The hint of future troubles began to emerge because of just that aspect of the show. At the 1994 winter Television Critics Press Tour, a twice-yearly hoopla when the networks' stars and shows are introduced to TV columnists and critics, Ellen was visibly uncomfortable being put in the position of having to defend the barker. At a press conference, she repeatedly tried to joke her way out of the questions, but the reporters wouldn't let her off the hook.

"Compared to a lot of stuff that's on TV, it's very tame, you know, but I don't know if that's an area that we are going to keep exploring, people barking and whatever they do when they have sex. That's just what happened to be in the pilot. But I certainly don't want to keep going in that direction."

She was also concerned that the storyline might drive away some of her longtime fans. "They keep asking, 'Why were you clean for so long and now you're doing this?' I don't want people to think I'm suddenly doing something else or changing because I'm on TV. The thing is, I was totally out of the loop. I wish I were as powerful as Roseanne and knew everything that was going on and had a part of everything, but I'm certainly not that powerful."

But she would be.

8
Thirty Million Fans

Originally, *These Friends of Mine* was supposed to debut in the fall of 1993. However, sensing that they had a hit on their hands, ABC executives wanted to position it in the coveted post–*Home Improvement* time slot to ensure that viewers would tune in. Unfortunately, they also wanted to put another show in that slot: the new *Grace Under Fire*, a half-hour sitcom starring another woman stand-up, Brett Butler, as a single mom who works at an oil refinery. Produced by the people who made *Roseanne*—Carsey-Warner Productions—and who wield considerable clout around the network, *Grace Under Fire* won out. It became the highest-rated new show of the season, and Ellen was forced to cool her heels for six months, until *Grace Under Fire* went on hiatus and her show could be slotted.

Ellen weathered the wait as well as she could. As "executive consultant" for her show (a rather euphemistic title meaning that she wasn't writing the stories or producing the show but still carried a lot of weight on both fronts), she huddled with the writers and producers to make sure that the scripts were as good as could be. It was still a difficult experience.

"It's shooting in a vacuum. You have these audiences who are bused in—whoever we can get, whoever is on the street at the time. It's hard to get an audience when they don't know what the show is about yet," Ellen said while the six episodes ABC had ordered were being filmed.

She also worried about her fans. "People in the business know I have something going on. But to those who don't know what's going on, it's like, 'We haven't seen Ellen on TV for a year, maybe she's not doing well. Maybe something is wrong.'"

The debut of the show was finally scheduled for March 1994. Shortly before *These Friends of Mine* first aired, Ellen told reporters that she was confident the show would be a hit.

"I have grandmothers who come to my comedy shows, and I think they are going to watch my TV show," she joked with *Esquire* magazine. "Anyway," she added, "they've told me they will."

She also suggested some headlines for reporters to use with their reviews. "The first is, 'It's the best new show on TV. I've never laughed so hard in my entire life. Soon you'll be calling them These Friends of Yours.'"

In a somewhat more serious vein, she told *Entertainment Weekly* magazine, "I don't know why, but whenever I've had this gut feeling, I've always been right." She added for good measure, "Now if this is printed and I fail miserably, I'll be embarrassed." (She would add that her gut only works where her career is concerned: "I'm not like this in Las Vegas," where she loses a bundle playing cards whenever she's booked at one of the hotels.)

Feeling even more confident as the debut drew near, she went so far as to confess to *The New York Times,* "I told my friends it would be the number three show." Why not number one? Ellen didn't say, but she probably felt that it would have been just a little presumptuous to suggest that she could beat *Roseanne* and *Home Improvement*.

Early in 1994, a smiling, buoyant Ellen DeGeneres is showing television reporters around the set of her new show, which is being filmed at Sony Pictures Studio in Culver City. Formerly the Metro-Goldwyn-Mayer Studio, once the home of Elizabeth Taylor, Gene Kelly, Mickey Rooney, Judy Garland, Fred Astaire, and *Gone With the Wind,* the lot would now be home for *These Friends of Mine*.

One of the crewmen, an old-timer standing by a doughnut-and-coffee cart, tells a reporter, "We've got a street named after Stallone here, which seems a little ridiculous, but at least he's in movies. If you'd told someone back in the 1950s that the biggest shot at the studio would be a comedian who's got a television show and dresses in sneakers, jeans, and sweatshirts, no one would've believed it."

"Shit," says another crewman standing nearby. "Lucille Ball had to build her own studio [Desilu] to get things done the way she wanted. And even then, her name came second, after Desi's." But in this day and age, more people would see Ellen DeGeneres every week than ever saw Liz or Judy or even Stallone in movie theaters. Such is the powerful medium known as television.

There are several standing sets for the show. (Standing sets are those that are never taken down during the season while a show is in production. After the season, the props are carefully stored, and the flats that make up the walls are pulled down and stacked so the sound stage can be used to shoot feature films.)

Leading the reporters on their tour, Ellen walks through the apartment set, the kind of combination living, dining room, and kitchen endemic in sitcoms. She is particularly pleased with the decoration: "People love to see puppies and kids, so I have photos of them all around my apartment."

As they are for all sitcoms, the different sets have been built wall to wall in a row. This saves space as well as time because the cameras simply roll from one set to the other. In addition to the apartment, the show's standing sets include the Buy the Book bookstore and coffee bar where Ellen Morgan works, and her boss's office.

The sets are built in front of a long grandstand, which can accommodate approximately two hundred audience members. (Tickets to sitcom tapings are free, but after *These Friends of Mine* premiered to raves, tickets suddenly became very difficult to obtain. Even network executives and friends and family of the crew—all of whom would normally be seated in the first row—suddenly had a tough time getting seats at all.)

In sitcom studios, the three cameras, which film the show from different angles, are situated between the set and the grandstand. The actors know which camera is filming by looking for whichever one has a glowing red light on top. Because the cameras often block the audience's view, large monitors hang in front of the grandstand so the audience can watch the scene that is being filmed.

Ellen leads her group into the green room, which is located behind the set. There stars and their guests can relax and have a quick meal prior to the taping. For Ellen, that meal is a salad, with no croutons, and either iced tea or water. From time to time, she pops open a bottle of Veryfine juice (a drink for which she was a spokeswoman at the time).

"You know, when you're on television in any capacity you're offered a lot of money to do a lot of different things. I had been offered commercials before, but I turned them down because I didn't believe in the product for whatever reason. But the Veryfine people allowed me to do what I wanted on those commercials and kind of write them myself."

(As proof that Ellen was a lot more business-savvy than

she usually let on, it had been written into her contract that if her series were in the top ten, she would get a huge bonus. It did, and the juice company backed a Brink's truck up to her house. "My manager's a smart man," she said.)

Among the cast and crew, Ellen quickly became known for her energy. "She seems to store it," noted one staffer. "She'll be real quiet for a while, then get incredibly active, revving from zero to sixty in a heartbeat. It's amazing the way she does that."

For the cast of *These Friends of Mine,* the green room would also be virtually the only place where the actors socialized. It's not uncommon for costars to shy away from socializing outside the workplace. As *Home Improvement*'s Pat Richardson notes, "A successful show is like a marriage: You'll be working together for many, many years, so you have to treat your relationship with respect and caution. You don't want to find out if the old saying about familiarity breeding contempt is true. The worst thing that can happen is that you start hating one another for some reason. You just don't want to risk blowing the on-screen chemistry you have."

Ellen's next stop is the makeup area. The makeup chair is one of her least favorite places to be, and she comments that she never wears makeup off-camera. Her attitude can be summed up by an observation made by fellow comic Cathy Ladman: "Makeup is such a weird concept. I'll wake up in the morning and look in the mirror: 'Gee, I really don't look so good. Maybe if my eyelids were blue I'd be more attractive.'"

Ellen, in fact, has commented more than once that "I really don't like the way I look." She doesn't like the shape of her nose or her hangdog eyes or her posture and describes her facial features as "too rubberized." But on this day, she looks positively radiant.

On hand to help woo the press is Betty, who is not shy in

front of a camera. When Ellen asks her mom if she thinks people should watch the show, Betty flashes the camera a big smile. "Oh, puh-lease," she implores viewers. "You won't want to miss it. It's going to be so funny. It's wonderful, just great."

"That's right," Ellen says, then looks from her mom to the camera. "She wants a condo."

Not far from the set is Ellen's dressing room. On the door is her name, but instead of the traditional star underneath it, Ellen has put a sunflower decal. This will be her sanctuary during the coming weeks. A place to relax and a place where she can have solitude while memorizing the weekly scripts, which run over fifty pages and are rewritten constantly up to the day of filming.

Unlike the plush motor homes movie stars are given while filming, television stars' dressing rooms tend to be more modest, in part because the occupants don't spend all that much time in them. Most of the actors' workweek is spent on the set, blocking and rehearsing. Doing a sitcom is much closer to doing a mini-play every week than to making a movie.

The walls of Ellen's dressing room are a bland yellow. There's a white sofa on one side and a wooden chair opposite it, a lacquered table, a dresser, and a standing lamp. When *Entertainment Tonight* comes for a visit, they find pinup posters of the show's hosts: John Tesh, Mary Hart, and Leeza Gibbons. Ellen couldn't find a poster of *ET*'s respected movie critic, Leonard Maltin, so she's drawn a picture of him in Magic Marker and taped it to her dressing-room door.

While the *ET* cameras roll, John Tesh's *A Romantic Christmas* CD plays in the background. Ellen assures viewers that she is wearing her *Entertainment Tonight* underwear. But the centerpiece of her homage is the top of her dresser, which has been turned into a mini-*ET* shrine with burning candles in front of small framed photos of the show's three hosts. Ellen kneels down in front of her "altar" and prays to the *Entertainment Tonight* gods that her show will be a success.

The point of all these shenanigans is more than a simple stab at humor. While giving the *ET* people terrific sound bites for their show, Ellen is also making it clear that she sees the whole process as a bit absurd. But she manages to play the promotion game in such a way as to stay true to herself.

When one of the *Entertainment Tonight* reporters comments that Ellen is being called the Mary Tyler Moore of the nineties, she counters by saying that actually she's the female Shaquille O'Neal. "It's flattering. So long as I'm not compared to *McHale's Navy* or *F-Troop,* I don't mind. I think what took me so long to get on the air in the first place is that I don't fit into the housewife role. And I don't feel like somebody's mom, and I think people would worry for the children if I were. I'm a single woman and wanted to play a single woman. So they finally figured out, 'Hey, why don't you just hang out with friends?' *These Friends of Mine* is about my obscure take on life."

Then someone else notes that *These Friends of Mine* is being compared to *Seinfeld.* Ellen simply shrugs. "It's closer to *Seinfeld* than it is to *Bonanza.*"

ABC decided to try something unusual with the show, both to give it a one-two punch and to see how it would perform in two different time slots. After pulling *Grace Under Fire* temporarily to provide a berth for it, they scheduled the first episodes to air on two successive nights: March 29, where it would follow *Roseanne* in the lineup, and March 30, where it would air after *Home Improvement.*

The network promoted *These Friends of Mine* extensively. During the week before the debut, it was virtually impossible to turn on an ABC program and not see a plug for the show. Of course, that really put the pressure on: if she bombed after all the hoopla, in those two plum spots, the two most coveted time slots on television, she would be washed up on TV.

She joked that to ensure ratings, "if I have to hurt somebody to get a controversial thing going, it doesn't matter. Because now I see that gets ratings. I'm thinking of kissing an animal of some sort, because that's never been done."

Ellen was nervous but excited. Fortunately, they were in the midst of shooting the first batch of six episodes for the show, so she had the work to keep her busy. But it was difficult to concentrate. Ellen had always liked putting her talent on the line, and this was high-stakes poker indeed. She tried to temper the enormity of it all by not weighing herself down with too much self-imposed pressure.

"Whenever there's an opportunity, there's a risk involved. A lot is resting on me, but it's not like it's just me onstage. There are a lot of other actors who are involved. There are producers involved. There are networks and studios. There are so many people making decisions, it isn't all on my shoulders." Plus, Ellen hadn't quit her night job. "The good thing about what I do is that I have my stand-up to go back to."

More than just her reputation and ego were at stake. In the few weeks she'd been working on the lot, she'd grown to love the studio environment. Who wouldn't? It's Disneyland, it's a living museum of movie history, it's glamour, it's wealth and fame, it's a daily creative outlet. And it was different from *Open House* and *Laurie Hill,* where she had a tiny trailer for a dressing room and little contact with the movers and shakers.

More than when she first started on *These Friends of Mine,* she wanted to keep it. And overnight, with just this roll of the dice, she could lose it all or it could be hers for years to come. As it was, Ellen felt as if she were fighting the fates. In January 1994, while *These Friends of Mine* was in the middle of shooting, Los Angeles was devastated by a major earthquake.

"I thought, 'You know what? I finally get my chance and we're all gonna die.' I really could have cared less the world was blowing up. It was more that my show would never get on the air."

Then, two weeks later, Ellen developed a medical problem that forced production to close down again. The day before her thirty-sixth birthday, Ellen was on the set working when she doubled over. "My stomach suddenly felt as if it were full of battery acid. I drove home, screaming in pain."

Even though she's no longer a practicing Christian Scientist, because of that upbringing it didn't occur to Ellen to just drive herself to a hospital. She called her manager, and he got her admitted to Cedars-Sinai (where, coincidentally, her mother worked as a speech pathologist).

Eventually, the doctors discovered the cause of her pain. "A cyst the size of a golf ball on my ovary," explains Ellen. "I didn't know what that meant until I learned your ovary is the size of a grape."

She was soon back on the set, and as the cast and crew filmed the episodes, they all kept one eye on the calendar. The premiere date was approaching.

That Tuesday, March 29, was nervewracking. It seemed as though early evening would never come: 6:30 p.m. Pacific Time, 9:30 p.m. Eastern, when the show would debut. She half-jokingly asked someone on the lot to explain to her again why they couldn't get the ratings at 10:01 p.m. Wasn't all this stuff computerized? How come a computer could be so fast that if you made a phone call from your hotel room and then rushed to check out, the call would be right there on your bill—yet they couldn't do simple addition and tell her right away how many people had just watched her show?

They just couldn't, she was told. Network executives had to wait until around 8:00 a.m. Eastern for the "overnights."

Okay, Ellen figured. At least if she couldn't sleep, she knew just where she'd be at 5:00 a.m. Pacific Time: on the phone to New York.

Though the wait was agony—even though she was unable to sleep—the results were worth it. Ellen didn't have to eat her words. Not exactly, anyway. *These Friends of Mine* was a smash on its debut night, landing at the top of the ratings, though only in the number seven position.

Typically, instead of freeing her to celebrate, the good news only served to raise more questions in Ellen's mind. Was that good enough? Were the demographics close to what the network wanted? Was the studio happy? Would C-Span have scored in that time slot just because it came after *Roseanne*?

The second overnights erased all her fears. The show scored even higher; it landed in the number three position, to be exact. Even more encouraging was research conducted by ABC showing that *These Friends of Mine* wasn't just a one-night hit due to "sampling"—that is, viewers tuning in to see what the heavily promoted show was about. The samplers enjoyed what they saw enormously; a large number of viewers said they intended to watch the show again wherever it turned up.

Ellen had her hit. And that's when the trouble began.

Ellen's comedy had never been as socially relevant as Lily Tomlin's or as biting as Whoopi Goldberg's. But it was often brilliant, and it assumed that the audience had some level of sophistication, which is something that TV rarely does.

When she first agreed to do the show, Ellen had expected that she would be able to retain a fair share of her personal, intelligent style of humor—despite the fact that she would be playing to a prime-time television audience. And she wasn't the only one who saw how important that was. Two months before *These Friends of Mine* debuted, columnist James Brady wrote in *Parade* magazine that "Ellen is beautiful. She's smart. And—most important to her current success—she is very, very funny." He said that if *These Friends of Mine* "has halfway-decent scripts and lets Ellen do her stand-up thing, it ought to work."

The truth is, about thirty million people did like it—including her old friend Gladys Johnson. After watching the first two episodes, she said that not only did she love the show, but she was amazed at how much Ellen Morgan and Ellen DeGeneres were one and the same. "She's totally herself, the way she looks, the way she acts, and the way she dresses. That's totally Ellen."

That sense that what you see is what you get, of course, is part of her appeal. Audiences sense honesty in a performer, whether it's Roseanne or Tim Allen; they know when a performer believes in the character she or he is playing. The trouble was, as the weeks went on, Ellen began to feel less and less honest. She began to think that a lot of the "comedy" got lost in whatever "situation" she and her friends found themselves. And she began to have second thoughts about some of the scripts, especially as they went into rehearsal.

At first, she didn't do anything about it. In those early weeks after the debut, what was most important to Ellen was to get out there and promote the show, to fortify her position in the Top Ten before she started worrying about fine-tuning or even overhauling the series. So to the press, she maintained an optimistic front.

"You know, I think the writing is great. That's one of the reasons I wanted to work with Neal and Carol and David in the first place, because they knew me so well and we just clicked immediately."

She pushed the show with her characteristically zany

public face. "You'll laugh, you'll cry, you'll sneeze, you'll dance," she told one reporter. "Wait a minute. That's the side effects of taking too much cold medicine."

Within four weeks, she said, she was interviewed "easily two hundred or three hundred times. My days have been crazy. Every single day my lunch hour is filled with interviews. I can't believe there are that many people out there who still want to talk to me." Sometimes she'd be up at 3:30 in the morning to do 6:30 interviews in the East. Sometimes the interviews bordered on the absurd—a condition she parodied in her *Us* magazine self-interview when she asked the classic "bad interview" question: "If you were a tree, what kind would you be?" (Her answer: "A sticker bush." Reconsidering, she said, "Joshua. They live to be 150 years old, and no two are alike.")

"On my hiatus week, every day I had a photo shoot. Some days I have two photo shoots. I've done every magazine you can imagine. The first photo session I did I had three looks— a smile, a stare, and a kind of smirk. Now I'm like a supermodel up there. I'm learning all the tricks."

Showing that she was a good sport and a network team player, she even agreed to cohost, with Joey Lawrence, Jerry Van Dyke, and others, a treacly ABC special, *Before They Were Stars,* which showed clips and photographs of superstars when they were just starting out.

Only once did Ellen complain about the grind, and with good reason. Shortly after *These Friends of Mine* debuted, Ellen went to New York to appear on *The Late Show with David Letterman*. She was hot, she was in demand—and she was bounced. While Ellen alternately cracked jokes and stewed in the green room at the former Ed Sullivan Theater, just north of Times Square, guest Jack Lemmon reminisced . . . and reminisced . . . and reminisced.

Staff members of the show helped to keep Ellen calm, especially when it became obvious that her spot wasn't going to be small—it wasn't going to be, period. When the late-afternoon taping ended, Letterman hurried backstage, apologized profusely to Ellen—whom he has known for years—and literally begged her to stay in New York and do the show the next night.

"Sorry," she said with uncharacteristic curtness. "I have a career waiting for me."

Letterman and his staff didn't give up. They did what one press report called "some pampering—including a 'small shopping spree,'" and Ellen softened. After all, he's one of Ellen's idols. She came back the following night, and after he introduced her, Letterman was effusive in his praise of Ellen and her show.

But the sense of accomplishment Ellen felt was fleeting as she became more and more concerned about the show. For if the character was totally Ellen, the show wasn't. Even though subsequent episodes featured Ellen, in almost every scene, allowing her to serve as a Greek chorus as she paired with one or more of those friends of hers, the situations in which they found themselves tended to range from the absurd to the contrived and predictable.

Among the former was an embarrassingly inane and unlikely episode in which Ellen and the gang are blackmailed into helping young Maria (Sully Diaz) smuggle her children out of Mexico under the pretense of having gone south to buy some artwork. Ellen ends up getting caught by a border guard (Patrick Mickler) and thrown in prison.

Another utterly improbable episode—written by coexecutive producers David Rosenthal and Warren Bell, who should have known better—has Ellen's "sweet and innocent" cousin Tracy (Joanna Daniels) paying a visit from Missouri. When biker-author Nester Biggs (Steven Gilborn) does a book signing, Tracy runs off with him, and Ellen vows, "I'll . . . I'll . . . take his books off the New and Noteworthy table!"

This episode wasn't *Lucy*; it was *Pee-wee's Big Adventure* without the benefit of Pee-wee. The best part of the show were the outtakes that ran under the closing credits: Gilborn misspeaking as he tried to do a reading from one of his books, and Ellen cracking up as a cheerful young woman (Jill Talley) invites her and Tracy to the taping of an infomercial.

Among the better shows—albeit one with lots more sex than Ellen wanted—was the one in which Susan needs a date for a wedding. Ellen wants to help and considers getting Susan a date, first with a strip-club operator, then with a transsexual, and finally with Adam, who proves to be a sexual dynamo but a bore and gets dumped.

The stories weren't the only problems in the early shows. There were never enough moments when Ellen could do what she did best: the short, honest, stand-up "bits." Despite everyone's best efforts, Ellen's stand-up asides usually ended up seeming shoehorned into the scripts—which, of course, they were.

For example, she'd be sitting in a restaurant, signaling to the waiter to bring the check, and would suddenly ask, "What am I doing? What is this kind of gesture? Am I writing something, am I making a check mark?" It's supposed to be one of those "things that everyone does but never thinks about" moments, but it came across as forced.

Or, unbeknownst to Ellen, after Susan and Adam have just met and slept together, Ellen runs into Susan in the kitchen. Caught off guard, Ellen fumbles through: "I've been meaning to have you over. This is like a slumber party except that, y'know, someone forgot my invitation. Not that I would've wanted to join ya. Two is company, three is sick. It is. Ménage-a-yuck, if you ask me." What should have been comedy springing from an awkward moment—something we've all experienced—became uninspired babble, and it stopped the show dead in its tracks.

Where was the "DeGenerese" truth in this false and predictable progression: "In high school," she says, "when my hair was longer, people were always telling me that I looked exactly like Farrah Fawcett." Pause. "Not always but, y'know, now and again." Pause. "Once."

Many of the jokes on Ellen's show relied on the classic comedy setup of "threes." That is, the comic makes two believable statements, which allows the listener to become complacent, then follows it with a surprise statement, the "zinger." Ellen used the device successfully in her act—for instance, the club soda bit, or this rack-of-lamb line:

It's so weird all the different names they have for groups of animals. They have pride of lions, school of fish, rack of lamb.

Unfortunately, the show's threes here weren't funny. For example, when Ellen has to break the news to Adam that Susan doesn't want to see him again, she tells him that Susan "couldn't stop talking about you all day long. Fabulous dancer, fabulous lover, never wants to see you again."

Or, following a visit to the beach with cousin Tracy, Ellen laments, "Spoilsport scientists don't want you to have any fun anymore. Don't lay out in the sun, don't eat fatty foods, don't swim in raw sewage."

Not every scene and gag was weak, of course. In the kidnapping episode, Ellen makes a phone call to her mother. After some everyday kind of chitchat, Ellen says, "One more thing real quick. I'm in a Mexican prison and I need you to send fifteen hundred dollars to post bail. om . . . Mom . . . don't 'Oh, Ellen' me." For everyone who's ever had to call home for help in a bad situation, it was one of the show's few moments of truth.

Another funny exchange occurred between Susan and Ellen at the bookshop. After Ellen has set up a display of books about fun things to do on the weekend, Susan comes in and complains, "What is this obsession with having fun on the weekend? Why can't it be enough to just sit at home and wonder whatever happened to your life?" Ellen looks at her and replies, "I'll see if we have a book on that!"

The good moments, though, were too few and way too far between. Ellen wasn't happy, but the producers told her not to worry. The show was working with viewers, and she would be crazy to mess with something that was so successful.

She tried to go with the flow, but the drag was becoming more pronounced. She was already thinking of what life would be like after *These Friends of Mine*. Roseanne had fought for the integrity of her show, won, and could retire with the fortune she had made from creating a viewing public—in spite of network reservations about her sitcom's more controversial episodes. Would Ellen be able to do the same? Not if she wasn't funny, or if she ended up—as was more and more the case—as a "straight woman" for the antics of Adam and Holly.

Settling for something that wasn't quite right gnawed at her more and more. So what if the show was popular? In her heart, she knew she had to make a stand. What she didn't know was how extensive the fallout would be.

9
The Big Switch to *Ellen*

Six episodes into the midseason order of thirteen, weeks before the premiere of the series, Neal Marlens and Carol Black abruptly left *These Friends of Mine,* citing the all-purpose "personal reasons" and causing the production to go on an unscheduled six-week break. During that time, David Rosenthal was promoted to coexecutive producer and was joined by Wendy Goldberg and Warren Bell. Marlens and Black refused to discuss their departure, and almost immediately rumors started swirling that Ellen had thrown her weight around and forced ABC to replace the producers.

In truth, ABC executives themselves had reservations about the kinds of friends Marlens and Black were creating for Ellen. In one episode, Adam fakes a neck injury to collect insurance money. In another, he won't come to the aid of a woman getting mugged. They also questioned the focus of the show; their position was, they had a talented comic in the lead and wanted her to be front and center. Everybody denied there had been a coup of any kind.

"It wasn't as if there was a massive conflict," explained

then-president of Walt Disney Television, Dean Valentine. "What happened, basically, is that the network was pressuring the show to go in a certain direction by putting Ellen in front and making it clear these people were really friends. I don't think Neal or Carol completely disagreed, it just wasn't their vision."

The "personal reasons" cited apparently included Black's pregnancy and the couple's recent loss of their home in the terrible Malibu fires of 1994. Undeniably, though, there had been conflict between Ellen and her producers over the direction the show was going in.

"When I first got this show, I was just so grateful and I thought, 'Well, they know what they're doing. I should just shut up,'" Ellen would later reveal. "And then slowly you start realizing, I've been on the road for thirteen years, I've developed a persona and a style. I don't do off-color jokes. I don't do things that are in bad taste. I don't do sexist humor about men-bashing. Because the show was created around me and because in essence I'm playing myself, I'm really sensitive to things like that. And I started thinking, 'I'm allowing myself to be portrayed as this person that I really don't want to be portrayed as.'"

After six weeks of going with the flow and giving herself every chance she could to feel more comfortable with the show—its relatively soft comedy and its relatively hard sex—Ellen was feeling worse than ever about the quality of the material and the content of the scripts. That frustration drove her to suggest—or insist, as some report—that the stories focus more on her and less on the ensemble and that she spend more time "executive consulting" during the writing process. Although she avoided talking directly about her disagreements with the producers, she once let slip, "He doesn't like to collaborate and that's an important part for me. They really wanted it to be their show, and I was a hired hand."

Concern with quality and subject matter was certainly a

large part of Ellen's motivation. But was she also driven by the desire to make herself the unequivocal center of attention? Was she desperate to keep Ellen Morgan, the linchpin of the show, from being overshadowed by frankly more quirky and interesting characters?

Anytime a TV star becomes successful, he or she tends to take greater control, either in name or in fact, of the vehicle that brought the success. Sometimes the actor has the show's best interests at heart, wanting to make sure that writers, directors, or network executives—some of them newly hired—do not come in and muck with a formula that works. By and large, that's what happened on *Roseanne*. It was also the case with Ellen's early prime-time stablemate, *Grace Under Fire*.

As Brett Butler, star of the latter show, explained it, the scripts were lame and "people weren't agreeing with me at the script meetings. I stood up and said, 'You should use me, you should let me help. I can't sing or dance, but I am really good at this.' So I went in at night and on weekends to work with the writers." When one of them protested that she wasn't a writer, Butler says, "I resisted the impulse to say, 'C'mere, I've read more books than you even know the names of.'"

She might have been speaking for Ellen, who has said, "It's a difficult fence to be sitting on where you want to state your opinion but you don't want to be considered difficult."

Sometimes a creative takeover is amicable; more often than not it's hostile and occasionally litigious. And once in a rare while the star loses: In 1991, when Delta Burke reportedly tried to wrest *Designing Women* from creators Linda Bloodworth-Thomason and Harry Thomason, CBS backed the Thomasons.

To many people who worked at the production offices, at the studio, and at the network, the power struggle with producers Black and Marlens seemed prompted more by Ellen's ego than by her desire for quality control. While some measure of ego cannot be completely ruled out, it was a small part of the forces at work, because Ellen really did have her fans uppermost in her mind.

"I would hope *These Friends of Mine* would be a hip show but not too hip and not too urban that we're gonna alienate people who go to work and they're bus drivers or whatever. I want them to come home and laugh. Honestly, I would love to appeal to everybody."

Also, Ellen did, quite naturally, feel that this was her show. Meanwhile, the other actors had been hired with the promise that this was going to be an ensemble series. Otherwise, *These Friends of Mine* was not a notch that either Arye Gross or Holly Fulger needed on their belts. They'd already done the supporting-role bit. So the seeds of discontent were planted early.

When Ellen was asked to do virtually all of the publicity for the show, Fulger and Gross were hurt, but they kept their disappointment pretty much to themselves. Ellen was funny and made for good copy, so they let it slide. But after a few weeks, the read-throughs started to take on a confrontational atmosphere. One of the regular attendees says that it was common for Ellen to zero in on all the good lines Fulger was getting, wondering why they weren't hers. Also, she failed to understand why the writers were promoting Fulger as the cute, funny one.

"Isn't that supposed to be my role?" she once asked.

When the star of a hit TV show asks that question, the only possible response is yes.

One of the production company employees griped, "Roseanne was smart enough to surround herself with good people, like John Goodman and Laurie Metcalf, and let them have as many jokes and good scenes as they could. Roseanne understood that their success would make her look good, especially in the early days when she was learning how to be a good sitcom actor. Ellen isn't like that."

What, then, was she like—a control freak driven solely by ego?

"Not at all," says a representative of ABC. "Her appeal is central to the success of the show, so why shouldn't we focus more on her? Besides, the situation isn't comparable to *Roseanne*. That's a show about a family. Everyone is expected to share the spotlight and the laughs. This is a show about Ellen."

Another view, voiced by an actor who appeared on the show, was that unlike Fulger and Gross, who had done dramatic work, Ellen wasn't "secure enough as an actress to stand there and not get laughs. She doesn't feel comfortable 'serious,' so of course she wants the jokes for herself."

A spokesperson for Ellen said that was absurd, and one is inclined to agree. At times, she's done some very dramatic and moving material in her act.

The fact remains, at the end of the day, it is the star's face and reputation on the prime time line and a show as marginally funny as hers was becoming could have destroyed that reputation—even if people tune in because they're amused by what the star can do with a dull line.

No one knew what was funny for Ellen the comedian better than Ellen. As Rosenthal pointed out, "Pound for pound, Ellen is the funniest person in the room." She had every right to make sure that people who shared her sound stage shared her vision. And being "nice" often only gets you run over roughshod. Even though Ellen was loath to assert herself, she finally realized this wasn't Mickey and Judy putting on a show in the backyard.

"This is a huge business for a network and a studio. Everybody's trying to make money off this show. What I have to realize now is that I've become this product. For Disney. I would love to think that everybody really, really likes me a lot and that's why I get work. But I have to realize this is a business. All I can try to do is maintain some integrity. Even though Ellen Morgan is certainly not me, I should never say or do anything on the show I don't believe in."

However much or little Ellen had to do with Marlens and Black leaving, once the changes started, they seemed to take on a life of their own. Shortly after the producer changeover, ABC directed that Maggie Wheeler's character, Anita, be written out of the show. Those who believed that Ellen had anything to do with this were unaware of how Wheeler got the role to begin with.

"It was Ellen who pushed for Maggie to be hired," says a source familiar with the casting. "The network was luke-warm about her and thought her character was dragging the show down. But Ellen fought tooth and nail to get them to keep Maggie on. It was only after the network was forced to scrap a couple of the episodes, in part because of their un-happiness with the Anita character, that Ellen relented."

"The shows were kind of going in a direction that wasn't really where we wanted to go, so that was one reason we made some changes," Ellen said.

Wheeler was released, and Anita disappeared without any explanation given in subsequent episodes. But the upheaval didn't stop there. Both Gross and Fulger were put on notice that their characters would no longer necessarily appear each week.

Now, cast changes are not new in TV. Meg Foster, the ac-tress who'd been originally slated to costar on *Cagney & Lacey,* was unceremoniously canned in favor of Sharon Gless, who went on to win several Emmys for the role; the late Jeffrey Hunter had William Shatner's part in the original *Star Trek* pilot, which failed to sell; Mike Henry and Lyle Waggoner were both up for the role of TV's *Batman,* only to be passed over in favor of Adam West. Usually, how-ever, these changes occur before a show airs. This was dif-ferent.

These Friends of Mine was a bona fide hit; why change it? "That's what I used to ask about Tide," Ellen wryly said at the time. "Because I thought it worked just fine on clothes, so why mess with it? I had the same questions.

"It scared the hell out of me. We never explained to viewers what happened to my old friends when the show changed from *These Friends of Mine* to *Ellen*. And it was so hard because Maggie and Holly were my friends. They're still my friends. I was really attached to these people. I told ABC, 'Don't you understand we're going to be torn apart for doing this? Why are we doing this?' I don't know. They thought the show could be improved.

"Everyone assumed I had all the power. But there was really nothing I could do about it except trust the right thing had happened."

In her stand-up act, Ellen once noted:

This is my assessment of life: people are stupid. Not us. It's all the others. Ever notice whenever you're with someone and they eat something that tastes bad they always want you to taste it, too? And we're stupid—"All right, I'll taste it . . . You're right, I'm gonna vomit."

It wasn't that she disagreed that the show could be better; she just didn't think tinkering with the cast was a way to improve it. Certainly it was bad news for Holly Fulger and Arye Gross. Not only would they have less to do, but they would get less money. They would only be paid for episodes in which they appeared, and they were tentatively set to act in just six of the thirteen shows ordered for the first half of the season.

It was reported that at least one of them asked to be released from contract and that the request was turned down. If it were demonstrated, after a few shows had been shot, that

Ellen couldn't carry the series more or less on her own, the "friends" could always be brought back—but not if they had already taken parts on a different sitcom or were shooting a movie.

Though one of the actors suggested that Ellen may have been behind the firings—motivated by jealousy over who was getting more laughs—a spokesperson for Ellen said that Touchstone Television, not Ellen, ordered the cutbacks for budgetary reasons. "Many TV shows are cutting back," he said. "This season 1993–94 a number of half-hour network sitcoms had to cut roughly one fifth of their budgets, about $200,000 a week, or face cancellation. That happened to *Evening Shade. These Friends of Mine* is no exception.

"You can't very well drop Ellen from her own show, and production costs are standard. So where are the cuts going to come from? It has to be from the cast."

That naturally bugged Fulger and Gross to no end, as it had to have bothered Wheeler. They had all suffered through the stages of "Will I get the part?" then "Will the pilot sell?" and finally "Will we be a hit?" Now they were on a show that had turned out to be a smash, on which a supporting player could make $20,000 or $30,000 a week in addition to millions more in residuals.

Instead of that, however, they were going to be earning relative peanuts. This just weeks after Holly Fulger had celebrated by going out and buying herself a new home.

"Ellen could've taken a cut," said a spokesperson for one of them. "I think all of the actors would have agreed to salary cuts to make up the deficit. They were loyal to the show. And they were also loyal to each other."

Another rumor to make the rounds as conventional wisdom was that once the original team at Black/Marlens company relinquished hands-on control over the show, they were replaced by Ellen's handpicked people. That move was widely rumored to have been made to keep the ex-producers from crossing swords with Ellen. As one employee said, "They've moved from out of the background to out of the building. We've been joking that we can start planning a spinoff, 'These Ex-Friends of Mine.'"

However, the producers finally denied any friction with Ellen and pointed out that they had relinquished hands-on control over *The Wonder Years* after a single season as well. They said that they enjoyed concentrating on new projects once a hit show had been launched.

After the March premiere, the critical response was as positive as the audience's had been. Matt Roush of *USA Today* noted, "Ellen a star, her friends aren't strangers and this is the warmest, smartest ABC comedy since I don't know when."

People magazine was equally complimentary. "Every time you start feeling that the network system is bankrupt, up pops an irresistible treat like this japery, which combines the bent appeal of *Seinfeld, Mad About You,* and the best parts of *Anything but Love. These Friends* has something those series don't: stand-up comic Ellen DeGeneres as the star. With her pop-eyed innocence and self-aware goofiness, she's a sitcom natural."

But the praise wasn't universal. *Entertainment Weekly*'s TV critic, Ken Tucker, was underenthused almost to the point of sounding offended. "I don't know about you, but Arsenio, dogs, and intercourse are three concepts I never want to have running together in my head at the same time," he said, referring to Roger's passionate yelps. He went on, "There's this knowing wink behind every joke in *These Friends of Mine* that just wasn't there in, say, your average *I Love Lucy* or *The Dick Van Dyke Show* episode. Part of the problem here is that the people who made *These Friends of Mine* want you not merely to laugh at but to identify—nay, mind-meld—with these characters. God bless Lucille Ball—

at least she never asked me to think of her as my doppel-ganger."

This kind of criticism only added to Ellen's distress. "It was so mean. That's what surprised me. I had a sick feeling. I can never let things roll off my back. When I'm onstage, if the whole room is laughing and there's just one person star-ing at me, I'm gonna go home thinking, 'How come he didn't laugh?' I'm wondering why I didn't get through to him."

She admitted she wasn't like her pal Jay Leno, who re-fuses to get caught up in the frenzy. "Jay doesn't take this all so seriously. If it all ended tomorrow, he'd go home and work on his motorcycles. I think as much as I appreciate all the good reviews, I'm always thinking about the bad reviews. I'm always thinking about what if people don't like the show. I'm never really satisfied that I'm doing anything re-ally outstanding. I don't think I'm ever going to achieve that kind of satisfaction of feeling pompous."

Ironically, the thing Ellen most worried about—the funny-light, sex-heavy scripts—seemed to escape the reviewers' notice. Perhaps, being television critics, they were accus-tomed to the banal. Rather, it seemed as though almost every critic who wrote about the show felt that it was a reverse clone of *Seinfeld*: instead of three young, funny, oddball guys and a girl dealing with daily frustrations in Manhattan, *These Friends of Mine* was three young, funny, oddball girls and a guy doing the relationship-career shuffle in Los Angeles.

TV Guide accurately summed up the differences between the shows by noting that the characters lacked "the easy, am-plified idiosyncrasies" of the *Seinfeld* crew, that Ellen and her friends were "quieter, saner—truer," and that Ellen her-self was "incredibly engaging" instead of "amusingly whiny" like Seinfeld. But that didn't stop the comparisons from dominating the press.

Disturbing as this was, none of these comments were new

to Ellen. She's been called "the spiritual daughter of Bob Newhart and a distaff George Carlin," in addition to "the female Seinfeld."

"I've always been compared to Jerry, even though we're not alike and I don't think our stand-up is that similar. It's just that I'm more like him than, say, Gallagher. We both do observational humor, that's where the similarity lies. I think it's because he's been around longer than I have. If I had been around first, people would be saying that he's a male Ellen DeGeneres. But I'm flattered by the comparison, because it's a successful show. But it's not like we said, 'Let's do a Seinfeld.'"

For the record, when asked what he thought of Ellen and her show, Jerry replied sincerely, "They're both terrific. I'm glad she's not on opposite me."

The *Chicago Tribune*'s Allan Johnson noted in a 1994 club review of DeGeneres, "Both comics work clean. Their TV sitcoms definitely are alike in that being-about-nothing kind of way. But DeGeneres is an animated storyteller, working jokes in while reacting to her audience. The cooler Seinfeld does a lot of one-liners and tends to stay a little detached."

Since the comedians were always being compared, Ellen says, it was not a surprise to her that the shows would be, too. At first, she tried to dismiss the comparisons with humor.

"Well," she told one reporter, "our kitchen is on the other side of the set." She added that, yes indeed, the shows were so similar that "they're even trying to get me to dress more like him."

Another time, she pretended ignorance. "*Seinfeld*? What's that? It's on Thursdays, right? I'm usually watching *Matlock*. We have friends over and we discuss *Matlock* for a while and by the time we switch the channel, it's over. But I just can't understand how a show with that bodybuilder Jake Steinfeld can be so popular."

Another time she revealed, "What's different about this show than *Seinfeld* is that my character is an alien and no one knows it. And I don't even ever reveal it on the show. It's just something I walk around knowing, that I'm an alien on this planet and I'm just blending in."

In more serious moments, her exasperation began to seep through. "It probably was written with *Seinfeld* as a huge influence," she commented, then added pointedly, "I wasn't in the room."

David Rosenthal, who was in the room helping create *These Friends of Mine,* said, "It was not a conscious choice. I think it was just the natural evolving of the show. But I think the strengths of that show and the strengths of this show are very different. And Ellen is a very different performer than anyone on that show."

At the end of the prime-time day, it didn't really matter how similar or different *These Friends of Mine* and *Seinfeld* were. What mattered to Ellen and what she wished people would realize was how well the individual shows were executed. "It's not the number of shows, it's how good they are."

Ironically, after the critics got tired of comparing her show to Seinfeld—or realized that the comparison wasn't valid—they took a different tack. As Ellen told one reporter, "Now people are comparing it to *The Mary Tyler Moore Show.* Pretty soon it'll be *Flipper.*"

In a very short time, comparisons with any show began to get on Ellen's nerves. She didn't understand why critics had to pigeonhole her or anyone. Hollywood entertainment attorney Steve Burkow was right on the money when he pointed out that it had nothing to do with Ellen, really. Rather, the post-*Seinfeld* airwaves were "like the post–*Die Hard* action movies. You had *Under Siege,* which was described as "*Die Hard* on a boat," *Passenger 457,* which was called "*Die Hard* on a plane," and *Speed,* which was "*Die Hard* on a bus.""

"Maybe," he said, "Ellen should be thankful for the

Seinfeld comparisons. Otherwise the critics might've described her show as '*Die Hard* in a bookstore.'"

But Ellen wasn't thankful. Because of the frustrating perception of the show, and scripts that weren't quite what they should have been, she grew increasingly annoyed as each week passed. Adding to her anxiety, two months after joining the production team, Wendy Goldberg left, prompting a whole new round of speculation about just what was going on behind the scenes of *These Friends of Mine*. Still, as the 1993–94 season drew to a close, Ellen's show stood out as one of the season's new hits, and she looked forward to the next season with the hope it would be smoother sailing.

It wouldn't be.

Samuel Goldwyn once said, "I don't want any yes-men around me. I want everybody to tell me the truth even if it costs them their jobs." Sometimes network television must seem, to those who make their living in it, to embody the spirit of that sentiment.

More dramatic developments were in store for Ellen and her series throughout May and June of 1994. First, before filming resumed late in the summer, Ellen asked (some say demanded) that shooting be moved from the Sony lot to Disney Studios in the San Fernando Valley. That put Ellen's work much closer to her home and, with the roads still clogged with post-earthquake traffic, much easier to get to, because she wouldn't have to use the surviving freeways. Not everything was better on Dopey Drive, though. The sound stage to which they moved her didn't have a dressing room. Unlike at Sony, Ellen had to retire to a mobile home next to the sound stage whenever she wasn't needed.

Next, the name of the show was changed from *These Friends of Mine* to *Ellen*. Naturally, that provided even more grist for the mills of those who viewed Ellen as a prima donna. But to many, the name change was long overdue, and Ellen herself pled innocence.

"ABC decided it was going to be a good block to have *Roseanne* and *Ellen* versus *Roseanne* and *These Friends of Mine*. And plus," she added with a smile, "the name sucked anyway."

The switch to Ellen was also intended to underscore who the show was going to be about—or who the star was, if you ask some of Ellen's coworkers. This was one of the names the producers had originally considered, and, an ABC representative said, "It fits in with popular shows like *Roseanne* and *Dave's World* which use names in the title." Nevertheless, the timing of the change was terrible. It only added logs to the fire that was already raging over whether Ellen's ego was out of control—a controversy, it should be noted, that was propagated mostly by unnamed sources in the media.

What did Ellen say in her own defense? Not much. The only thing you can do, she believes, is "be true to yourself and hope there are people who like what you do."

Ellen also shrugged off all the rumors of a feud with the producers without actually addressing whether one had broken out. She maintained in *Entertainment Weekly*, "I've heard all kinds of rumors about that, but we're all still good friends."

Going into the 1994–95 season, she expressed confidence that the show's future was as bright as ever, even with all the drastic changes, including yet another cast change. In June, Holly Fulger was officially released from her contract. Relative newcomer Joely Fisher, the offspring of Connie Stevens and Eddie Fisher, was cast as Ellen's new best friend, Paige. Arye Gross would stay on board, but his role would be considerably diminished. Susan, played by Cristine Rose, was also written out.

"It's not so much an ensemble anymore," Ellen acknowledged. "It's kind of following my character. It's about trying to fit in but not quite making it and not caring because I'm not sure if I want to."

Ellen admitted she felt the same way about her own life. "I don't care if I fit in or not. If I want to make a joke at something and the person behind the counter at Bullock's doesn't understand my joke, I look like an idiot, but it's something I choose to do."

Then, making one last swipe at the idea of Ellen the Egomaniac, she added jokingly, "Eventually, what I want is just nobody but me. Five years from now it'll just be a half hour of me talking to myself. I was kind of thinking about it the other day. It'll be on A&E but they'll watch it."

At the 1994 summer Television Critics Press Tour, Ellen discussed how she thought some of the changes, which included her buying the bookstore she once worked at, would benefit the show. "I think owning the bookstore gives me more of an investment in that I probably, in reality, would have just quit the bookstore and worked somewhere else," she joked. "But it also gives me more excuses that I can have other things happening besides being at work all the time.

"The thing that's so funny is that because things have been changing every day, my mother's like, 'What's going on now with the show?' The other day I said, 'Now I own the bookstore.' She goes, 'Really!' She was so impressed, like that's a huge deal. Like, now, I've finally made it, I own the bookstore."

Executive producer David Rosenthal was surprisingly blunt in his take on the cast changes. "We all felt Ellen was wonderful and that the show was working, but that she could just use some more support, comedically and personality-wise. Holly did terrific work for us. It was just a matter of chemistry and what this show needed in terms of characters to surround Ellen with."

There were some critics who openly questioned how it was possible for Ellen to have completely clean hands as far as the cast changes. She responded, "That's really funny. I truly am an innocent bystander. I just read in *Esquire* magazine, I'm under a column of 'Women Who Can't Be as Wholesome as They Seem.' And I don't know what people may think, that I'm this tyrant. But ABC made a decision, and I was just praying that we get picked up again.

"As crazy as that sounds, we were neck and neck with *Grace Under Fire*. I mean, we were doing better than her for a little while, but she had a whole twenty-two weeks to prove herself. We had seven weeks. I didn't know if there'd be a time slot for us. I was talking to a critic who said the only place to go is after *Roseanne,* but then they'd have to move *Coach*. I just didn't think it was possible that we'd even come back until the midseason. So I certainly am not saying, 'I want this and I want that.'"

One admitted bone of contention was the theme song. At one point, Ellen had told reporters that her close friend Melissa Etheridge was writing a theme song. She did, but it never aired.

"It was on there until the last minute," Ellen explained, "and they took it off and changed the music. Disney didn't think it was the right music for the show, that it wasn't upbeat enough.

"I disagreed. And I still think she should have the song. But now I think they're going to change to not even having opening titles, instead going the way *Frasier* has where it just kind of goes right into the show. So we're talking ten seconds of music. I don't think Melissa's really challenged by that. I mean, I think I could write that."

The lyrics of the ditty that was ultimately used were supposed to be a jab at the sappy theme songs sitcoms typically have:

You know I'm close
I'll keep my promises
I'll always listen when you talk to me
I'll always hear you.

Looking back at her first half season, Ellen singled out some of her favorite episodes. "I liked a little bit about a whole lot of them. I think my favorite show was 'The Hand That Robs the Cradle,' which was about dating a younger man and trying to get into a club and not being hip enough. And working really, really hard to be hip, and as a result, I become entirely too hip and scared the guy away."

When asked if she felt she was now more in control of her show, Ellen was quick to back away from the implications of the question. "I don't know how to write a show. As soon as I feel like I know how to write a script I think I'll make an attempt at that. But I'm going to let the writers do what they do. And what I'm best at is playing around with a situation. Sometimes it ends up in, sometimes it doesn't. That's also the freedom of having this kind of job where the show is created for me, so I can really just go with it and take chances and hopefully end up with stuff that isn't typically on TV already. But they respect me, I think, a great deal and ask for my opinions and give me a lot of freedom to do what I want. So I don't think I need to have power and control in any other way than what I have."

Ellen seemed genuinely grateful to be where she was. "I can't thank ABC enough. To be given this time slot after *Roseanne* and to change the name is more than I could have asked for. You know, there are a lot of people out there struggling that don't have this kind of opportunity. I'm really grateful to everybody.

"I got lucky because, I think, women are now getting more opportunities, and there wasn't a woman doing what I represent. And," she added, "anybody who has a sense of humor likes me.

"What I love about doing a television show is just the challenges and getting new things every week and trying to find new directions that I can go in that I haven't gone before. I just enjoy what I'm doing. I pretty much always have.

"Having this series is a huge validation and vote of confidence after thirteen years of doing comedy," Ellen acknowledged, then added ruefully, "But I'm not kidding myself—this is a weird business. Everyone wants to be your friend as long as you're successful and making them money."

All Ellen wanted was the chance to make the best series she could, with no more backstage upheaval, no more whispered accusations, and, most important, no more mediocre scripts. Now she knew just how precarious that dream could be.

When told by one reporter she had a skyrocketing career, Ellen seemed pensive. "Skyrockets," she noted, "blow up sometimes."

10
The Diva du Jour

In early 1994, at thirty-six, Ellen was just beginning to savor the taste of true celebrity. "It's sporadic but it's starting to happen more and more since the show's been on the air. When it does happen, it catches me off guard. Reruns and Comedy Central kept my career going before my show came on."

At that point, she had concluded that the worst part of TV stardom was "probably the fact that people see you play a character or see you on a talk show for about a five-minute interview, and they project some personality or image onto you from what they see. And it's probably not who you are, whether it be good or bad. That and the invasion of privacy. Everything else is an upside. Anyone who complains should get out of the business."

Within a few short months, Ellen's philosophy would be sorely tested. "I've always wanted to get to Celebrityville. And now that I'm here, I realize there's no finish line."

Now she equated fame with living in a fishbowl. "I'm a huge people person, and what does scare me is the loss of my privacy. I love watching people. I love doing things. And it's really going to be hard for me. It's already kind of starting to be that way, where it is hard to go places and do things the way I used to. And the more famous you get, the more people tap on the bowl, but they are the same people who feed you.

"I used to be out in public and people would just look and say, 'You're that comedian.' They weren't scared of coming up. And then it was slowly where they'd stare at me and hit their friend with their elbow and point at me. Most of the time now they just stare, like I'm an animal who got out of the zoo somehow. 'She's in a restaurant! Quick, call somebody!' That's not right.

"At first when that happens, you're uncomfortable with it. After a while you get used to it. It becomes part of your daily routine—you go out, you get looked at."

Typically, Ellen tried to cope through humor. "People always ask me, 'Is your life as a performer that much different than ours? The little people. The nobodies. The scum?'

"Everybody thinks my life has changed since I've become successful, but I don't think so. I was talking to the woman who brushes my teeth for me, Pantry, and she said, 'I don't think so either.'"

But it had changed, in ways both good and bad. "People around you change. I think if someone is a certain personality, if they seem pompous or if they seem like these control freaks, they were probably like that all along. They'd be like that if they worked at the Broadway department store or if they were on television. You know, this is who I am. This is who I will remain.

"Suppose today some salesperson may give me an attitude and I'll be a bitch, then she'll tell all her friends I'm a bitch and probably that I look better on TV, and then those friends will tell their friends and so on. Next thing you know, three thousand people think I'm a bitch, and by that time the story will be so blown out of proportion, it's now I've slapped a saleswoman who was pregnant and that I'm fat and an alcoholic.

"But if I go home and tell a friend this salesperson is rude, I doubt they'll call anyone and say, 'Hey, there's a woman who works in the shoe department at the Broadway who's mean.'"

As she started to do more and more publicity for her series, Ellen found herself constantly bombarded with questions about her personal life—questions every celebrity is asked as part of a standard interview. It wasn't that she was being singled out, but whenever a television celebrity becomes noticeably secretive about his or her private life, it naturally sends a certain message to veteran entertainment journalists.

"It's hard enough to have a private life when you are not a celebrity," Ellen complained in a 1994 interview. "It's amazing to me that everyone thinks I have a responsibility to divulge my personal life. I'll try to hold on to that and keep it separate as long as possible, but people will speculate and do what they may."

At other times, she tried to answer without really answering. "I'm in a relationship now and I'm happy. And I'm not hiding some secret like I'm really an Hispanic male. I'm probably more normal than anyone I know who's a comic. But in this business, I feel like you're exposed enough. And for the longest time, my career was everything. The more people know about me, the harder it becomes for them to accept me in different roles."

In a self-interview printed in *Us* magazine, Ellen addressed her frustration at always being asked about whether or not she had a boyfriend. "Let's say I do. What's next? What's his name? What does he do? Are we happy? It's hard enough to have a healthy relationship without all the pressure of people watching you, scrutinizing every step.

"Now let's say I don't have a boyfriend. What's the next question? Why not?

"My private life is just an area I choose to keep private. Hence the name private life. Maybe someday I'll change my mind, but not yet."

Ellen's tendency to keep her personal life in general close to the vest, however, actually preceded her TV stardom. Fellow comedians who have worked with her say she's never really been "one of the guys."

"Most comics, male and female, will spend a lot of time sitting around clubs after performances, shooting the breeze and just hanging out together," said an L.A. comic in 1994. "But Ellen has always just sort of gone her own way. She usually shows up with several other women who she spends most of her time talking to. It's not that she's rude—if you go over and talk to her, she's pleasant enough. It's more of a shyness, like the neighborhood kid who stands off to the side because they're too shy to say they want to play unless they're asked—or begged—to."

According to her friends, Ellen isn't someone who seems to fit in automatically. "She doesn't really bend to the situation; she finds situations that fit her," says one. "But her tendency to travel in groups is one thing that's always been kind of weird—for a stand-up, anyway. Having people hovering around you certainly keeps others away and keeps them from getting to know you. And yet Ellen has made a career out of exposing herself onstage. It's like she wants to let us see her and love her, but is afraid if we get a really good look, we'll reject her."

On one hand, Ellen's worry was reasonable enough. As debates on hot-button topics like gays in the military and gay marriage have shown repeatedly, in the United States views on homosexuality are polarized. While within the entertainment industry and in most major metropolitan areas someone's sexual preference is rarely a concern, in the rest of the country the issue is divisive. So her fears of repercussion were in no way imaginary.

As early as 1994, the rumors about Ellen's true sexual preference were so widespread that DJ John Walton asked his listeners, "Has anybody ever known this woman to be associated with a man in a romantic way?" Later he reported, "Everyone said no!"

Being the butt of this kind of attention is certainly incentive to run and lock the closet door, but doing so only makes things worse.

"If you act like it's something to hide and be ashamed of, other people pick up on that," says Ellen. "I'm not saying go on talk shows with graphic updates of your latest exploits, either. But you pop the balloon if you say, "this is who I am, so what?" You can be honest without rubbing people's noses in it. Besides, who wants to spend their life looking over their shoulder, or cringing when they open the paper out of fear 'it' will be mentioned and their terrible secret will be out?"

That said, it still just seemed easier to try and keep her private life from being public fodder. But it wasn't as if the idea of coming out hadn't occurred to her. In an *Advocate* interview, DeGeneres says she used to discuss such a possibility with close friends k.d. lang and Melissa Etheridge. "They both came out before I did. We used to talk about coming out all the time. Melissa and k.d. wanted me to come out, but they never pressured me in any way."

If anything, it was Ellen who gave herself the most grief about being in the closet. "I remember crying, wishing I could be a part of the march on Washington in 1993. I thought, *This is a huge group of people that I belong to. And I can't do that because I'm not out!* That was a powerful thing to watch the march and to not be able to be there—it impacted me and just tortured me more. I wanted to be able to be out. My friends were out! And I kept justifying why I couldn't—because music is different from television. If you sell 6 million albums, you're a huge star. If you have 6 million viewers on television, you're canceled."

So concerned was Ellen over her public image that she requested one episode be changed. In "Ellen's New Friend," which aired in December 1994, Ellen wants to become friends with a woman introduced to her by their mutual friend Audrey, but she doesn't want Audrey included. Some of the scenes in the original script bothered Ellen because she thought they were too suggestive of Ellen Morgan's being possibly romantically attracted to the women, so they were rewritten.

"I try not to, but I worry about everything," Ellen admits. "I care way too much what other people think. If the show is successful, then you're reaching millions of people. But you're also standing there naked, saying, 'What do you think of me?' And there are mean people who just want to tear you apart. That kind of frightens me."

For good reason. As soon as Ellen became a household name, she discovered that not every journalist was going to treat her privacy with kid gloves. In fact, some—particularly those who worked for the tabloids—were about to make the pernicious television critics seem like her biggest fans.

As her career continued to expand and she ventured into the world of prime-time stardom, Ellen began to realize that even though her whole act and career was based on honesty, continued success might necessitate creating a dishonest double life. She worried about what middle America would think and wasn't so sure viewers would welcome into their homes every week a gay woman who was blatantly "out there" with her sexuality.

In her stand-up routine, Ellen did a bit about her cat.

My cat is sneakin' out at night. 'Cause the other morning I found a stamp on her paw . . . I wouldn't

*have noticed it myself but I just bought this new black
light.*

At times she must have felt like her poor feline who had
to go out under the cover of darkness. But at least she wasn't
alone. Most of Ellen's friends during that time were, in fact,
gay women, many of whom were rather high-profile
Hollywood types. Even though on one hand she was worried
about how the public would react to the truth of her life,
Ellen still frequented gay bars/clubs, the Palms and the She
Club, where she was often seen having candlelit dinners
with an unidentified girlfriend.

As opposed to being a risk, these clubs were safe havens,
places she could go and truly be herself. "Before she became
a TV star, Ellen thought nothing of going out to lesbian bars
and hanging with her friends there," one associate said. "Up
until last year 1993 it wasn't unusual to see Ellen at gay
women's places like the dance club Girl Bar or eating at
places like Little Frieda's and the Abbey, which also cater to
a gay clientele. The gay community in West Hollywood is
very casual and laid-back, so it's no big deal. People are used
to seeing famous faces at local gay clubs, and most gays are
very protective of gay celebrities."

But once *These Friends of Mine* ended the 1993–94 season as the fifth-ranked series of the year, Ellen had to reassess her social life.

"That's why Ellen has started going underground, just a
little bit," a woman who traveled in the same gay social circles reported in 1994. "She's not as familiar a face in the gay
bars anymore. Instead, now she's a part of the 'private house'
scene.

"There's a whole group of successful, famous gay women
who have learned it's better to stay out of public places and
socialize privately. In the old days, there was a group of famous, powerful men—like Rock Hudson and producer John

Epstein—who did the same thing, and they called themselves the Velvet Mafia. So these women call themselves Crushed Velvet, and basically their social world revolves around each others' houses. It's very private, and since the gatherings move around it's very secure."

This woman also said Ellen's ascent to the top professionally had been reflected in her increased status socially, particularly among gay women. As Ellen's star rose, so did the number of invitations she received to join this elite social group of gay women.

"Now, Ellen is the queen bee among the upper echelon of gay women in L.A.," said the woman. "When she walks in— never alone, always accompanied by someone—every eye in the place turns her way. It's like Princess Di walked in. Ellen is attractive and funny and has everyone eating out of her hand. She's the diva du jour. But even though she's gracious and engaging, you can't help but get a sense that Ellen is vaguely uncomfortable with how cliquish this group is.

"Plus, Ellen has other dilemmas to worry about. There's a certain danger in closing yourself off from the world at large because you're so afraid of being who you really are—and denying who you really are. It's one thing to keep your private life private and simply keep it off limits during interviews. Quite a few celebrities do that, gay and straight."

Many of her friends and associates within the gay community understood Ellen's reluctance to be outed. Others worried that she was ultimately doing herself more harm than good.

"Ellen has definitely changed over the past couple of years," said the woman. "Especially since starting the television series, Ellen has developed that entourage mentality, where she comes and goes surrounded by a gaggle of people in the hopes they'll keep the big, bad world away. . . . But what it really does is tell others you're inaccessible, which isolates you from finding new friends. And a siege mentality stagnates you."

While the members of the gay community were determined to shield Ellen, they were no match for the tenacious tabloid press. That Ellen is gay was common knowledge within the industry and among entertainment journalists—many gay themselves—long before she had a series on the air. But because she wasn't a big enough television or film name, it wasn't newsworthy. Thus, when Ellen was chosen Best Female Comedy Club Stand-up in 1991, reporters didn't have an urge to go through her garbage or to examine her lifestyle very closely.

Once the series became a hit, however, in her heart Ellen had to know that it was only a matter of time before her life would play out in the papers—and that it probably wouldn't be pretty. She already felt that she had been burned by the legitimate press on a couple of occasions.

One prompted her to muse, "Most of the time I do interviews, I read them and just shake my head. It's so misconstrued, so out of context. I'm sitting there thinking, 'This isn't what I said at all. I've never wanted to braid LaToya Jackson's hair.' I've never met Julia Roberts, but I'd like to braid her hair. Just kidding."

Another time, when she was photographed at an industry function beside Brett Butler, who towered over Ellen, the comedians were dubbed the winners of "the Mutt and Jeff fashion award."

So she could only try to brace herself for what the tabloids would reveal. Considering that Ellen had always been someone so accessible and so diligent in her dealings with the press, it was especially difficult for her to accept being such a target.

"I miss stand-up terribly," another target, Tim Allen, has said. "Life was much easier then. I knew that rustling in the bushes was a cat, not a photographer trying to take my picture when I go to the mailbox. Like that's newsworthy. 'Peace in the Middle East . . . and comedian gets swimsuit issue in mail.'"

"The first time it happened, I was freaked out," Ellen recalls. "I wondered, 'How can I get on television and tell everybody this isn't true?' Now I realize it's not personal. They have a job to do and that's how they sell papers. That's what they do. They make up stories, and I'm flattered that I'm a big enough name that they're making up stories about me. They found my house and somebody was trying to take a picture of me from a hill overlooking the yard. I was just freaking out. I said, 'Can we put a dome over the house? Can't we just dome it?'"

Ellen has also joked that she has the book *How to Kill an Intruder in Your Home* on her nightstand. "I haven't read it yet, so I'll just throw it. It's heavy."

Stars and their handlers work very hard to promote the idea that most of what the tabloids print isn't true. Sometimes it is, however, and they know it. Tabloids such as the *National Enquirer* or the *Globe*—have teams of attorneys who go over every story and who demand verification, corroboration, and very specific data from sources. While it is true that an unscrupulous reporter can fabricate sources and data, or can be the victim of a scam, such chicanery doesn't happen nearly as often as celebrities would like the public to believe.

So why all the lawsuits? Because by suing, celebrities can maintain that they are the aggrieved victims. And it's a way to try and find out the source of a story. What they don't publicize is that they later quietly drop the suit. Why? Because the gist of the story is most often true.

While promoting her show in March 1994, Ellen told reporters that her biggest fear was that someone would publish her high school senior photograph. Of course, within two weeks the *National Enquirer* had found and published the 1976 photo.

"Ellen will just die when she sees it in the *Enquirer,*" said a former classmate. "She once told me, 'If I ever become famous, the first thing I'm going to do is hire a private eye to track down every copy of the yearbook, buy 'em up, and burn 'em.'"

Julie Battenfield, another friend of Ellen's from high school, told the *Enquirer,* "In the picture, Ellen's hair flipped out at the side. She was such a joker, everyone thought she'd done something to make the picture look funny. But she hates that picture to this day!"

That drove the point home that she was fair game. As someone living a closeted life, all she could hope was that the public wouldn't believe everything they read, even if it was true.

In May 1994, the *National Enquirer* ran a story with this headline: "TV's newest funny girl warned: Stay out of gay bars. *These Friends of Mine* star told to watch those friends of hers."

In other bold print, the tabloid claimed: "Producers fear her lifestyle will turn off viewers." And: "The show's producers told her to tone down her lifestyle in public to make her heterosexual character more believable."

Friends were quoted as saying they hadn't "seen her date a guy since a football star Ben Heath broke her heart in high school."

Crystal Neidhart, a gay woman who lives in New Orleans, said she frequently saw Ellen at a certain French Quarter lesbian bar with a beautiful woman around 1982. "Ellen always had her arm around the woman's waist or shoulder. I saw them slow-dance very close."

When later asked about her relationship with singer Melissa Etheridge, Ellen told a reporter, "I was a fan first. I saw her on Melrose Avenue and approached her and we laughed and laughed and laughed. We became friends and continued laughing."

Another member of Ellen's social circle commented, "It's also no secret that she's very close with Melissa Etheridge, who is very openly gay. Melissa refuses to live in the closet, and most people in her crowd don't think it's hurt her career at all."

The implication was that Ellen shouldn't worry about whether coming out would hurt her own career. But there's a vast difference between a musical performer whose CDs you buy and the television star you let into your home—a difference Ellen's representatives were acutely aware of.

Ellen's publicist at the time, Lori Jonas, adamantly insisted that the story was untrue and denied that Ellen went to girl-only bars. She also denied that Ellen's producers had ever asked her to tone down her lifestyle.

However, associates of the producers admit that there was some talk about how best to respond to the article. Some wanted to ignore it, others wanted to vehemently deny it, and still others wanted to counter with interviews in other magazines and newspapers. In the end Ellen decided to do nothing. Although she wasn't anxious for her private life to be grist for the public mill, she didn't want to blatantly lie.

"For Ellen to pretend to have a boyfriend or feel the need to create a life for public consumption that doesn't really exist is very stressful," noted a friend. "Leading a double life wears you down—as many women in the Crushed Velvet group can attest. Ellen seems torn between just saying, 'The hell with it,' and being who she is without trying to hide or make excuses or staying in the closet so middle America will love her unconditionally."

Not that her coworkers didn't know the truth. An ABC representative admitted, "Ellen is very comfortable with who she is, and she has never made a secret about her lifestyle. It would be sad if she had to change to appease anyone else. I think Ellen's personal life is her personal business. Case closed."

When reporters kept niggling at her about the *Enquirer* story, Ellen felt compelled to call it sensationalistic and untrue. Privately, Ellen's handlers floated tentative negotiations. They let the tabloid know that Ellen might cooperate with them on innocuous stories like "At Home With . . ." or "My Most Embarrassing Moment." They didn't admit there was anything to hide; they maintained they just didn't want Ellen's family and friends being harassed.

The agreement unraveled when the tabloid refused to tell Ellen's people the names of the sources who were helping them get information about the star's private life. Later one of Ellen's representatives went back to the tabloid to try to revive the deal, but the *Enquirer* declined.

All of the deceit obviously preyed on Ellen's mind. "I'm such an extrovert. Why would I want to expose myself to the world if I didn't like people and care what they think? Maybe I care too much."

The realization that her sexual preference was being revealed in smarmy articles meant that she had lost control of that part of her life. Because she didn't feel confident enough or brave enough to confront the issue head on, her life would be sensationalized, painted—and tainted—by others. It frightened and worried her, but not enough for her to take control. Not yet.

All of my friends were seeing a therapist, and I thought something was wrong with me that I didn't see a therapist. So I went to a therapist to find out why I wasn't seeing a therapist. And it turns out I'm very screwed up. Thank God I found a therapist to tell me that for $125 an hour.

In addition to the swirling speculation about her sexuality, Ellen was also singled out for her looks in some unnecessarily sniping articles. The most bizarre was one claiming that Ellen "revealed for the first time that she has a chemical imbalance that makes her appear masculine."

The article alleged that Ellen had been heard to say, "A certain number of women have it. It makes them more masculine. I have always felt that way. I mean, I played with dolls when I was a kid, but I've always felt different."

In truth, like most of us, Ellen would like to improve some things about her body, but she had already come to accept herself. "I'm very comfortable with who I am, and there are people in my life who like who I am. But as far as the stereotypical, beautiful, sexy woman we have created in magazines, I certainly am not that. This business manipulates and screws up women's—and men's—views of what we're supposed to look like.

"I mean, if I could have a computer and change things, I certainly would. I don't show off my body, because I'm more comfortable with having a conversation than drawing attention to myself. I think I represent a whole lot of women who haven't been represented on television, and I think that's part of the success of the show."

She was also stung to be included on Mr. Blackwell's Worst-Dressed List. "My gender-bender style is apparently a bore," she said in response. She also went on to say she wasn't about to change. "People seem to like me, what I do, that I can help them realize that they don't have to act or look a certain way."

It was the best of times and the worst of times for Ellen. She was living out a professional dream and was struggling with trying to remain true to herself without losing it all. Her dilemma was apparent in the melancholy she sometimes exuded. "As I've found, living in L.A. is different from living anywhere else, and I certainly wouldn't be here if I didn't have to. It's a means to an end, and as soon as I'm wealthy enough, I'm definitely going to get out. At the moment, however, I have no choice. I look at it as a prison term. I'm serving my time. I'm doing it because I'm in this business. It's what I do. It's in my blood.

"I think my whole career up until now has been based on wanting people to like me and wanting to be accepted and proving to people I am a really good person. After a while, though, it's like I'm exhausted. I can't please everyone.

"In Los Angeles, I live up on a hill in a house that has a view of a lot of different things. And I have my dogs. So you know, I just hope I can keep doing what I'm doing, and when I get enough of it I'll move to Montana like everybody else."

11
Queen of the Emmys

No sooner had production of the first season's episodes wrapped in May 1994 than Ellen hit the road to perform a select number of engagements in several states, including Texas and Florida. Even though she had spent so many years doing stand-up, she was nervous getting back on the road after close to a nine-month layoff.

"I'm scared to death to go back out again, because I haven't done it for so long," she had admitted in January 1994. "It's going to take me a few weeks to get back into that kind of shape again. But I still want to do stand-up, because it helps create an audience and a bigger audience. And once they see the show, then I'm reaching more people that have never seen me before. So it's just a smart thing to do to keep doing stand-up."

Even though she was now a big TV star, Ellen didn't ask for any more contractual perks or treat anybody differently. She did have one new stipulation for this round of concerts—she wouldn't play in club settings anymore.

"I only want to work in theaters now. The environment is

so much better for a comic. Everyone's facing the same direction, you can build the act to a nice, strong finish, and you don't have to worry that you're competing with someone in the audience who's drunk."

Other than the venue restrictions, it was like slipping into an old pair of comic slippers. "I played bigger theaters. I could definitely sell a lot more tickets. But other than that, not much of a difference."

The shows were sellouts, and the audiences were wildly enthusiastic. Somewhat taken aback by just how much affection was being hurled her way, Ellen joked at one venue, "Boy, they must really like me. Or hey, did somebody forget to take Toni Braxton's name off the marquee?"

The only downside of the tour came in Buffalo, New York. A trio of tabloid reporters checked into Ellen's hotel, hoping to catch her doing something rude or being lewd with someone or getting herself into any kind of compromising position. But Ellen was tipped off about the surveillance, and her manager quietly had her change hotels.

The final stop of her brief concert tour was in New York, where she appeared at the venerable Town Hall on June 11. It was a key part of the tri-state Toyota Comedy Festival, which lasted eleven days and encompassed seventy-five events.

The Town Hall show may have been the most triumphant of Ellen's entire career. She sold out the nearly two-thousand-seat house, and when she pulled up in front of the theater in a stretch limousine, dozens of fans crowded around to get her autograph or pose for pictures with her. She stood in the street and obliged everyone with unflagging good humor and enthusiasm, despite her manager's obvious discomfort at how long it was taking her to do this.

Inside, Ellen took the stage and waited while latecomers hustled to their seats, teasing them to "Hurry up, hurry up. Run, run, run!"

When everyone was finally settled in, Ellen made the dramatic announcement that she was retiring from stand-up to write poetry, then read the hysterically awful "Oh How I Wish I Were a Bird." She also said she'd written others, including "What's There to Smile About?" and "What's the Use? We're All Going to Die."

After this, Ellen performed her now-classic routines: being sold to the Iroquois, shooting deer, airplane peanuts, the mating eagles . . .

They don't stop dropping until the act is completed. So it's not uncommon that they both fall all the way to the ground, hit the ground, and both of them die . . . I don't know about you, but if I'm one of those two birds, I would seriously consider fakin' it.

. . . the phone call to god, and many others.

She also surprised—and delighted—the audience when she admitted that whenever she's flying and hears a strange noise, her reaction isn't a silent prayer but a loud "Fuck! Shit! Damn! Hell!"

When the ninety-minute performance was over and a few audience members hurried out to beat the rush, Ellen thanked everyone for the "standing and walking ovation." Fans started calling out for an encore, and Ellen was happy to oblige, joking that she should do what Diana Ross does during her music concerts: start the routine, then hold out the microphone and let the audience finish.

As Ellen took her final bows, she let the applause thunder through her. A couple of months later, at the 1994 summer Television Critics Press Tour, Ellen stunned the critics by announcing she was putting that part of her life behind her.

"I've stopped stand-up," she said, almost as an aside. "I'm not doing it anymore. I think I've retired. I'm not sure. But I don't think I'm going to do it again. I've been doing it thirteen, fourteen years, and I just felt I hit a place that was it for me. I didn't think I was really growing anymore, even though . . . I thought I had a good show and I think I have good material.

"I mean, on one hand stand-up is harder. You're alone and you can't start again if you screw up. Well, you can, but it weakens the end result. I like what I do, but it just wasn't as challenging, and I constantly like to be challenged. I didn't get into stand-up knowing where I was going to go. It's what I enjoyed, and I had fun with it, and I found out I wanted to do television from there, and then I decided I didn't want to do stand-up anymore."

Ellen shared the feeling she had while standing onstage at that final performance. "I went out there knowing this was the last time I was going to do stand-up, so it was really an interesting tour for me. It was great. But *Ellen* keeps me busy, and I'm talking to people about doing films right now. . . . There's plenty to do beyond stand-up. There are a lot of people existing without stand-up."

That said, Ellen did admit that her decision wasn't without melancholy. "I'll miss just being alone. But I've never been one of those people who craves being onstage in front of people. If anything, I really do get nervous in front of big crowds. And as much as it doesn't seem like that, it's not like I can't wait to get onstage, like Robin Williams or Jerry Seinfeld. They love doing that.

"I really love being part of a team doing things. This is brand-new to me. And I hope to get better and better at acting and learn things, and so to me this is a lot of fun. Who knows, I may change my mind. I may miss it and I may want to do it again. I may actually just wait and do the Barbra Streisand thing where somebody offers me fourteen million dollars and I'll decide to come back. And I'm focusing all that kind of writing on the book."

Ellen had been commissioned to write a humor book, along the lines of Jerry Seinfeld's SeinLanguage. "It's on

O.J. Simpson," she laughed. "Seriously, it's just stuff. Not to even try and compare myself to Woody Allen, but it's like his early stuff when he used to write just short stories. It's going to be a mixture of a lot of things. I'm supposed to have like sixty thousand words or something and I think I have two thousand. I have a ways to go. Some days I feel like I have nothing to say, and other days it just flows out of me. It depends on how much I have to drink."

The book was scheduled to be published in October 1995. "It's good timing. The show will have been on a year, and I think that's a good amount of time to let people really be familiar with me. . . . It's right before Christmas. Books make great gifts."

Kidding aside, although the book wasn't due for over a year, Ellen would find the deadline tough to make, because she was suddenly in great demand. Other work beckoned, which is one reason she had scheduled such a short tour. First, she had been asked to host the VH1 Honors show.

Ironically, even though Ellen had spent the previous decade-plus working in front of groups of people, hosting the awards show was nervewracking. "I was dying. I really thought people could see the mike shaking. I was really so nervous, and because it was live I was really surprised that you couldn't see I was shaking. I guess through just years of doing something for a living you get better at hiding things. So even when I'm nervous now it never shows. . . . I think whenever you're nervous it ultimately hurts you. I try to tell myself that before I do anything.

"But the VH1 Honors were scary as hell because it was just me. It was me keeping it going for two hours. And because they had to keep making these huge changes with Prince's band and with Michael Bolton's band, they kept telling me, 'You may have to stall,' for like ten minutes. And I thought, 'What am I going to say for ten minutes?' I had some things to say, but I was so grateful I didn't have to say them, because they were so stupid. I was not prepared at all. But it was great. I thought it came off well, and I was really happy with it."

After the VH1 Honors, Ellen got busy with pre-production for the new season, which included interviewing writers. Pressing even more on her mind was her upcoming stint as co-host for the forty-sixth annual Emmy Awards show, sharing the duties with *Home Improvement*'s Patricia Richardson.

"I was outside at a pay phone and it rang and they asked me to host the Emmys," Ellen deadpans. "I'm kidding. Actually, I was the fifth caller."

The day of the ceremony, Ellen was at the Pasadena Civic Auditorium early, rehearsing for that evening's broadcast, especially the backstage bits that would be among the comedy highlights. Ellen was dressed in her usual style—jeans, shirt, and newsboy cap worn backward. Following her around were members of the production staff, several friends, and her girlfriend at the time, a short, pretty, slightly zaftig brunette who watched Ellen with what could only be described as adoring looks.

While working during rehearsal, Ellen was in her element, comfortable and in control. Having hosted the VH1 Honors would prove to be invaluable experience. Ellen was mentally prepared for the Emmys and determined to be on top of her game.

It wasn't the hosting job that worried her. It was the wardrobe. The Academy of Television Arts and Sciences views the Emmy Awards as a black-tie event. Even members of the press are required to attend in formal attire. Although she wasn't under any sort of official mandate, Ellen still felt pressure to at least make an appearance in a dress.

"I hate dresses. I'm too muscular to wear a dress. I had not worn a dress since like 1980, and I wasn't going to wear it," she admits. "It was so much pressure. 'Are you going to wear a dress? Are you going to wear a gown?' And I didn't even think about it, because I always wear suits. That's what I feel comfortable in. Some people don't feel comfortable in pants. But then I thought I would, just to show people I could. So I thought, 'Okay, I'll wear a dress when I come out and that's it.' Most people would be in their trailer, petrified of what they were going to say. The most terrifying thing for me was walking across that stage in a dress."

Watching Ellen, it was almost painfully obvious how uncomfortable she was walking out to join co-host Richardson. But despite her awkward steps, her face was beaming. "I looked out into that audience, and I've never seen my dad so happy. He was so proud. I know that wearing that dress made his life complete. I haven't seen the show, but I saw a picture of myself in *USA Today*. I thought I looked big. I'll probably wear a dress again in about ten years."

But the dress would be the least memorable part of the evening for the television community in attendance. It was indeed a show to remember. The broadcast opened with Bette Midler singing a biting rendition of "Rose's Turn" from *Gypsy,* a performance for which she had been nominated.

Ellen took control from the first minutes of the show, commenting to Richardson about the dramatic way Midler ended the song, "You know, that was my idea for her to crumple to the ground at the end."

For once, the banter between two co-hosts was actually funny. In part this was because of Richardson's expertise at being a straight man, which Ellen played off of skillfully.

DEGENERES: (*to the nominees in the audience*) You should feel no pressure at all. It's your night. And it is a big night. It's big. Big, big, big.

RICHARDSON: Big Stars. Big limos.

DEGENERES: Big hair, big shoes. I'll tell you actually how

big it is: literally, there are thousands of people watching us right now.

RICHARDSON: Thousands? Ellen, this show is being watched by over six hundred million people in eighty-five countries.

DEGENERES: (*laughing*) Right . . . like there are eighty-five countries. That's crazy. I mean, there's America, and Canada, Micronesia . . . ten tops.

RICHARDSON: Ellen, you're forgetting Europe . . .

DEGENERES: All right. Eleven.

Ellen stayed in her dress for another segment, to introduce John Larroquette. Then she rushed backstage and changed into a tailored suit and, keeping the formality of the occasion in mind, black high-top sneakers. Thereafter, Ellen became a sort of roving reporter, taking both the home audience and those in the auditorium on a behind-the-scenes adventure. Her first stop was outside. Under a sizzling September sun, she spoke to the fans sitting in the bleachers, who stake out territory to watch both the stars' arrivals and departures.

"I'm just curious," Ellen asked the cheering spectators, "did you have any idea these were such bad seats?" After Ellen did her own version of "Rose's Turn," she confided to the fans, "I guess the big news is, Jane Seymour showed up with Ja'leel White, TV's Urkel. They're dating now. Spread it around."

Her next stop was the director's truck, with its wall of monitors showing what each of the sixteen cameras being used was seeing. "Oh! This almost looks like the security room for Whitney Houston's house." The Emmys' director, Lou Horvitz, let Ellen take over the reins of the show for a few moments. "Okay, cue music. I don't like that, take it off. You have anything like Pearl Jam?"

Then she started scanning the audience to see who was

laughing at her jokes. "Okay, Kirstie Allen is laughing. Candice Bergen's laughing. Everybody's laughing. I'm not going to say the people who aren't, but I can see you, though."

After Jason Alexander's clever salute to television theme songs, Ellen was up in the farthest regions of the balcony, seats "reserved" for the public. "Oh, this is so exciting. Who was that? It's kind of hard to see from up here. I'm not sure if that was Marlo Thomas or Pat Morita. Anyway, it's exciting. I'm here in the balcony. You can see what a huge place this is. It's big, but it looks bigger on camera. That's what the camera does. I'm actually very thin. I weigh forty-two pounds. Wait until you meet me.

"Okay, I actually have a couple of questions for you right here, ma'am," Ellen said to a woman sitting in an aisle seat. "First of all, I'm sorry, who don't you know? Aren't you concerned when you win, how are you going to get down there in time? It's people like you who makes these shows run long. You're so high up that by the time the show reaches you, it's over."

Ellen led cameras into the press room, for a prearranged encounter with Michael Richards. Her girlfriend stood in the back of the room, excitedly taking pictures, then followed discreetly behind as Ellen left to return backstage. All through the evening, Ellen looked relaxed, attractive, comfortable, and very, very natural on camera. Her impish smile was extremely appealing, and one got the sense that here was someone with an amazing wit and an ease on-camera that people would pay to see.

"It was probably the biggest night of my life," Ellen would say later. "I'm brand-new to this, so I was very impressed. I've been watching the Emmys for years . . . then I'm onstage hosting, looking at all these heroes: Candice Bergen giving me a thumbs-up, James Garner, Angela Lansbury, and Carol Burnett sound asleep. No, they were all encouraging me, smiling at me, winking at me. And the next day Paul Reiser left a message on my answering machine, 'Yes, you are the funniest person in show business.'"

Ellen recalled that during one commercial break, "all of a sudden I hear this 'Hey!' And I could tell it was Roseanne. She was in the front row, and right before we go live she goes, 'You're funny.' Which was very nice, except she said the same thing to John Lithgow later on when he was standing there. I thought, 'She's just throwing that out to anybody.' It's still very nice, but it was right before I went on, so it kind of threw me a little bit."

Nobody noticed. In one memorable performance, she made people look at her differently. "Before the Emmys, I was just another actor on TV. What I did on the Emmys is what I do—I'm a comedian. And that was so easy. So suddenly I was in my element, and people were shocked, like, 'Who's this?'

"I think if I would've really realized what a big deal it was, I wouldn't have been able to pull it off. I wasn't thinking about eighty-five countries tuned in. I was thinking about that room. Because everybody in show business was there. And for some reason, everything clicked."

Within the industry, it wasn't just television people who were tuned in that night. Film executives were also watching, and nobody had to tell them there was untapped potential in Ellen for the big screen.

"Minutes after the show, I could tell that something marginally had shifted," recalls her manager, Arthur Imperato. "There'd been interest in Ellen for feature films all along. It's just that at the Emmys, people saw her as a very, very special talent."

Ellen's agent, J. J. Harris at United Talent Agency, said that although there had been "a daunting awareness" of her client ever since her series went on the air, it ballooned after she hosted the Emmys. "Most of the studios called and said they'd like to have a meeting with Ellen and get her to do a movie" during hiatus.

And when her mother told Ellen she had read an ad in one of the Hollywood trade papers that a movie company was seeking an "Ellen DeGeneres type," Ellen figured her time had finally come.

I've been up and I've been down, and up is better. Unless you're sleeping, in which case down is better. Especially goose down.

If indeed she was going to get the chance to do movies, she wanted to be in as good shape as possible. Earlier in 1994, she had taken up kickboxing, and she had lost fifteen pounds prior to the Emmy telecast. "Watch out, Oscar de la Hoya," Ellen joked. She also said, more seriously, "I want to feel great about my body because I never have. I have never felt sexy. I was looking at myself on tape the other day, thinking, 'I'm fat.' I have a trainer now, and he has me on a no-fat diet and boxing four times a week. I'm really trying to transform myself." In fact, the only drawback to her dressing room was that there wasn't enough room for any exercise equipment, like the Nordic-Track and Lifecycle she would exercise on daily at home.

But first Ellen had a series to film. While she planned to take advantage of whatever opportunity arose from her Emmy duties, Ellen's number one priority was the show, for which she had the highest aspirations. "The thing that's frustrating me so much is that I want the show to be number one. I'm not lighting candles, but I pray once in a while to the Nielsen families."

Number one shows uniformly share one feature—outstanding writing. And although the cast changes did seem to be an improvement, and making Ellen the bookstore's owner did open the storyline possibilities up, Ellen was still concerned about the scripts. She hoped that better communication and increased collaboration would help the show find its groove.

"They ask my input," Ellen said early during the second season. "They call me if there's an idea that they have that they're questionable about. I call them when I have ideas for shows or just even little tiny things I want to put into a show. I give them ideas and listen to theirs. And other than that, that's it. I don't sit in the room when they're writing.

"When I get the script on Monday, we come up with different ideas, and then all week long when we're rehearsing, until Friday when we shoot, I just keep playing around with it. Sometimes we shoot two different ways. We'll shoot the way it's written, and then I'll just come up with different ways."

Ellen was trying hard to balance her vision with the creative suggestions of the writers and was willing to try just about anything. "The writers are coming up with more and more ridiculous things—I'm in a ballet wearing a tutu and dancing all over the place. I think it's the awkwardness that everyone relates to, that sense of not fitting in."

In November 1994, one anonymous on-set source noted, "What you've got is a hit because of the time slot and because Ellen just jumps off the screen. But the different factions are still fighting over what the show should be. One camp still wants it to be *Seinfeld*. Another wants it to be *I Love Lucy*. And a third wants it to be more like *The Mary Tyler Moore Show*."

What Ellen wanted was for it to be Ellen. "I'm trying to portray a strong, single woman in the nineties, which I am in real life. But I don't think that I act or behave anything like a thirty-seven-year-old woman is supposed to act. I really think of myself as a girl, not a woman. I know some women will be offended by that, but I just feel it's a matter of redefining our sex."

She was getting impatient for everything to finally fall into place. "We haven't quite hit our stride. I'm such a perfectionist. I feel like I'm getting close to that David Letterman syndrome. He's never happy with his shows, and I get that way. I'm always thinking, 'That just wasn't right.' I think we have so much further to go for it to get better. I think Arye's character can be developed more, for instance. It's not like I'm too timid to speak up or that I'm too nice. But I've learned that you can be nice and still exert some pressure to do things the way you want them done."

Privately, Ellen would admit that she wished she had what Jerry Seinfeld had, a Larry David. "Jerry is lucky because he has someone who is on the exact same wavelength and who can help Jerry create the show they want. They are the show, and it must be great to have that kind of collaborator."

When asked if she had any special casting wishes for her show, Ellen didn't hesitate. "Tom Hanks would be great. I would love to have him. I don't really have anybody in mind right now, and it probably depends on the story ideas coming up. I'm interested in having as many cool people as we can on. Whoever will do our show that would enhance the show."

As the series moved into the second half of the 1994–95 season, Ellen found that she had little time for anything except work, even her beloved dogs. "I explain to them, 'I'm successful now. I'm doing well. Somebody has to bring home the bones.'"

Whenever she felt herself starting to cave under the stress of her life, though, time with her animals was decidedly regenerative. "The best therapy is to take my dogs out for a long walk. We go around the neighborhood for an hour or two at a time. When the walk is over, I'm happy and refreshed."

Ellen says that cooking helps cheer her up, too. "I go into the kitchen and shut the rest of the world out. I spend an hour making the most delicious Caesar salad in the world."

Those days, Ellen was cooking for one. "One day Ellen came onto the set very upset," reports a crew member. "She told everyone her girlfriend had broken up with her. It really threw Ellen off kilter. I don't know if it's the reason why, but not long after, she started therapy."

Around that time, Ellen made a telling comment. "We are bombarded by the message that your life isn't complete until you find the perfect person. And no matter how much you try to say, 'My life is fine without it,' when you're raised with that all your life, it's bound to seep in."

Since Kat, it seemed as if Ellen had been on a fruitless search for her perfect person, going from relationship to relationship. She wanted more stability in her personal life and needed to find out what inside her was preventing that from happening.

This was one area where her mom was of little help, says Ellen, with Betty not yet having truly come to terms with her daughter's sexual identity. "When I would have problems in relationships, she would say, 'Now, you see, why don't you just give this up and meet a nice boy?' She has never understood it. She really just kept thinking it was a phase."

"Well, it certainly would have been easier on her if it was," countered Betty. "This is not an easy thing. It's not an easy way of life, but it's who she is."

As painful as her private life was, her career had taken on a life of its own. She was offered the female lead in the sequel to *My Cousin Vinny* after Fox Studios couldn't reach an agreement with Marisa Tomei, but she turned it down. Then she came close to committing to *Runaway Bride*, a film that had been previously attached to Demi Moore and Sandra Bullock. The film, about a woman who had walked down the aisle three times and been unable to say "I do" even once, had been kicking around the studios since 1992, when Harrison Ford and Geena Davis were supposed to star in it.

But Ellen wanted to be very careful about her selection, knowing how important the decision would be. In the end, she opted for a black comedy called *Mr. Wrong,* being produced by Disney—at whose studio, where, not so coincidentally, her series was being shot. The movie was scheduled to begin shooting no later than June 1995, during her next summer hiatus, and to be released in winter or spring 1996.

She was so excited, it took her mind off her constant worry that she was being misinterpreted by people who chose to base their opinions on her TV character or her stand-up persona.

"I think I'm a little hipper than I come off. I like to experience life in many different ways. I'm a very open-minded, very liberal, very strong woman. I think that I'm a little stronger than I let people know because I realize how much it scares them. In my life, I've found that people are frightened of strong women."

Some are; others seek them out. In February 1995, Ellen was asked to be grand marshal of the Endymion Mardi Gras parade, the Big Daddy of pre-Lent celebrations. She was genuinely dismayed when she learned that it conflicted with a planned appearance at the White House. "People in Los Angeles don't understand why this is a problem. They laugh, they say, 'How could a parade be as important as the president? You get asked to be in parades all the time.' They don't understand about Endymion."

It was a small glitch in an otherwise fabulous time. Even Ellen seemed somewhat awed by all that was on her plate. "I've got my own TV show. I've got a book deal. I've got a film. I've gotten nominated for a Golden Globe. It is just amazing to me that I've achieved all this. What do I do now?

I've got everything I've ever wanted. I don't know if I should just go into politics now, or wait. I don't know if I should become a mass murderer, just for a change, just to do something different.

"It's going to be a really amazing year."

12
Hollywood, Two Degrees of Separation

As the second season got underway in September 1994, Arye Gross was the only remaining original supporting cast member—just barely. After debating about whether to start with a completely new slate, the network asked him back at the eleventh hour. Adam was originally intended to be Ellen's primary comic foil and, indeed, initially served that purpose well enough.

"In *Ellen*'s most endearing flip of the *I Love Lucy* formula," said one review, "Adam is Ellen's Ethel. Ellen is strong and agile; Adam is a flabby weakling. Nervous Ellen can still put on a (momentarily) convincing show of confidence; Adam is a hopeless wimp. Like all the best sidekicks, Adam makes Ellen look good."

As the season wore on, however, Gross would find his sidekick role increasingly diminished. It wasn't that Gross had changed his characterization. It was just that when Ellen and Joely Fisher were on the screen together, they seemed to generate more crackle and snap. As Paige edged closer to center stage, Adam seemed less important and, in fact, was often a bit of an energy drain with his lazy voice and laid-back demeanor.

Joely's character, Paige Clark, is a childhood friend of Ellen's who takes the concept of self-centeredness to a new level. Vivacious, ambitious, and voluptuous, Paige has her sights set on a producing career in entertainment—and on most of the men in Los Angeles County.

Wendy Goldberg once described Paige as "a person who's very much the kind of friend who will nudge Ellen into things that are way over her head. And she's the kind of person who likes to poke the cage. She takes a lot of risks and gets Ellen into situations that Ellen will then have to im-provise to get out of."

Even though Joely was a relative newcomer when she was cast as Paige, she had literally grown up in and around the business. Her mother is actress Connie Stevens, and her father is crooner Eddie Fisher; the couple's relationship is part of Hollywood gossip lore. His marriage to American film sweetheart Debbie Reynolds broke up over his scan-dalous affair with Elizabeth Taylor. Ironically, after he left his wife and children to wed Taylor, she unceremoniously dumped him when she had an even more scandalous affair and fell in love with Richard Burton.

Fisher's first big break came in 1992 when James Brooks cast her in *I'll Do Anything,* which he intended to be the first original movie musical since *Fame.* The film starred Nick Nolte and a host of unknowns, including Fisher and future *NewsRadio* star Vicki Lewis, cast on the strength of their singing. (Coincidentally, the film also featured the future love of Ellen's life, Anne Heche. In Hollywood, it's more like two degrees of separation.)

In the movie, Nolte plays a down-on-his-luck actor who suddenly finds himself driving a limousine to make ends meet and raising his young daughter after his ex-wife is sen-tenced to a two-year jail sentence. The production filmed for four and a half months, and Fisher was in heaven. "I thought it was a kick, really off-the-wall."

But the good times wouldn't last. Brooks, an Oscar winner for *Terms of Endearment,* dismantled his ambitious film, with songs by the likes of Prince and Carole King and choreography by Twyla Tharp, after test audiences lynched it. It was reported that one hundred people walked out of a test screening. The opinion cards showed utter loathing for the songs—or, more specifically, for the way the songs were sung by some of the less-than-vocally-trained cast. "At the test screenings," Joely reports, "people laughed out loud when Nick Nolte sang."

Brooks cut all the songs, leaving some of Joely's work on the cutting-room floor. Scenes deconstructed by the removal of the musical numbers had to be reshot so the release of the movie was delayed two months.

I'll Do Anything was supposed to have been Fisher's big break. In fact, the movie did receive several positive reviews. However, audiences were less enthusiastic.

Even though it might not have catapulted her into being the next "it" girl, *I'll Do Anything* did open some doors. Joely caught the eye of the *Ellen* producers, who saw her as Paige. It took a moment, though, for Joely to visualize herself as such a self-obsessed character.

"I think of myself as buxom and brazen," she says, "but I said, 'Oh my God, how am I going to do that?' It's so awful, but she's so much fun to play."

It can also be awful to be an actor called upon to replace another performer. But Joely understood that this was strictly a creative decision intended to improve the show, so she was able to set aside whatever qualms she had about the cast changes.

"They felt the chemistry wasn't right before. They loved Ellen and the idea of the show, but they needed to make some changes to make it a hit. They wanted to find someone

The photo Ellen didn't want fans to see—her high school senior picture. (Seth Poppel Yearbook Archives)

Ellen, who briefly considered going pro, shows her form on the tennis court. (Seth Poppel Yearbook Archives)

Ellen with her varsity tennis team. (Seth Poppel Yearbook Archives)

Ellen has always been a huge music fan. Here she poses with
singer Joan Osborne. (Ramey Photo Agency)

Ellen and her mom, Betty, coming back to Los Angeles after a trip.
(Ramey Photo Agency)

Ellen's preference for man-tailored suits such as this one caused some viewers to write in wanting to know why she didn't dress in a more feminine fashion. (Ramey Photo Agency)

Since her daughter's public coming out, Betty DeGeneres has become a best-selling author and an outspoken activist. She encourages parents of gay children to offer acceptance rather than criticism. (Sue Schneider/Shooting Star Agency)

Ellen at the Grammys with Sammy Hagar and an unidentified man. (Ramey Photo Agency)

Ellen's costar Arye Gross was often her "date" to Hollywood functions before behind-the-scenes turmoil convinced Gross to jump the series ship. (Ramey Photo Agency)

Ellen and her brother Vance. (Ramey Photo Agency)

Ellen credits *Finding Nemo* with helping revitalize her career. In the film, Ellen plays a memory-challenged fish named Dory. Here, Ellen and Alexandra arrive at the film's 2003 premiere. (Sue Schneider/Shooting Star Agency)

Ellen and Alexandra Hedison met through mutual friends several months after Ellen's painful breakup with Anne Heche. Ellen credits Alexandra with "saving my life." (Sue Schneider/Shooting Star Agency)

Ellen, sans date, cools herself off with a portable fan at the 1996 Emmys. (Ramey Photo Agency)

Ellen and Anne Heche arrive at the Emmys. (Ramey Photo Agency)

Ellen admitted that after winning the Emmy, she finally felt as if she had been accepted by Hollywood. (Ramey Photo Agency)

After Ellen won an Emmy for "The Puppy Episode," she and Anne caused a scandal with their overly affectionate kisses with Bruce Willis and Demi Moore.

(Above) Bruce greets Anne Heche while Ellen looks on from behind. (Ramey Photo Agency)

(Above left) Betty DeGeneres looks on in utter shock at Demi and Anne's passionate kiss. (Ramey Photo Agency)

(Left) Bruce and Ellen, Demi and Anne, will set tongues wagging, so to speak, when news of their kiss fest is reported in the press. (Ramey Photo Agency)

After the announcement that Ellen and Alexandra had split up, it was reported that *Arrested Development* star Portia DeRossi was Ellen's new love interest. (Barbara Binstein)

With the success of her new talk show, Ellen has proven there indeed are second acts in American lives.
(Sue Schneider/Shooting Star Agency)

Ellen accepting the People's Choice Award on January 9, 2005, for Favorite Daytime Talk Show Host. (Frank Micelotta/Getty Images)

who butts heads more with Ellen. They needed bigger energy that goes against what she is doing. So I read with Ellen and made her laugh, and that helped. I had three auditions, and then I went in front of all these 'suits' from the network. That was at four o'clock, and at six o'clock I got the call that I got the job. Just then everything in my life changed."

Including her hair color. The producers asked her to dye her naturally blond hair red. Actually, they insisted. Ellen was also blond, and they didn't want the viewers to be confused. (Duh!)

In asking Fisher to mess with her hair, they were treading on one of her most prized assets. "I have the thickest, curliest, craziest hair. I call it fusilli. It's a phenomenon."

Actually, though, Joely says that she quickly grew to like her change of shade, feeling it fit her "big mouthed, wise-cracking New Yorker" persona better. "I was blond my whole life until this show. But I really like the red—it seems to suit my personality and direction."

According to Joely, who has since gone on to star in her own Lifetime series, *Wild Card,* working on *Ellen* was an enjoyable experience. "It was a busy place, a comfortable place. There were no egos allowed."

That kind of atmosphere and tone, whether on a television sound stage or a film set, is always set by the star. Ellen had made it clear that she wanted "everybody on this show to have their own spark and to add something."

It didn't take too many episodes into the second season to see that Joely was adding her own brand of spark. In a 1995 interview, she commented on her new relationship with TV fans. "When I go shopping, people know who I am. And people yell, . . . 'Hey, girl from *Ellen.*'"

It certainly helped Joely and Ellen's on-screen chemistry that they became off-screen friends and would often go out after tapings with the rest of the cast. The two would also socialize individually and in fact Fisher credits Ellen with playing matchmaker and setting Joely up with the man she would eventually marry, special-effects cinematographer Chris Duddy, whose work includes *Terminator 2.*

"It was a couple of days before my birthday," Fisher recalls. "I went to visit Ellen, who was shooting a film for Epcot Center. Chris was up on the crane, and I saw his profile. He has a magnificent profile. I thought, 'Oooh, you have to introduce me. He's cute,' and asked who he was. Ellen said, 'You gotta go for him.' But I had to go to a meeting. She called me later and said, 'Here's the deal: He noticed you, too, so you gotta come back.' And we've been together ever since." Duddy and Fisher married in 1996 and five years later became parents to daughter Skylar.

Fisher wasn't the only co-star to jump to Ellen's defense over speculation that she was turning into a tyrant.

"Nice is often a misused word," says David Higgins, who played Coffee Joe on *Ellen.* "In Hollywood, after you slam someone, you say, 'But they're a nice person.' But Ellen really *is* a nice person."

So how come everybody was so anxious to brand her the next Brett Butler or Roseanne? Mostly because a series that has what's perceived to be a revolving door for producers is more often than not a series whose star's ego has gone wild. When Wendy Goldberg became the latest producer to leave the show, just a few months after joining the production team in the second season, it prompted a whole new round of speculation about just what *was* going on behind the scenes of *Ellen.*

In part, it was true that Ellen was becoming more assertive. But being forthright is not the same as being tyrannical, as producer David Rosenthal pointed out. "At the beginning, I think she was just grateful to have somebody creating a show for her. Now I think she's realized, 'You know what? I'm the star of the show and I've got a lot to say and boy, I'd really like to be heard now.'

"When we started out, it was very much an ensemble show. By the sheer force of Ellen's talent and personality, it's evolved into a show about her, and the others are satellites around her."

But as Ellen was well aware, sometimes the brightest stars burn out the fastest.

13
The Sitcom That Dares Not Speak Its Name

When the rankings were released for the series' second season, 1994–95, *Ellen* came in thirteenth for the year. Considering all the behind-the-scenes upheaval, Ellen had reason to feel optimistic. If it could settle into some kind of consistency, it had the chance to be a perennial top ten show—and maybe even realize Ellen's dream of holding down the top spot, which for that season was held by *Seinfeld*.

By March 1995, Ellen was acting as a producer, attending script-critiquing meetings and sitting in on the editing. She already had ideas for the 1995–96 season, the show's third, including having Ellen Morgan see a therapist, as well as hiring more female staff writers. Ellen thought it was as silly to have a male-dominated staff on her show as it would be to have all-white writers for *Martin*.

"They were focusing on me dating all the time. And they said, 'Well, you're a single woman and that's what single women do.' And I said, 'There are lots of women who don't date this much.'"

This is not to say that Ellen believed there was a difference in the sexes' humor, per se. "If you read something on paper, I don't really think you'd be able to tell the gender of who wrote it," she said at the time. "But I think to get into a woman's head exactly and write it from that perspective, it's beneficial to have a woman writing it. We have male writers, and I don't think it really needs to be a full staff of women. But I do enjoy working with women, and they understand when once a month I get cranky."

As the series progressed, so did the amount of physical comedy performed by Ellen. "That's something that evolved from my stand-up. Like when I talked about how people react when they trip while walking, they go into that fake jog for just a second.

"The first thing we did physically on the show was a scene in *These Friends of Mine* where I was trying to get a new water bottle into the container and spilling it everywhere. I did that in one take, and they thought, 'Well, this is something she can do.'

"I think it gets to be too much if you do it every single show, and we don't want to force it into things, but it's a kind of humor that I really enjoy doing"—even though she often paid a price for the pratfalls. "Every week a different part of my body gets injured. They say I can get a stuntwoman, but I don't want to. It's too much fun. But I'm thirty-seven. Some weeks, just for my own well-being, I can't be doing that stuff."

Much to Ellen's annoyance, in March she learned that her show was being moved out of its post-*Roseanne* 9:30 cradle to the 8:30 time slot on the same night. Aware how important it was for a young show to develop a core audience, Ellen expressed some of her disappointment. "I wish we had a chance to just be after *Roseanne* or *Home Improvement* or *Grace Under Fire* and grow like most shows."

But in the context of the overall series picture, changing time periods wasn't worth stressing over too much. More important to Ellen was finding a consistent voice for her character, which at times still exuded a vagueness that translated into a feeling that something was missing. To *San Francisco Examiner* television critic Joyce Millman, at least, the missing piece was obvious, as she detailed in a long, pointed, and stunningly prescient critique in the spring of 1995.

The Sitcom That Dares Not Speak Its Name

Once you look at Ellen as a closeted lesbian, a very funny show makes perfect sense.

When Ellen DeGeneres's sitcom These Friends of Mine *debuted a year ago, it seemed like a pale imitation of* Seinfeld, *riding on the coattails of one of TV's cushiest lead-ins,* Roseanne. *But several changes of cast and focus later, the rechristened* Ellen *has hung in there as a genuine hit, often outranking* Roseanne. *Not bad for a prime example of a don't-ask, don't-tell sitcom. . . .*

As a single-gal sitcom, Ellen *doesn't make any sense at all, until you view it through the looking glass where the unspoken subtext becomes the main point. Then* Ellen *is transformed into one of TV's savviest, funniest, slyest shows. Ellen Morgan is a closet lesbian. . . .*

If Ellen *were to lay all its cards on the table, so to speak, could it still be a hit? Well, the pro-gay attitude of* Roseanne *hasn't hurt that show. The pressure to be a role model, though, coupled with the inevitable conservative protests might squeeze the life out of an upfront* Ellen.

And that would be a shame, because Ellen *is at its best when it's being utterly silly, when it drops any pre-*

*tense of realism and lets DeGeneres show off her gift
for physical comedy.*

The article was the first in a mainstream publication to obliquely question *Ellen*'s, and by extension Ellen's, sexuality. Although the article failed to make any national waves, it wasn't lost on either the writing staff or Ellen herself. To those who knew Ellen it was logical that the part of the show that was missing was the part of Ellen's life that nobody could allude to openly. Her character would be stilted and awkward for as long as Ellen and *Ellen* had to pretend to be something they weren't.

But Ellen wasn't ready even to contemplate such a bold, radical move. For one thing, personally and professionally, life was going so well that she didn't want to jeopardize all that she had worked for. Besides, she didn't have time to think about making any more significant changes to the series. She had a book to write, and filming on her movie, *Mr. Wrong,* was scheduled to begin June 1.

For Ellen, the most obvious change resulting from having a hit series was that she wasn't as anonymous as she used to be. "I always get surprised when people know who I am. I'm just constantly amazed at that. I was at a party and—I'm not dropping names, I'm really not, but Steven Spielberg was at this party and I'm thinking, 'He doesn't know who I am.' And he walks over to me and grabs my hand and goes, 'Thank you so much for putting your feet through the blinds at the barre where you're doing that ballet thing.'"

She was kidding, of course—although she did notice that stewardesses were more attentive to her. "Actually, they'll give me a case of club soda and a case of peanuts. And I've got to walk off with this thing. It's ridiculous. They're getting better, but it's still the whole upright-recline thing that really bugs me," she joked.

Although Ellen was just a few years shy of forty, she often still felt like an adolescent, in part because she lived like one, relatively speaking, by Hollywood standards. "I just don't think to live like an adult. People like my house, but it's not as grown-up as other people's homes that I see. Like in *Style* magazine."

She admitted that her decor included curling posters on the walls. "I want to start buying art because it's an adult thing to do. I go to parties of people who are in the business and I'm thinking, 'Well, I'm probably making that much money. And how come they have nice stuff?'

"Even Tom Arnold. I look at Tom Arnold's house and I'm thinking, 'His house is nicer than mine? Tom Arnold has better taste than I do?' You know, I can afford this stuff. But I just don't buy. I don't. My house is just average."

However, Ellen's closets were well furnished. "I buy clothes a lot. I always end up wearing jeans because I don't go out much. I put something on at the store and I'm like, 'This is cool.' It's in my closet and I go, 'Oh, I don't go anywhere, do I?' So I just have cool clothes that look good in the store."

One of Ellen's biggest pleasures was being able to treat her friends and family. "I like giving gifts, and I've given some things to people, like I've bought cars for my family. I like being able to share."

Especially with someone she loved. And as the second season ended and she prepared to shoot her movie, Ellen was indeed very much in love. Earlier in 1995, she had met a slender redhead named Teresa Boyd, who's been described by acquaintances as a commercial producer.

"They were introduced by a mutual friend at Muse," which at the time was a trendy restaurant in Hollywood. "They struck up a conversation and talked the entire night. At the end of the evening, Ellen asked Teresa for her phone number, and she called her the very next morning to invite her to breakfast. From there, the relationship quickly became serious."

There's an old joke in the homosexual community:

Q: What do two gay men do on a second date?
A: What second date?
Q: What do two gay women do on a second date?
A: Rent a U-Haul.

While stereotypical, the humor is less apocryphal than it might seem at first glance. Even in lesbian publications, the phenomenon of fast-forming relationships is often a topic of discussion, with many gay women wondering why the nesting compulsion seems to be expressed so vividly in female couples. Thus few in the community were surprised when, after dating for only a couple of months, Teresa moved in with Ellen and the two became seemingly inseparable.

Ellen and Teresa were photographed numerous times while out together either for private evenings alone or at Hollywood-related events. At Melissa Etheridge's birthday party on May 27, 1995, Ellen and Teresa were seen by many in attendance openly holding hands and kissing. When Ellen went on location to San Diego for *Mr. Wrong*, Teresa went along and could be seen hanging around the set.

Although Ellen still refused to answer questions that delved too much into her personal life, she did once describe what she looked for in a romance. "The same thing anybody looks for. I think intelligence, a sense of humor, a sense of fun, someone who's very strong and independent, and just somebody who you totally get and who gets you."

For a while, that person she got was Teresa. But suddenly being seen in public with the same woman repeatedly was bound to cause speculation in the tabloid press. While Ellen was working on *Mr. Wrong*, the *National Enquirer* published an article that claimed she and Teresa were planning on raising a child together, although "neither wants to get pregnant. So they're talking about adopting a baby."

The paper quoted Ellen as saying, "We're taking things one day at a time but I definitely see us with a little one running around. What's a home without children?

"Teresa has made me want to settle down. She's shown me what real happiness is."

Importantly, from a legal standpoint, what the article didn't say was that Ellen and Teresa were lovers or that they were sexually involved. They might be a "cozy couple" and "gal pals," but nowhere in the article was the word *gay* or *lesbian* used. That's because those are considered "red flag" words by the libel attorneys who vet the tabloids. In a carefully worded piece such as this, the point would be made quite clearly without actually printing anything that could be considered libelous. The angle of wanting to adopt a baby was merely a device to run a story about Ellen having a live-in lover, a fact that happened to be true.

Ellen's strategy for dealing with such stories was to comment on the aspects of them that were stretched or false. "It's so ridiculous now. I'm getting faxes of all these tabloids now saying things that are total lies—places I've never been, things I never did, all kinds of things."

Probably because Ellen had admitted in legitimate interviews that she would like to have a child someday, it was often the topic of tabloid gossip. It was also something Ellen found she could joke about. On *The Rosie O'Donnell Show,* Ellen laughingly informed the host that "I found out that you and my pal Madonna, who I've never met, talked me into having a baby. So I'm gonna have a baby by December. So I'm thinking, 'I gotta get busy.' I mean, I'm gonna need a nanny, so I start looking for a nanny."

Ellen said that once she read Hillary Clinton's book, *It Takes a Village,* she realized one nanny wouldn't be enough. So "I put an ad in the paper, 'Live-in village wanted. Must bring own towels.' I found one, but they were nomadic, so I'd have to come home from work and look for my kid. But there's like five hundred people to a village, and I have a small place and don't have that kind of room. So I may not have the kid after all."

The constant scrutiny by the tabloids was one reason Ellen often talked about moving away from Los Angeles— that, and the police helicopters that frequently patrol the hillside areas. "I was walking one night and I heard a helicopter, it was kind of close and I thought, 'Okay, there's someone in the area,' and the light is searching around and I thought, 'Oh, I better run to my house because they're looking for someone.' So they see me running and the light starts following me. I'm trying to explain to them, I point to my key, the light followed me into the house. I'm thinking I want to show them my cat. They're probably thinking I have a hostage and think I am saying 'I'll kill the cat.' I'm trying to show it's my cat, but my cat's flipping out so it doesn't look like it's my cat. I thought it was going to get shot."

L.A.'s company-town personality also bothered Ellen. "In L.A. it is all about the business. And you get so caught up in it. I do not belong in this business, I really feel that way, because I don't fit in."

Even when her series was at its most successful, Ellen complained that her social life was anything but the stuff of Hollywood dreams. "I never get invited to anything. Premieres and things like that, yes, but not parties. I hear Rosie O'Donnell talking all the time that she's hanging out with Penny Marshall and all those people, and I have a friend at the Gap. And that's fine, but how come I don't meet people in the business?"

On the rare occasions when she *was* included, she felt even more the outsider. "I once got invited to Goldie Hawn's house for a Gucci fashion show. And I'm looking at the envelope, I swear, for about twenty minutes thinking, 'They meant to send it to Ellen Barkin. There's no way they really sent this to me.' I don't know Goldie, I've never met her. So I'm thinking, 'Okay, I'll go.' This could be fun. It's a fashion show and they say it's an intimate, small thing.

"I agonized forever what to wear to that, and I picked some white pants and a vintage shirt which I thought would be fine. But I didn't know what time to go and—this sounds like I'm dropping names, but I happened to be talking to Mary Tyler Moore that morning on the phone, so I asked her, 'It doesn't start 'til one, so does that mean I get there at twelve-thirty because I want to be early?' And she starts laughing at me like that's the most ridiculous thing. She goes, 'No, you get there after one.'"

Not wanting to be rude, Ellen showed up at five after one and was mortified to discover nobody else was there. "I'm the first one there, and there are like forty valet people out front waiting and they're all dressed better than me. I said, 'Please tell me I'm not the first one here,' and they said, 'You are.'

"I walked in and I just wanted to find a leaf-blower and keep going to the next yard. The staff is in black pants and bow ties walking around serving champagne and hors d'oeuvres, and the whole lawn is done, there's a stage for the Gucci fashion show, and everyone, once they showed up—an hour after I'm there with the staff, helping them chop cucumbers and putting cold cream on them. Not cold cream; that would be cruel. Anyway, everyone is wearing gloves and hats and dresses.

"Some paparazzi guy says to me, 'You're caj,' and I'm like, 'I know.' I did not fit in."

The best part of being in Los Angeles for Ellen was her house, nestled in the Hollywood Hills. It was the opposite extreme from her first apartment in Los Angeles after moving from San Francisco, which she rented merely on the basis of an ad in the *L.A. Times.*

"I'm driving and I'm getting further and further east. I ended up in East L.A. I didn't know the area, but the paper said 'New York charm.' Which I discovered meant the murders and rapes of New York are in the area. They shot *Hell Town,* the series with Robert Blake, in front of my building. And any *Cagney & Lacey* where they had to be in a bad neighborhood was shot in front of my building.

"If you have to live in L.A., though, there are nice places. There are a lot of trees, I don't know how they still live there, but there's wildlife—raccoons and possums and coyotes.

"The other day . . . there was a deer in my backyard. I thought this was amazing, I'm in L.A. and it was so close. A mother and a little tiny baby deer and I thought, 'Oh, I wish I had a gun' . . . That's a joke. I just don't understand how anyone could look at that and go, 'Ooh, I wish I had a gun.' They're just so beautiful."

Her love for animals was so encompassing that on the rare occasion when Ellen was able to spend a quiet night at home during that summer hiatus between the second and third season, she would usually pass the time watching her favorite channel. "I watch the Discovery Channel a lot. Mostly for me, but also for my dogs. It's the only time they're interested in television. They really don't care about my show at all, but on the Discovery Channel there are animals moving around."

In the summer of 1995, however, Ellen didn't have much time to watch TV because she was too busy being a movie star. And while filming *Mr. Wrong* was exciting, Ellen found the process strikingly lacked immediacy. "It is slow and I'm a very impatient person. And it's a real hard thing to do a film when you're impatient, because you're sitting around for hours waiting for a new shot, or something happens and they have to relight."

But she wasn't complaining. "It was still a whole lot of fun. I've been really fortunate because I was able to do stand-up, which is immediate, and television, which is fairly quick, and now film. And then a book. I've done about every single thing except my exercise video . . . which is coming out."

Another difference between doing a film and her series was that in a significant way, she had less riding on the movie because "there are so many people involved. If I would have written the movie and directed it and produced it and starred in it, if it was *my* project, then I would have a lot of pressure on myself and expect a whole lot."

Shortly before the film was due to be released she said, "I hope the movie does well, and I hope my work was good, and I think it's funny. But I don't think it's going to make or break me. I feel pretty good in my life with or without a film career. But we'll see."

14
Squeezing the Pigeon

As the third season began production in August 1995, there were more changes behind the scenes on *Ellen*. Out went executive producers Warren Bell, who accepted a development deal of his own with Disney, and David Rosenthal, who announced he planned to quit and go work for Dream-Works. In came Eileen Heisler and DeAnn Heline, who had worked together as partners on *Murphy Brown* and *Roseanne*.

"Yes," Ellen deadpanned, "we've had like forty-three producers. They keep spontaneously combusting. Nobody's safe with *Ellen*."

Actually, Heisler and Heline were merely the third set, albeit in three seasons. It just seemed like there had been more. And as everybody involved with television knows, it is not uncommon for a series to have new producers from year to year. The ultimate goal of most writers is to be promoted to a producer's position on a show and from there to get a lucrative development deal with a studio or network, and that is often achieved by leapfrogging from series to series. After a writer makes a name for themselves on one series, another series offers her a better title and more money. If they are associated with a successful enough show, they will then be offered a development deal, meaning they can create and executive-produce their own show.

Although in film, writers usually aim to become directors so they can control their scripts, in television, writers aspire to be producers, because that's the best way to be in creative control. Film is a director's medium, but television is controlled by writer-producer hyphenates.

Ellen said she had no problem with the changeover to Heisler and Heline, even though she was not consulted by the network or studio beforehand. When she met with her new producers, she simply hoped they would be open to collaboration and would bring a better female sensibility to the series.

"I think she liked the things that we were talking about for the show," Heline says. "And we just really clicked."

Heisler adds that Ellen was someone who had been on their wish-for list. "When we saw she had a show, for us personally, we had always thought, 'There's someone we'd really like to write for sometime.' When the opportunity came up, we just sat down and mutually talked about our ideas for the show. It was an easy connection."

Because both Rosenthal and Bell had, according to *TV Guide,* "avoided public comment" about leaving the series, there had been widespread speculation that their departure had been less than amicable. Bell later denied the rumors as mere industry conjecture. "I always laughed at the trade papers when they ran stories about the show having a revolving door of producers," Bell said. "I had a great experience there. It elevated my place in the industry tremendously. Ellen was wonderful and generous to me."

In addition to the new producers, *Ellen* was also introducing yet another new regular character and bringing back the recurring character of Audrey in a full-time capacity.

Dean Valentine, then Disney's president of network television, tried to explain the changes this way: "We're just one rocket booster away. The show was incredibly funny, but it was incredibly funny only because we had Ellen DeGeneres. We want a show that's funny in all of its many parts."

Midway through the second season, the writers had moved Arye Gross's character, Adam, out of Ellen's apartment, leaving her without a roommate, although Adam seemed to spend just as much time there as before. For the third season, Heline and Heisler, who thought Ellen needed a stronger personality to play off of, created Spence Kovak, Ellen's hotheaded cousin who moves in with her after getting kicked out of medical school.

"You're always looking for the best counterpoint to Ellen," Heisler explained. "I think that Spence and Paige both serve to drag Ellen into uncomfortable situations. Spence with his hot-headed, occasional loose-cannon attitude, and Paige with her whole Hollywood scene. I think Ellen's character is most fun when she's in those awkward situations."

(Not to be too cynical, but there's another reason new writer-producers tend to create new characters. Even after they leave a series, they continue to get paid residuals for characters they created every time that character appears in an episode.)

The actor they hired to play Spence was Jeremy Piven, who at the time was a relative newcomer to television, having done mostly film and theater. He had been drawn to the small screen by simple entertainment-industry reality.

"I wanted to do this one movie script," Jeremy recalls. "The director wrote it for me and I felt very close to it, but the people financing it wouldn't approve me. I later saw a list of the people they would approve, and they were all on TV shows. So when *Ellen* started knocking on my door, it seemed the logical move. Now the next time I hear from these people, I can say, 'Turn on the TV, man.'"

Heisler and Heline didn't care why he wanted to do television, they were just happy to get an actor of his quality. "Jeremy adds this great urban energy and great *maleness*," Heisler said. "He's just got that sexy charisma about him that both men and women respond to. He's just so quick and funny and goes totally out on a limb. Makes the ensemble stronger."

Being no newcomer to the business, Jeremy was not awestruck joining the cast of an established show and didn't worry about holding back. He brought an instant energy to the series that Arye Gross's Adam simply couldn't match. As for stories about *Ellen*'s behind-the-scenes difficulties, Piven was adamant they didn't emanate from the star.

"She's not a diva," he asserted shortly after joining the show. "She wants to make the best show possible, and she tries to solve problems by working hard. Her input comes in many forms, from dialogue changes to suggesting story arcs. She always has a point of view, but she doesn't get in your face. I think the writing's really great, and I'm having a blast."

So was Clea Lewis. When she was hired to play Audrey in the second episode of *These Friends of Mine,* she thought it would be just another one-shot deal. "Audrey was so obnoxious," she said, she never thought the character could be brought back. "But I hypnotized Ellen without her knowing it," Clea jokes.

The truth was, Ellen enjoyed Clea's comic ability, so the producers revamped the character to make her less obnoxious and more well-intentioned. "It was a complete surprise to me. I did a one-shot guest-star appearance. And then the following season, I had actually fled L.A. and was in New York being incredibly depressed because a lot of things had fallen through, and I was just drinking a lot of coffee and wearing black, and then I got a call saying, 'Come back. They want you to do two or more episodes as Audrey.' So I came back, and they kind of kept adding them one at a time."

After she appeared in eight episodes in the second season, she was made a regular in the third season. When asked why she pressed to have Clea join the show on a permanent basis, Ellen didn't hesitate. "She's hilarious. And I had so much fun with her, and she compliments me. She brings me things every day, so why wouldn't I want her around? I just think she adds something so special, and so unique. I saw that and said, 'Let's grab her.'"

As it entered its third season, *Ellen* bore almost no resemblance to its original incarnation, prompting Ellen to comment, "The show's gone through such a transformation that it's almost like we need to get reviewed again."

Also gone were the opening titles. "We were going to have opening titles and had a whole thing planned that we were going to shoot, and then we ended up coming on the air two weeks early, so we didn't have time to shoot them," explains Ellen. "So we were going to go on with just me saying, 'They'll be here next week.' And then we started thinking that it would be funny if every week we have some excuse and we don't have them so we're just filling time every opening title."

In one example, Ellen brings her mom, Betty, on.

BETTY: Why don't you sing? You've got such a pretty voice.

ELLEN: I'm not going to sing, Mom.

BETTY: Well, if you've got all this time on your hands, why don't you say hi to your Aunt Helen and Aunt Audrey?

ELLEN: I don't want to s—

BETTY: You never write them.

ELLEN: Hi, Aunt Helen. Hi, Aunt Audrey.

But the most important change going into the third season was one Ellen had absolutely no control over—and the one that would affect her show the most. For the 1995–96 season, ABC moved *Ellen* yet again, from its 8:30 time slot to the Wednesday leadoff spot at 8:00. It was hard for Ellen to conceal her dismay, even under a veil of humor. "It's our third season, and we've moved like ten times, we're now at eight o'clock, and I really believed the network when they said that studies show that people stop watching television after eight-thirty. So I said, 'Okay, let's move to eight then.'"

While most of the cast was happy with the way the third-season episodes were going, there was one notable, glaring exception. As Jeremy Piven's presence became more pronounced on the series, Arye Gross's profile had diminished. It seemed almost a foregone conclusion that his character was being slowly, but inevitably, eliminated. So it was hardly surprising that Gross chose to jump ship before being pushed off.

However, when news of his departure leaked out, it was assumed by many that Gross was being fired but being allowed to save face by announcing it was his intention to quit. But Ellen maintains, "It was his choice. Arye wasn't really happy where his character was going, and he wanted to go off and pursue other TV and film projects instead of doing a television series.

"I don't think anybody knew what to do with the Adam character," Ellen says. "It had changed so much because of the changes the show has gone through. So it was a mutual agreement—he wanted to go off, and we were fine with understanding that. It wasn't like there was anybody mad at anybody. I love Arye."

His last episode, "Hello, I Must Be Going," aired in January 1996, amid continuing speculation he had been forced out of the series. That impression was fueled by Gross's silence regarding his departure. At the January 1996

Television Critics Press Tour, Ellen was offered the opportunity to set the record straight.

"The most important thing is that I never fired anybody," she said, exasperated. "That's absolutely false. Whenever I see stuff like that it's upsetting. But people are going to assume what they want to assume."

In fact, Ellen may have been partly to blame for the rumor that she had fired Gross. While attending a party, Ellen was talking with a group of associates when someone asked why Gross had left the show. She quipped, "I don't know. I guess some people just can't take a joke about being fired."

While Ellen might not have fired Gross herself, according to Dava Savel, who co-executive-produced the fourth season and was a writer during the third, Gross was indeed let go before he could jump ship.

"It was icky as far as I was concerned," Savel said later. She added that the only saving grace was that Gross had seen it coming. "I have been on shows where the actor didn't even know he was getting written off until he sat down at the table reading the read-through and saw that he was out. That's horrible."

When one journalist asked her why she was the continuing target of power-gone-mad stories, Ellen seemed at a genuine loss. "I wish I knew. It's the same when I read things I never said and it's in quotes. I think that sometimes people don't want to believe that things are actually fine on the set. We have such a great atmosphere and a great working relationship."

A short time later, she would turn this perspective on its comic ear and announce that she was going for a new image because "the nice thing is not working for me. I have this reputation for being nice, and I think I am nice, but people are going to talk no matter what, and I've heard that now I'm supposedly not nice. So I decided, 'Why not stir up a little controversy?' Maybe it can help the ratings, to become a bitch."

She described her first attempt at having a new 'tude. "Everyone knows I love animals, so I thought, 'If I kill a pigeon, this will show how wild I can be.' So I grabbed a pigeon, brought it in—everyone was stunned—and I started squeezing it. But it made a little peep, and I got scared and I rushed it to the animal hospital. I bruised its spleen evidently. It's costing me a thousand dollars a day to keep this pigeon alive."

Ellen said she decided to leave animals alone and concentrate picking on people. "Brett Butler fires people on *Grace Under Fire*, and I've never fired anybody . . . well, I'm going to fire some people. So I fired a guy, I don't even know if he worked on the show or not. But then I found out the guy had a family, so he's living in my house now with his family. I'm in a hotel, and that's costing me money."

Since the direct approach wasn't working, Ellen decided to go for the subversive. "I'm always on time, so I decided to stay in my trailer all day and not come out. I guess I was in there until four or five o'clock 'til I realized it was Saturday. The electricity was off, I couldn't use the toilet, and now I have a bladder infection which is costing me a fortune. I've lost so much money being a bitch."

All joking aside, Ellen was confounded by the impression many had of her—people who had never worked with her: that she was being difficult, that she was forcing out cast and producers left and right. All Ellen wanted was for the show to be the best it could be, and she always conducted herself respectfully and honestly.

"This is who I am, it's not a conscious effort. I don't look at anybody and say, 'Okay, I'm going to be like this; I'm not going to be like this.' I am who I am. Everybody has a different way of dealing with stressful situations. I don't like to yell. I don't like to be mean to people. I respect other people and their feelings. I wouldn't ever want to be treated like that myself."

That, some might postulate, was actually the bigger problem. From the beginning, Ellen had deferred to others, occasionally in direct contradiction to what her comic gut instinct told her. It was a case of damned if you do and damned if you don't.

"I cannot control everyone's opinion of me. I can be the best person I can be and there will *still* be people who just don't like me. I cannot make everybody love me and believe I'm a good person. I've read too many things that are totally false, and you get to the point where you just let it go, go home, and get on the Lifecycle for three hours."

Yet, at the same time, Ellen admired the ability of others to get what they wanted without feeling the need to make apologies. "Brett and Roseanne don't pull any punches, and I think that's great. I deal with that in therapy all the time, to try and get to that point."

By the midpoint of the 1995–96 season, *Ellen*'s ratings took an inexplicable tumble. Part of it had to be attributed to ABC's overall faltering, with that season marking a downswing during which the network would eventually slipslide to third place, just barely ahead of Fox. One unnamed series higher-up suggested that perhaps the series' troubles might be solved if Ellen Morgan got a puppy.

As nervous television executives looked for answers, word began filtering out that some of the network brass were worried that Ellen's appearance might be part of the problem. As the series had progressed, Ellen's look had indeed changed. In the first half season and subsequent full season of 1994–95, she had been partial to pants outfits with vests. While not particularly "girly," the outfits had still been tailored and stylish.

However, over the course of the third season, Ellen's manner of dress had begun to evolve into more of a butch look, for want of a better term, with flannel shirts and jeans her usual style. Perhaps the choice of wardrobe that resulted in the biggest response was her decision to wear a powder-blue suit to Paige's would-be wedding in the season finale. According to one article, executives decided to feminize Ellen after "viewers called in droves wondering why she wore a man's-style suit to a wedding."

To Ellen, the flap over fashion was astonishing. "I could not believe someone took the time to write in and ask why I always wore pants and never wear dresses or skirts. So my answer was 'In a drunken stupor, a long time ago at camp, I tattooed both my legs with bougainvillea, and so now I'm constantly bothered by bees whenever I wear dresses.' It's like, that it matters so much."

Ellen didn't understand why she couldn't dress in a style that was comfortable for her; dresses and high heels were unnatural. "I don't get it. I mean, I see transvestites, men who love dressing up as women, and I'm thinking, 'What is wrong with you that you would wear high heels and you don't even have to?' I mean, to be on that angle, it's like you're downhill skiing."

Another noticeable change in the storylines was that Ellen Morgan had, for all intents and purposes, stopped dating. And in many regards Ellen Morgan became more of an enigma. Why would someone so attractive and funny find it so difficult to find romance? In addition, the plots didn't allow the viewer inside the character's head. That's because Ellen herself didn't want to let her public inside her own life.

Not coincidentally, it was that exact fear of revealing and exposing herself too much that was most telling in both Ellen's big-screen and publishing debuts.

15
Right Book, Wrong Flick

In 1994, after her series had established itself as a hit, Ellen was approached by publishers about writing a book, and she signed on with Bantam Books. However, she immediately nixed the idea of doing a straight autobiography. She knew that to write about her life and exclude her sexuality would be dishonest and self-deflating. The lie she was living to her public would be forever etched between the covers of the book, a testament to denial and fear.

Instead, she asked to write a comedy book and was given the hardy approval of her publisher. Ironically, she was once again following in the footsteps of Jerry Seinfeld, whose *SeinLanguage* had started a stampede of comics writing about their lives. But even Jerry, known for keeping a distance from his fans, revealed substantial bits about himself in his book. Paul Reiser would make his life the star of his book *Couplehood,* and Drew Carey would stun his readers by discussing, between hilarious bits and observations, his suicide attempts and being molested as a child.

Ellen wanted none of that. When she said she wanted to write a comedy book, she meant just that. And she meant to do it largely from scratch.

"It's not an autobiography in any way," said Ellen of *My Point . . . and I Do Have One,* as her book was ultimately called. "People are very disappointed by that, I don't know why. And in some bookstores it's in the biography section. I don't know why that is, either. And there are people who are just angry they're not getting an autobiography. Woody Allen wrote *Without Feathers,* and that was just some funny stories."

Some of the confusion stemmed from the structure of the book, which was written with tongue firmly attached to cheek. "I write everything seriously, as if it's true. There's a journal that I keep when I race the Iditarod," she says, referring to the yearly race on dogsleds across Alaska's frozen tundra. "I trained with my two dogs at home in L.A. at four in the morning on the streets just because I think I can do it. One dog is smaller so we go in circles a lot. But because I didn't write 'Ha-Ha' in parentheses after everything, people are like, 'Oh, she races the Iditarod.'"

It was more work than Ellen ever imagined it would be. "The stand-up is easier for me because that's what I did for so long. I wrote stories that I'd never told before anywhere else. A lot of people believed a lot of the stories, too, which was scary. The whole book was just comedy, nothing was real, and yet people would come up and say, 'Oh, you went back and interviewed your people to find out who you were.' And I was like, 'No, none of that was real.'"

Even though Ellen was used to writing her own comedy material, putting it in book form was a new experience. "I would sometimes write at my desk, sometimes in my living room, sometimes in bed. Actually, mostly in bed. And I would just write. I never knew from day to day what would be there.

"The book is slices of my brain. There are daily affirmations—simple ones like 'At least I'm not as fat as her,'" because you have to start small. There are journal entries, like when I train for the Iditarod, and all the entries begin, 'Uh-oh, this was not a good idea.'

"The way the whole Iditarod chapter started was I just thought it would be funny to have a journal entry following my life and I just thought, 'What am I going to come up with that I do every day?' And I thought about training for the Iditarod and came up with how I would start doing that. I wrote one journal entry, and I thought the next day would be a different thing. But then I decided that'd be a fun thing to follow through all the way to the end of the race."

Among the eclectic topics covered are dance lessons, recipes, and cures for diseases, "all made up. (Cure for Walking Pneumonia: Sit Down!) And if something happens to work, I could win the Nobel Prize." Ellen also does faux interviews, "like with a woman in New Orleans who makes jewelry out of crawdads and drinks a drink called chocolate thunder which is Ovaltine and vodka. But that's not true, either. All the interviews are fabricated," Ellen sighs, somewhat amazed that so many people didn't get the joke. "But if you wish to believe it's true. . . ."

There came a point when Ellen wondered if she would ever finish. "The scary thing is, I almost strangled my editor, because I probably wrote about seven books," Ellen says. "I just kept sending him stuff. I would write and send it and send it, because I wrote longhand. I didn't want to count and didn't do it on a computer, so it wasn't counting. So I was just sending stuff, and he was hating me because it wasn't on disk. He had to transfer everything.

"I kept writing to make sure I had enough. And I said, 'Can I stop?' And he said, 'Stop when you feel like you have to.' I finally said, 'Look, I'm blocked. I can't think of anything more.' And I wrote the last chapter," which says the one thing you should never do is write a book.

Ellen felt her hands start clenching when her editor came over and showed her a manuscript the size of "a Webster's dictionary. I wanted to kill him. I was like, 'You could have told me to stop a long time ago.' And he said, 'Well, we wanted to make sure we had enough.' He also said, 'People like small, easy things.'"

My Point . . . and I Do Have One came out in September 1995 and, in a bit of irony, knocked Newt Gingrich's book out of the top spot of the *New York Times* bestseller list. Ellen came up with the title because "there really is no point. I've always thought that when people say, 'My point is . . .' they never have one."

But for those who got the joke, Ellen's book did have a point—to be funny. One reviewer, who admitted that he hadn't been particularly interested in reading the book in the beginning, said that "as I continued reading, I found the material to be a lot more humorous. An entire chapter is dedicated to Ellen's aspirations to win the Iditarod race, a word she hears on television and can't find in the dictionary. Ellen is determined to win the dogsled race with the help of her two dogs and newborn kitten. I won't tell you the outcome, but I guarantee you won't be bored."

Shortly after the book's publication, Ellen joked, "The book is doing very well. My goal is to outsell the Bible." She also noted that now that the book was finished, "I have things to write about now, but I didn't before. Funny how that happens."

She also got a lot of comic mileage out of the cover photo, a headshot of a short-haired Ellen smiling at the camera, which she admitted not everybody, particularly her mother, liked. "I had a reporter say, 'Herb Ritts did the cover. . . . When you think of him you usually think of fashion and sexy and hot.'" Ellen laughed at the not so subtle slam.

The next media she set out to conquer was the recording industry, with her comedy CD, *Taste This.* "I'm pretty happy with how the CD turned out. It's a lot of what I'm known for, it's show tunes and some of my favorite Bible stories. There's a juggling section and a tribute to menthol cigarettes."

While her book had been hard work in an unfamiliar territory, her CD was a walk down a bittersweet memory lane. "That was so fun for me. That was a theater, three thousand people who made plans to come see me specifically, they weren't just in a minimall getting yogurt and I just happened to be next door at Chuckles, 'cause that's how a lot of people saw me when I first started out. I played for twelve people and nine were drunk. It was so horrible in the beginning."

But her final tour had been surreal. "That was a special time. It was magical to be onstage and have that kind of energy of people who really, really enjoyed me and liked me. I miss doing that. I hope one day I do it again."

Although she performed live on the series, Ellen explained, "it's not nearly the same as doing stand-up, because it's an amazing energy to put something out there and get it back, and you get into this rhythm. I live for the show. We shoot on Fridays, and we have an audience of three hundred people. That's my only chance to be with people live any more. Other than that, I'm holed up in my house watching Discovery Channel."

Curiously, even though she missed the intimacy of standing in front of thousands of people, she also had developed an aversion to watching other comics. "I can't bear to watch it anymore," Ellen admitted in 1996. "After I stopped doing stand-up it was just too much. For a while it got to be where every time you changed the channel there was a brick wall and somebody standing in front of it. I just got tired of seeing and hearing that same rhythm and same kind of delivery. There was nothing new. It was just everybody suddenly trying to get a shot at getting a sitcom.

"So I have no idea what's going on with stand-up. I have no idea who the comedians are out there right now. Sometimes, if I come across somebody really, really bad I'll watch for a few minutes just because they're just so bad I can't even believe it," she laughed. "I just like watching really unbelievable things."

Ellen seemed to be such a successful multiple hyphenate that she jokingly pondered what mountains were left to conquer. "Synchronized swimming—I just want to wear the nose clip," she suggested. "Then maybe I'll sell some Amway products."

However, Ellen's triumphant all-media march was about to develop a pronounced limp. When Ellen had signed to make *Mr. Wrong,* it was the culmination of a long-held dream. "I've been waiting a long time to do a film. When I first moved to L.A. people told me I'd get a series and a movie right away. But it didn't happen right away."

It didn't happen until Ellen's turn at the Emmys piqued the interest of the studios, including Disney motion pictures group chairman Joe Roth. "I saw her series and thought she was great and would be entertaining in any medium. And I don't distinguish between TV and film in terms of performers. They either make you laugh or they don't. But the trick is to get them in a part playing close to the persona of their TV character but not necessarily playing themselves."

Ellen was wooed by Roth's laid-back, nonsuit demeanor. "When I met Joe, I really connected with him. He didn't seem to be b.s.-ing me at all and genuinely sees something in me. He thinks my movie career will be bigger than my TV career. I've always thought so, too.

"Ultimately, I think film is what I should be doing. It's

just more real. Television is so fast and immediate that you can't really take the time to play out moments with your character. I've always wanted to play more of a real character, because Ellen Morgan is sort of a caricature. She's not a real person."

On paper, it's easy to see why *Mr. Wrong* appealed to Ellen, who earned in excess of $2 million for the film. It wasn't a brainless comedy (think any *Saturday Night Live* alum). "It was really important that my first film be right, not a silly comedy. And this is not a mainstream comedy. I have a kind of twisted sense of humor. I like dark humor. I have a little bit of an edge to me and I like taking chances and I have a little weirdness but," she amended, "I'm pretty normal. As comedians go, though, I'm very normal. If you spent any time with any other comedian you would think that I'm like a dental assistant."

So normal that when she read the original version of *Mr. Wrong,* she was stunned. "When my manager gave me the script to read, I stopped. I mean, it was *so* sexually explicit. It was like reading a porn script, with these unbelievable positions. I said, 'Are you out of your mind?' I cannot imagine, you know, faking an orgasm or really simulating sex. That's such an intimate thing to share."

The script was rewritten so it was less erotic and more hearts-and-flowers. Once the movie was tailored to fit Ellen's parameters, the lead character was someone Ellen would be believable playing—a successful white-collar worker—and the movie's acting demands fell within Ellen's range. The premise had plenty of comic promise, and the film would have the mighty Disney marketing machine behind it. Choosing *Mr. Wrong* was as close to stacking the odds in favor of having a successful movie as is possible when making a film.

In the movie, Ellen played Martha Alston, a talent coordinator for a San Diego talk show. Martha is intelligent with a successful career but is still seen by her well-meaning friends and family as a bit of a failure because she hasn't found her Mr. Right.

The character "is pretty satisfied being who she is," Ellen said. "I think she is a person like a lot of women out there who find themselves in their thirties and haven't really met the right person and they're single and they have a career they're happy with and they go to work every day and they're lonely at times and they're happy at times. She's intelligent, she has a good job, but she's pressured by the people around her—her family and friends—who keep asking her why she's not married and making her feel bad she's not. There's a lot of pressure from society to find that perfect mate."

When Whitman Crawford, who on the surface appears to be a modern Renaissance man, comes into her life, even Martha thinks she's found the man of her dreams. "She meets this guy who seems to be incredible, just perfect." It turns out, however, he's about to become her worst nightmare. "Everybody has had that experience of meeting someone, in the beginning they seem like they're everything," Ellen suggests. "But then you just start seeing little tiny signs and you think, 'Wait a minute. That's not right.' And in the movie, we slowly see he's insane. It's hysterical. Pretty sick things happen." No matter what havoc he causes in her life, ironically, everybody still thinks she's better off with him than to be alone.

Of course, Ellen's costar, William Pullman, had a different take on his character. "He's the Evel Knievel of romance. He's a daredevil. He's a passionate individual and is ready to go to any lengths to be with Martha. Now, some women find that objectionable, and apparently, the title of the movie, *Mr. Wrong,* suggests that that's not the right idea. I'm starting a crusade for all those people who are willing to believe in this kind of obsessive love. And by the time the movie's released, we're actually going to have more people who agree with

Whitman Crawford than agree with Martha Alston's distance from Whitman."

As loquacious as Pullman was about his character, he became curiously vague and flip when asked what it was like working with Ellen. "The curse of these kinds of interviews before the movie is out is you're going, 'Oh, we are the masters of comedy together. We're the Rogers and Astaire of the funny. Oh, we tickle each other's funny bone,' so endlessly, without any proof. Then the movie comes out and you go, 'So what? That didn't get off the ground.'"

Such sentiments didn't sound like a rousing endorsement of their film. When pressed about Ellen herself, Pullman said, "She's a very interesting kind of talent, for a certain kind of funny. She can do a lot with very little. She can be reactive and be funny. And she can say very normal things and be funny."

The film's director, Nick Castle, called the movie the "nightmare version of *Sleepless in Seattle.*" (Castle had been hired to direct *Sleepless in Seattle* but left because of disagreements during the writing stage.)

Son of Hollywood choreographer Nick Castle, the junior Castle won an Academy Award when he was twenty-three years old for Best Live Action Short Subject, *The Resurrection of Billy Bronco.* Castle later temporarily dropped out of the Hollywood scene to become a political activist. Prior to *Mr. Wrong,* Castle had directed two uninspired comedies, *Major Payne* and *Dennis the Menace.* He had also worked as a screenwriter, writing *Skatetown U.S.A.* and *Escape From New York.*

As the movie's opening date neared, Ellen hit the promotion trail once again, but not to the extent she did with the series, partly *because* of the series. *Mr. Wrong* was released while *Ellen* was in production, which limited the amount of time she could spend talking up the movie. But she did the requisite rounds on the talk shows, and segments about her and the movie appeared on most of the television entertainment magazines. Her overall attitude was somewhat fatalistic. "People who like what I do and like my comedy will come see my film."

Mr. Wrong opened to disheartening "mixed reviews."

Among the more positive reviews was the one in the *Boston Herald.* "Ellen DeGeneres makes an unconventional and appealing comic heroine in her movie debut, *Mr. Wrong.* Although the ads make this look like a tasteless comedy about stalking, *Mr. Wrong* turns out to be a smart and absurd take on the mating game."

The venerable entertainment industry trade paper *Variety* also heaped praise on her. "Ellen has found a movie vehicle that is sui DeGeneres in *Mr. Wrong.* The saga of how the perfect mate evolves into the date from hell has an underlying darkness that may surprise and put off some of the actress's TV fans. That edge spells commercial success domestically and should open up international horizons for the rising screen star."

Others, including influential critic Janet Maslin, thoughtfully pointed out that the movie just missed. "Unlike the mismatched lovers they play in *Mr. Wrong,* Ellen DeGeneres and Bill Pullman actually do have good chemistry, but they don't have a movie to show it off. Good-humored but mostly flat, *Mr. Wrong* wastes an amusing premise and two likable stars."

The Internet site Mr. Showbiz thought the problem was that the material was below Ellen's ability. "In outline, *Mr. Wrong* has promise: *Fatal Attraction* redone as nightmare comedy. But the comedy as a whole just doesn't gel. Here, director Nick Castle never finds the right tone and Bill Pullman never quite finds his footing. DeGeneres has an instant, three-dimensional screen persona. She's a great reactor. Unfortunately, no one else in this film has been brought anywhere near as much to life."

The *Hollywood Reporter* was more blunt. "Hoping to follow fellow Touchstone Television star Tim Allen's successful leap to motion pictures, Ellen DeGeneres takes the big-screen plunge with *Mr. Wrong,* but in this case *plunge* seems to be the operative word. This pressure-cooker comedy starts off promisingly enough but, like DeGeneres's ill-fated relationship, *Mr. Wrong* goes seriously wrong, hopelessly spinning out of control, never to regain its agreeably quirky footing."

Another review agreed. "What more could a girl hope for?" it asked rhetorically. "Actually, a sense of comedy that doesn't insult the intelligence of a railroad tie would be nice. When the inevitable occurs and Crawford turns into a psychopathic cretin, what was merely icky becomes cruel.

"As if defying you to smile while your mouth opens in sheer stupefaction, the movie has him issuing racial insults, assaulting a street person, and engaging in stunts too puerile even for juvenile delinquents to enjoy. The script oozes a barely muffled rage that is less humorous than it is horrifying, and all the amiable DeGeneres can do is wait it out."

The most pointed review came from the *Advocate,* which zeroed in on the real reason *Mr. Wrong* lacked tangible chemistry. "No one's saying DeGeneres is obliged to discuss her private life. She's a terrific talent and we can all respect the right to privacy. Besides, she's already performed a service for lesbians just by looking like one every week on prime-time TV.

"But DeGeneres seems uncomfortable by her own silence. . . . She keeps dropping hints in her work. Take *Mr. Wrong,* her first venture onto the big screen. . . . Wouldn't we laugh all the more if she could bring herself to tell the whole joke?

"As it stands, *Mr. Wrong* isn't awful. . . . The script packs a few good laughs, and the supporting cast boasts first-class troupers. It's all very competent. But there's DeGeneres at the center of things, guarded and self-effacing and determined not to let us in.

"In playing against her own sexual allure, DeGeneres is fighting a losing battle. A great comedian channels his observations of the world through his specific physical presence, and that includes a specific sexuality.

"Whether she actually sleeps with women, DeGeneres comes across as a real homo heartthrob. She and her handlers accept that on some level, or they'd present her differently. But they don't write situations for the character we see. Instead, they keep trying to reduce a star with real sex appeal to a sexless, straight wallflower."

Ellen simply wasn't a good enough actress to be convincing as a character with whom she had little in common. As long as she denied her sexuality, or put herself in situations that were alien to her frame of reference, the result would be performances that lacked the visceral emotion that is so important in film.

The *Advocate* review also made clear that Ellen's sexual preference was hardly a secret. Maybe TV viewers in the nation's breadbasket and Bible Belt didn't realize it, but those who were even remotely involved in the entertainment industry certainly knew or assumed she was gay. That wasn't the issue. The issue was that Ellen's discomfort with herself was stilting her performances, both in film and on television.

Despite the obvious challenge posed by the *Advocate* critic, Ellen refused to take the bait and address the inferences posed in the article. Although *Mr. Wrong* was an undeniable disappointment—Ellen had been hoping to match Tim Allen's success in *The Santa Clause*—she chose not to dwell on it and instead immersed herself in the series again.

On the other hand, even though *Mr. Wrong* hadn't lived up to anybody's expectations, it hadn't been a bomb, and Ellen had projected a likable screen persona. She would al-

most certainly get other film offers, which was really all she
could ask for.

"I like films a lot. So depending on how the show goes,
either I'll keep doing the show and films in between or I'll
not do the show anymore and just do films. Or I'll just work
at Macy's in the lingerie department. Anything is fine with
me. I'm very easygoing."

Too much so at times. Only those who understood that in-
trinsic trait of Ellen's could answer the question of how—as
happened again in the spring of 1996 as the third season
came to a close—so many changes could occur on her own
series without her input. It was a fact that many in and out of
the press often found hard to fathom. Was it just ABC coming in and dictating?

"Sometimes it's coming from CBS, which I don't understand," she joked, before turning serious. "You know what?
Sometimes things do happen. I *do* find out about things after
the fact, and all of a sudden I go, 'Wait a minute, what's
going on here?' I think that's because sometimes I don't
exert this power that everybody believes I have. And sometimes I really just want to have a life. I want to go home and
I don't want it to be a twenty-four-hour day. I want to just do
my work and do the best I can."

16
An Act of Courage

Ellen ended the 1995–96 season ranked at thirty-eight, a disappointment for the year. The end of the season also marked the end of the line for Heisler and Heline, who left the show. And for the first time Ellen assumed a producer credit. Several critics openly wondered why ABC didn't pull the plug on the show, even though it was still one of the floundering network's more successful programs. In the current world of network television, with over one hundred shows competing on six networks, that ranking is more than respectable. The problem was one of perception. *Ellen* had been touted, by the media at least, as the next coming of *Seinfeld*. Anything short of that would be viewed as a failure to live up to the star's potential.

"I think that we've had such a struggle," Ellen said wearily at a press conference. "I thought the pilot was so funny, so good, we had a great start and a lot of attention. Because we got so much attention initially, the focus has been on seeing if we could maintain that."

Ellen acknowledged that the much-publicized behind-the-scenes creative changes may have also added to the conventional wisdom that the show was off balance and out of kilter. But, as she pointed out, "writers and producers *do* change a lot and shows *do* struggle. When *Roseanne* started, it didn't start off with a bang. It had time to grow and for the characters to find out who they were. It was the same with *Seinfeld* and *Cheers* and with most shows. They had the time to grow."

Without wanting to offend Disney and ABC too much, she also noted that "we've been all over the place, then all of a sudden we were thrust into starting off the night at eight o'clock." Plus, she says, it was difficult to have a clear vision when "the studio and network and everybody has different opinions on what the show should be. It was a vague show to begin with, in that it didn't fit into a specific niche. We're still trying to find out what exactly the show is, who I am and what I represent."

However, Ellen took umbrage at the suggestion the show was so bad it didn't deserve to be on the air. "I think we have a great show, and I think people are always surprised when they tune in. I just did an interview with someone the other day, and he hadn't seen the show in a while and he watched it just to see what was going on, and he really, really liked the show and was surprised by it.

"I think a lot of people sort of gave up on us because we moved so much and changed so much. And they thought, 'Oh, well, what is this?' But I think if people would give the show a chance and watch it, it's a good show. Yeah, I want it to be better and better. I hope we keep working to find little things and keep adding things that make it pop out more.

"But you know, it's not like we're struggling more than any other show. The time they start resting on 'We've got it made, we know exactly who we are,' it becomes a caricature of itself. So there's nothing wrong with evolving and changing."

At least one Disney executive had high praise for *Ellen*, pointing out that it was only Ellen's talent that kept the show going and doing as well as it had. "Disney was willing to go with a half-baked idea and no great secondary characters because they love Ellen as a talent. Ellen herself was great, but there was never a reason for that show to be, or a big idea behind it or a real strong cast. Ellen has bought ABC and Disney a tremendous amount of time to figure that show out, by sheer force of her personality."

In the end, it would be Ellen who had to figure out what her show was missing and be willing to do something about it. The first hint her costars had that a dramatic comedic change might be in the wind occurred in spring 1996, toward the end of the third season. During a taping break, Ellen leaned over to Peter Bristow, an openly gay actor who played the equally out Peter on the series, and whispered, "I'm thinking of doing what you did."

With the voicing of that thought, an idea was set into motion that would soon take on a life of its own. That June, Ellen invited her writing staff to her house, ostensibly for a pre–new season get together. While the assembled group toasted the upcoming season with champagne, Ellen stunned her writers by asking, "What do you think if the character came out?"

New coexecutive producer Mark Driscoll admits the idea filled him with excitement, because it had long been a topic of discussion in the writing room but one with which "we would have never approached Ellen."

Dava Savel, another of *Ellen*'s new executive producers, says Ellen's suggestion filled her with relief because the writers were "running out of ideas." With Ellen's edict of no more episodes about dating, there was an obvious hole in the center of the show. What the writers didn't know was that by outing Ellen Morgan, Ellen DeGeneres would fill a gaping hole at the center of her own life.

"I made a decision during the summer that I wasn't going to live my life as a lie anymore," she said later. What took her so long to finally muster the courage was "the shame. I know what it feels like to try to blend in so that everybody else will think you're okay and they won't hurt you. I decided that this was not going to be something I was going to live the rest of my life ashamed of.

"You are bombarded early on that what you're supposed to do in life, if you're a girl, is meet a nice guy and get married and have kids and be accepted." In other words, be the girl next door. Except, as Ellen noted, "I'm the girl on the other side of you."

The one constant in her professional life had been the rapport she had with her fans. The thought that terrified her the most had always been that "if they found out I was gay, maybe they wouldn't applaud, maybe they wouldn't laugh, maybe they wouldn't like me if they knew I was gay."

Ellen was aware of how much was at stake, for everybody involved. "You know, it's a wonderful job. I am very fortunate. I love what I do, but as far as putting the kind of pressure on that I am an industry or a product, I don't even want to think about that because I'm a person and that's all I can handle.

"I heard that we have *Ellen* calendars in bookstores, which I had no idea about. It's really interesting, because you get into this and it starts out with stand-up or with whatever, then you suddenly get a TV show and you suddenly become this person that is watched and studied. It's a very interesting place to be. You go through different phases of what it means and how important it is to you. But ultimately I try to just really look at . . . what my priorities are in life."

Even after being in the spotlight for so many years, Ellen was still vulnerable to the critical barbs of strangers. That would be the most difficult obstacle to overcome if she were to follow through and out her character. It was the one part of the business she would like to change.

"I mean, one person's opinion in a newspaper, one person doesn't like me, and millions of people read it. The other day I was going to see a movie and my mother goes, 'Oh, I heard that was bad.' And I said, 'Where'd you hear that?' She said, 'Well, I read it.' I said, 'So, one person's opinion and now you heard that was bad.' Now, what if I said, 'Oh, my mother said that was bad.' Now suddenly everybody heard that was bad because of one article. It's a very powerful thing. So I understand somebody not liking me, but it . . . hurts when you read something really, really negative."

But that was now a risk she was willing to take, in part because she felt she had to. Sometimes, as Ellen noted, you just had to have a little faith. "Like when you give the guy in the red jacket keys to a forty-thousand-dollar car and just assume, 'Well, this is safe.' But he has that hat on, so you trust him. It's official, even though he could have bought it at the snack shop."

With her decision to give her character and herself the chance to live openly and honestly, a world of possibilities suddenly opened up for both Ellen and *Ellen*.

In July 1996, at an ABC party held at the House of Blues, Ellen floated the idea to several reporters in attendance that she was considering a drastic change of character for her television alter ego. "It's not just 'Ellen Buys a Table' this year," she told a writer for one national publication.

"Ellen starts reexamining her life. She goes on a personal journey. She finds out who she is, which I think was lacking from the show all along. The public may have to stretch a little." And after the 1996 Emmys, she tantalized reporters by posing this hypothetical: what if Ellen Morgan were to come out of the closet? From that night forward, there would be no turning back.

The fourth-season premiere episode opened with a 27 percent decrease in ratings from the previous season's opener, due in part to competition from *The Nanny,* which was now scheduled opposite *Ellen.* It seemed the perfect time to do something radically different with the show. But both Ellen and the writers knew that it was important to lead up to any revelation slowly and give the audience time to get used to the idea.

One way to do that was to include some veiled, and some not so veiled, references within the dialogue of the show. For example, in the season opener, while in the bathroom Ellen starts singing to herself, "I feel pretty, oh so pretty. I feel pretty and witty and . . . hey!!!"

But whatever hopes they had of working quietly behind the scenes were forever dashed in September as the tantalizing rumor that DeGeneres had decided to out Ellen Morgan first appeared in press reports. From there it became an almost instant media obsession, to the point of overkill. Ellen appeared on *Good Morning America* in late September to say slyly that the whole thing had been "blown out of proportion. We're adding another character, a guy, Les Bian."

That night, Ellen appeared on *David Letterman,* who let his audience know that he, for one, was all for lesbians. (A longtime friend of Ellen, Letterman was determined to be supportive.) Ellen offered the *Late Night* audience a different shtick, saying, "The character does find out she's *Lebanese.*"

Both ABC and Disney were determined not to make any rash decisions in either direction. They were aware of the enormous implications of such a move. "They're a little freaked out," suggested one source at the time.

Never a network to miss a shameless publicity opportunity, Fox announced it was outing a character on one of its sitcoms. It turned out to be Lucky, the cocker spaniel on *Married . . . With Children.*

* * *

It would be several months before any of those possibilities were realized. Once they were, to many both within and outside the industry, the biggest question was why she had waited so long.

The answer, of course, was that this was uncharted territory. Just a little over a generation ago, being known as gay could deep-freeze a career. *Dobie Gillis* costar Sheila Kuehl, now a California representative, says her career was ruined after a CBS executive described her as being "a little too butch."

While there is still the justifiable fear that being openly gay may hinder an actor's career, some, like *NYPD Blues* star Bill Brochtrup, feel it's only one of the pitfalls actors face on a daily basis. "People are typecast regardless in Hollywood," he points out.

It wasn't that Ellen was afraid simply of negative reaction; she had already experienced a lot of that. It was more a fear that she suddenly would face censure and criticism. Ellen's quandary was how to balance who she was in private with her public image and career. The answer, when she was finally ready to accept it, was surprisingly simple: just be herself and trust that the majority of people would accept her regardless.

"I'm really content with exactly who I am, whether that's normal or not. This is my normal. This is normal for me," she said.

Once that was clear, it was a natural progression to include Ellen Morgan in the equation; she wanted her character to reflect her own off-screen life. "This is me and this is how I want to be on the show," she explained. By having Ellen Morgan come out of the closet, she would lead the way for Ellen DeGeneres to do the same. And once set into motion, there would be no turning back.

The last thing Ellen wanted was to become the Jodie

Foster of television, someone always the object of endless speculation. Questions about Foster's sexual preference have long been the topic of conversation in Hollywood, often overshadowing her stellar career. At one point, one of the tabloids had a standing offer of $100,000 for any woman who could substantiate she had an affair with Foster. Although nobody ever came forward, Ellen dreaded the thought of a similar bounty being placed on her head.

"I always thought I could keep my personal life separate from my professional life," Ellen would later say. "In every interview I ever did, everyone tried to trap me into saying I was gay. And I learned every way to dodge that. Or if they just blatantly asked me, I would say, 'I don't talk about my personal life.' I mean, I really tried to figure out every way to avoid that question for as long as I could."

Although Ellen suspected there would be some cynics who would conclude that altering her character's sexual orientation was simply a ploy to boost the show's sagging ratings, in her heart she knew it wasn't being done for ratings or to rev up the show. It was the final stage of a lifelong process of learning to come to terms with who she was, of accepting herself and her sexuality and facing her fears of rejection head on. If she wanted to lead an open and honest life, she would have to confront her critics and her own fears.

Ellen says she drew inspiration from someone else who decided not to live in fear and shame anymore: Rosa Parks, one of the pioneers of the civil rights movement who mobilized a nation by refusing to give up her seat for a white passenger. "I'm sure everyone that was friends with her said, 'You know what? We think it's wrong you're sitting back here, too, but just don't make a big thing.' I wasn't going to sit in the back of the bus anymore. I belong with everybody else."

However, there was a lot more to consider than her psyche. What Ellen was contemplating would truly break new ground, more so than most people might have initially realized. While film studios can be as controversial as they want because they finance their own product, television is beholden to sponsors, who in turn are beholden to shareholders. All it takes is one disgruntled shareholder or one politically conservative sponsor to raise a ruckus, and networks tend to cave in.

What must be remembered is that there is a vast difference in the public's perception and attitudes toward television when compared to film. To see a film, we have to get in the car or walk to the theater, buy a ticket, and go in. Television comes into our homes—not unbidden, of course, but very often mindlessly. This, in a sense, is exactly why homosexuality on TV is so bothersome to some people: it comes into their bedrooms and living rooms. Those who are opposed to gays for whatever reason, from moral concerns to sheer prejudice and intolerance, can assert that it is unacceptable for alternative lifestyles to be broadcast over public airwaves. What is accepted and celebrated in one medium is frowned upon in the other.

If Ellen Morgan came out, would ABC and Disney allow her to be a three-dimensional character? Or, would her sexuality be shorn like a sheep in autumn? A lot depended on the advertisers, who wield an undue amount of clout in the broadcast world. However, at least one ad buyer, Paul Schulman, thought Madison Avenue would take a wait-and-see attitude toward the show if indeed the lead character had a change of sexual heart. "They'd like to look at the episodes. I think Ellen and a girlfriend hanging around the house would be fine, but I don't think they'd want Ellen in bed with another woman." Anything overtly sexual "would be a real problem."

But, as Schulman correctly pointed out, *"Ellen*'s biggest

problem isn't whether or not to come out. Its biggest problem is something called *The Nanny*."

The debate over whether *Ellen* and Ellen should come out of the closet consumed the television industry as 1996 came to a close. Peter Mehlman, a former writer and producer on *Seinfeld* (which had come under fire early on for being "too Jewish"), put the question into proper perspective. "I think you can have a gay character leading a show, but for it to be truly accepted, the sensibility of its leading character—whether they are gay or Jewish or whatever—has to be that of a citizen of the world." The only way Ellen knew how to do that was through her humanity and humor. Both would be sorely tested in the months to come.

When the writers returned from hiatus to start working on the scripts and storylines for the 1996–97 season, they tacked up a seemingly innocuous note on their bulletin board that said simply THE PUPPY.

The reference was to one of the writers' bleaker moments, when a network exec came up with the idea that Ellen get a puppy. Even more pathetic, the network was enthusiastic. "It was an indication of just how lost the show was that network executives would be excited by Ellen buying a puppy," Mark Driscoll—he and Dava Savel were the new executive producers for the fourth season—said wryly.

But THE PUPPY represented what the producers and Ellen hoped would turn the series from a show that in many eyes had failed to reach its potential to a groundbreaker with the first gay series star. "We all recognized there was something missing at the center of the show," Driscoll admitted.

Before they could implement Ellen Morgan's coming out, the new executive producers wanted to get a feel for the cast's reaction. "So one of the first things I did was to meet with every single actor. I had lunch with them and talked to them about the entire year, what they wanted to do, where they saw the character going. We wanted to make sure we were all on the same team."

But the actors were the least of the hurdles. Savel noted, "We really needed to sit down with Disney and ABC and convince them there was a future for this show with Ellen as a lesbian."

So in July and August of 1996, Savel, Ellen, and Driscoll approached ABC and Disney. Present at the meetings were Disney executive Dean Valentine and Jamie Tarses, president of ABC entertainment. Tarses had earned a reputation as a programmer with her finger on the pulse of popular culture and, it should be noted, was instrumental during her tenure at NBC in getting the *Friends* lesbian wedding on the air. To her, outing Ellen Morgan "seemed like a very bold idea. We felt this would perhaps give the show the creative soul and drive it was missing."

Valentine was more reserved. "I said it was only worth doing if it was a great episode. I told Ellen I'm not interested in standing on political soapboxes. First and foremost, it has to be great TV."

To Ellen's delight, she and her team were given a tentative go-ahead, although promised nothing. The concerned executives made it clear that the decision as to whether ABC and Disney would agree to have Ellen Morgan come out would ultimately be based on the creative content of the episode presented. And before Ellen had driven back to the studio, the programming chiefs had already passed the hot-potato issue to Disney CEO Michael Eisner, the man who runs the empire of the mouse and in whose hands the final approval rested.

Not everyone jumped on the bandwagon, though. One former staffer commented on what would happen when the series would air in syndication. *(Ellen* was sold to Lifetime for syndication at $600,000 per episode.) "I can't imagine watching it and saying, 'Here's the great episode where

Ellen goes out on a blind date. And oh, by the way, she's a lesbian.'"

Ellen's costars didn't know it when they showed up for the first table reading that the entire season was to be geared with the coming-out episode in mind, but they quickly found out. But once the cast realized what was happening, there was unanimous support.

"You know, as funny a group as we are and as distinctive a group of people, characters, that we are, it never really clicked," acknowledges Joely Fisher. "There was something always missing. And maybe this was it." If nothing else, Joely felt, it gave the show "a very definite point of view and a definite perspective."

All of the talk and speculation had raised public awareness and interest, and to those involved, it seemed like the time was right to go forward. However, final approval to write the episode was still being withheld. The reticence of the Disney and ABC higher-ups to give their blessing even to the preparation of a script—left Ellen and the writers feeling in a state of will-they, won't-they limbo. It was the beginning of what would become a litany of grievances Ellen would have against the network and studio.

DeGeneres was aware of the issues but in the end felt that the network's exposure was minimal because she was the one with the most to lose. "I'm in a business where I'm the commodity. I'm the product. Please buy me, you know? That's why when Disney or ABC were worried about boycotts or this and that, I kept saying to everybody, 'I'm the one who's going to get the biggest boycott.'"

She pleaded with the network, "You can cancel the show, you can go make another one. It's not going to hurt you. I'm the product here. You can go on. Life goes on for you. This is my life. I am taking the biggest risk here. And I'm willing to take the risk because that's how much it means to me."

In the meantime, there were other forces affecting the

show. In hopes of boosting *Ellen*'s ratings, ABC changed the show's time slot yet again. It was moved from 8:00 on Wednesday to 9:30, after the network's newest hit, *The Drew Carey Show*. Then, in the winter of 1997, Ellen's manager heard through the grapevine that ABC was planning on taking *Ellen* off the air for two months to try out Arsenio Hall's new show in its time slot.

Ellen was so angry, she walked off the set for a day. She also declined to participate in a Las Vegas–themed stunt planned for February sweeps, in which all the Wednesday sitcoms would be set in Las Vegas, with crossover appearances by the various cast members on each other's shows.

Ellen's behavior was explained by one observer as mostly frustration and anxiety. "She wanted to get to the story, and Disney was not being totally supportive." Walking off the set in protest and becoming uncooperative in network stunts "may have been her way to speed the process along."

At the January 1997 Television Critics Press Tour, Jamie Tarses fielded questions about whether Ellen Morgan was or wasn't going to come out. "I think that we are seriously considering going in the direction that everyone's speculating on *Ellen*. And we're also telling the truth when we say we have not yet determined, because there have been serious conversations. It's not a no-brainer. Truthfully, it's going to be based upon creative content. We have not yet seen the material that's going to help us with this decision as to whether or not we all want to do this together. But," she added, "it's a given that she'll be returning to that time slot."

In addition to the pressure of waiting on the wavering studio to make a decision, Ellen was under the additional stress of being in the middle of contract negotiations. (She would eventually sign a very lucrative deal with Disney's Touchstone Television, which included a salary increase from about $90,000 to $125,000 per episode and a co-executive producer credit for the fifth season.) Then, to compound her worries, her personal assistant quit, prompting pointed comments from some on the production staff who felt Ellen was overreacting to ABC and Disney's apparent reluctance to let her character come out of the closet.

But to Ellen the hesitancy was a personal affront and rejection, so the more the network and its owner wavered, the more determined, and angry, Ellen got. Finally, worried that their star might actually walk off for good, Disney and ABC finally gave the go-ahead to write a coming-out episode in late January 1997. But once given the green light, the writers faced a daunting task. "The writers are having a problem with this," said one member of the production team. "They are trying to make it light and not too dramatic. They don't want it to be a 'very special *Ellen*.'"

Both Driscoll and Savel were determined to make sure that the proposed subject matter was handled with sensitivity and humor. "I felt a tremendous sense of responsibility, to Ellen primarily," said Driscoll. "It's a story she cared very much about."

Added Savel: "And it's important for the gay community. We're not looking to make her some big role model, but this is something a lot of kids go through. And they don't know where to turn. If this episode helps some child in the Midwest with their sexual identification, we've done our job."

Savel also said it was important not to change the character. "It's still not going to be easy for Ellen. We want people to see the struggle."

However, Disney's Dean Valentine, then head of television development, rejected the first draft because he felt the script "didn't dig deep enough into the character." Instead, the primary focus was on the reaction of her friends to the revelation that she was gay. ABC made suggestions, too, and the writers went to work revising the script. On March 3, 1997, ABC formally approved the script for filming.

"She was beaming" after getting the word, recalls costar Jeremy Piven.

ABC also capitulated about taking *Ellen* off the air. It kept Arsenio Hall's sitcom in the 9:30 Wednesday time slot but moved *Ellen* to Tuesday nights. Although Ellen by now had lost count of how many times her show had been moved, it was a compromise she could live with, so on March 4, *Ellen* replaced *Life's Work,* starring another former stand-up, Lisa Walters.

If Ellen had thought that the media scrutiny was intense before, after the revelation that there would in fact be a coming-out episode, it quickly became a media firestorm. Everyone weighed in with opinions, both supportive and hostile.

Former *Dobie Gillis* star Sheila Kuehl saw it as "a courageous move. Advertisers, networks, producers, and fans have to haul out their prejudices and say, 'Does this make a difference in how I feel about this woman?'"

Bruce Vilanch, a flamboyant gay man best known for comedy writing, commented in his *Advocate* column: "Of course, having a lead character in a comedy series announce that she is a lesbian means that sooner or later she's going to have to have an encounter with—guess what?—another lesbian. This may not be as earth-shattering as we think, since it is well known that there are only five lesbians in the world: two couples and the woman who breaks them up. So there won't be a *lot* of those episodes. But their inevitability means that we're going to be visible in a big way. That's worth an award or two. If we're lucky, maybe even an Emmy."

"I hope it does what Ellen intends, and that's to send a positive message about lesbians and gays in general to the public," said her brother, Vance, who was now one of *Ellen's* writers.

Tim Allen asserted that he himself "would have done it a long time ago. I think it would be an interesting show to have a lesbian as a main character who is funny. Let the viewer in on it but have her play in her world like she's not. Let her have to fool people. It would be illuminating to show people how ridiculous it is to have to hide your sexuality and how society forces people to be uncomfortable letting it out. There's so much room for comedy there, I would have let it out a long time ago."

Marshall Herskovitz, producer of *thirtysomething,* said, "As far as I'm concerned, the two most dangerous influences are commercials and the news, more so than anything you'll ever see on a prime-time show. You have to put controversy in context. Things are controversial because people fear them."

Those opposed to presenting a sitcom lead as gay were just as vocal. Donald Wildmon, head of the socially conservative group American Family, put advertisers on notice that viewers would "reveal their true allegiances to themes which gnaw at traditional family values."

Another critic, Reverend Fred Phelps, warned, "It's a sign we're on the cusp of doom, of Sodom and Gomorrah."

Randall Murphee, editor of the *American Family Association Journal,* declared, "A culture that immerses itself in casual, illicit sex will become a culture adrift in a sea of moral irresponsibility."

L. Brent Bozell III of the archconservative Media Research Center said, "If Hollywood is driven by producing a product that the people want, then there would be no market for this. The only group that wants this type of programming is a very small, militant group in Hollywood."

Author Camille Paglia, never one to pass up a chance to irritate both sides of an issue, said, "As an open lesbian, I say that the entertainment industry has been exploiting the artistic talents of gay people throughout the twentieth century without ever giving them their due. But the objections of Christian ministers who believe in the Bible are well founded.

People on the left have got to accept that it is not simple bigotry that causes believing Christians to object to this kind of element in popular culture."

Bigotry did seem to be at the heart of Reverend Jerry Falwell's reaction. He denounced Ellen as simply "Ellen DeGenerate."

"What can I say to him?" Ellen asked. "How can I even respond? That's something a fourth grader would say to me and think is funny and giggle. How can you argue with that kind of logic? I know that there are people out there that are saying things because they don't understand. And it's all coming from a place of fear."

Ellen said that she understood that some people felt threatened, "but Jesus, as far as I'm concerned, he was nonjudgmental and taught love and acceptance. That's all I know about, and that's how I live my life." Ellen added to writer Judy Wieder, "I think whatever works for you is right. Heaven or hell is what you create right this minute where you are. You have a choice to live in joy or not. And that's my belief. If I'm wrong, then I'm wrong, but I'm not hurting anybody."

Although she might have had reservations about her daughter's lifestyle, Betty bristled at the personal attacks against Ellen. "I don't need to get on a soapbox here about people who say it's a choice or it's wrong. It's who she is. And it's who so many people in this world are who are creative and productive and wonderful, wonderful contributing members of society. I'd like to know how many people who spoke out against Ellen have relatives in their families who are gay. Ellen is such a good person. Now, I don't want to get weepy, but she's so good that she shouldn't have this directed at her."

Even Ellen's father was moved to affirm his support of his daughter, "because, you see, I love Ellen. She's somebody I've always loved and I always will love her. I don't have a whole bunch of great qualities, but one of them is loyalty. And that and love go together."

Some within the industry thought that it was ultimately unwise, from a strictly business point of view, to present a gay lead character. "What you're going to find is *Ellen* is going to take a hit on this," opined Dick Wolf, creator of *Law & Order*. "If it was my show, I probably wouldn't have done it. This is one specific area that a large percentage of the population is very uncomfortable with."

Producer Mark Driscoll said he understood why so many people felt the need to offer an opinion. "Even if somebody doesn't like the show, they generally like Ellen DeGeneres. She hosts the Grammys. She's not your regular sitcom star. The fascination is taking someone like that and totally splitting her open. And it's taboo. Her character is not secondary. We're taking a well-established, well-liked character who, after four years, says, 'Guys, this is why I haven't been dating.'"

Of course, there were some industry pundits who dismissed the entire thing as a publicity stunt, which prompted Disney executive David A. Neuman to respond, "That would be a silly and idiotic stunt on any level. You might get a great rating one week, but winning a victory in a series is about the next one hundred episodes. We have the rare opportunity to replicate something that happens in real life."

Ellen maintained that her reasons were firmly personal. "I did it selfishly for myself and because I thought it was a great thing for the show, which desperately needed a point of view. I didn't want to talk about it until after the show was done. I never wanted to be 'the lesbian actress.' I never wanted to be the spokesperson for the gay community. I'm not here to say, 'I'm gay, everybody be gay.' I did it for my own truth."

Beyond the danger of being typecast as "a lesbian actress" was danger of a more immediate—and physical—kind. On one occasion, Ellen was followed by a suspicious-looking stranger in a car to the studio, and the show received at least one bomb threat.

"That was one of my biggest concerns," she said. "If I did this, would something happen to me? It just became secondary to how strongly I believe in what I'm doing."

Ellen continued to make news, this time for her actions off the set. At the Los Angeles Gay and Lesbian Center's gala Women's Night '97 held in Beverly Hills on March 1, Ellen was on hand to present openly gay singer k.d. lang with a Creative Integrity Award. Standing before the predominantly gay crowd, Ellen joked that she had just discovered lang was gay. "I think I was as surprised as anyone when I found out two days ago she is gay. I should have seen the clues. Like the fact that k.d. prefers to sleep with women."

When accepting her award, k.d. ribbed Ellen back. "I'd like to thank Ellen for coming out . . . tonight," she said, causing the audience to erupt in cheers and applause.

Ellen later said, "When you have a phase and stick to it, it becomes a way of life, which is my motto. I hope to do the same." But she stopped short of making a public announcement that she, too, was gay. Not that there was much doubt, especially after k.d. and Ellen kissed each other with photographers madly snapping away.

"I'll never live that kiss down," Ellen sighed afterward. "She kissed me, first of all—k.d. knows, if you ask her—and it turned into *I* kissed her."

By that time, who kissed whom was almost irrelevant. For all intents and purposes, Ellen was living out and in the open. The only thing left to do was make it official. While to some that might have seemed redundant, one television executive explained why it was necessary: "You have to fulfill that expectation or you're forcing a distinction between public and private, which would be awkward for millions of people who view Ellen Morgan and Ellen DeGeneres as the same person."

Comic Lea DeLaria was more derisive. "What is she going to say? 'I'm not a lesbian, but I play one on TV?'"

DeGeneres made it official in April 1997 in a *Time* magazine cover story that ran the headline "Yep, I'm Gay," followed by a two-part interview with Diane Sawyer on ABC's newsmagazine *20/20*. Looking comfortable, appealing, and unthreatening, Ellen answered Sawyer's sometimes uninformed questions with an eager honesty.

"I hate that term *in the closet,*" Ellen commented. "Until recently I hated the word *lesbian,* too. I've said it enough now that it doesn't bother me. But *lesbian* sounded like somebody with some kind of disease. I didn't like that, so I used the word *gay* more often."

Ellen talked freely about her life and was acutely aware that she stood to lose fans in both her straight and gay audiences. "I'm letting down the straight community that is going to worry about their kids watching me. And I'm letting down the militant gay community that says, 'How dare you not be gay enough.' But it doesn't mean that I need to be some poster child for anybody. The main reason I never wanted to do this was because I don't want to become political and I don't want to become some gay activist. And that's the risk here. I think I'm going to piss off *everybody*. I can only hope that people are as fair-minded and as open and accepting as I am.

"For me, this has been the most freeing experience, because people can't hurt me anymore. I don't have to worry about somebody saying something about me or a reporter trying to find out information, because now I'm in control of it. Literally, as soon as I made this decision, I lost weight. My skin cleared up. I don't have anything to be scared of, which I think outweighs whatever else happens in my career."

The reaction to Ellen's *20/20* appearance was immediate and predictable. Those who supported her found even more reason to celebrate her honesty. Those who opposed what she represented were even more convinced she was a tool of the devil—including some in her former home of Atlanta, Texas. First Assembly of God pastor Van Venter declared that homosexuality was "demonic. I think the show is part of a diabolical plan to drag down society."

To which Ellen replied, "It just goes back to the fact there's so many more things on television that you should worry about your children seeing."

And Ellen's former English teacher, Ruth Trumble, said, "Even though I don't think anything bad about Ellen, I think she's making a mistake."

A more thoughtful analysis of what Ellen's personal admission meant to society at large was offered by Ariel Kaminer in *New York* magazine. "Ellen wasn't in the closet in the first place—at least not in any sense ordinary mortals might recognize. She's been out for years. She just hadn't mentioned it to *Time*.

"For those poor queers who aren't actually famous, the difference between being *in* and *out* is a simple thing. In the closet, people work hard to hide their sexuality, undertaking labor-intensive ruses—even fake marriages—and still living in constant fear of discovery and its consequences. Out of the closet, people are free to chase after members of their own gender without worrying about who's watching.

"But when famous people are involved, these distinctions tend to break down. In the mistaken name of tolerance, celebrities are routinely afforded the option of living an openly gay or lesbian life and still being officially coded as straight, with all the privileges that entails.

"Until she said otherwise, Ellen DeGeneres, despite all the available evidence to the contrary, wasn't gay, either. She was hiding in plain sight."

Critic Frank Rich noted that "the big unspoken, unexamined subtext of the entire *Ellen* circus" was that "many straight Americans, especially men, find lesbians titillating even as they deplore or are threatened by male homosexuality." He also pointed out the somewhat shocking fact that in forty-one states people could still be legally fired if they admitted to being gay.

That truth prompted others who had walked down Ellen's path to believe that one had to look at the big picture. "You can't diminish what Ellen is doing," said *Married . . . With Children* star Amanda Bearse, who had publicly come out in 1993. "Every time someone steps out in that way, especially with the power that is behind her, Disney and ABC, it's important. It was a long time coming."

Author Jacqueline Mitchard noted, rather poetically, that "though they don't say this on *Sesame Street,* a lesbian is a person in your neighborhood. And if television is a mirror as well as a window, then that's how it is."

As the April 30 air date approached, the fallout among advertisers and affiliates began. The only affiliate to refuse to run "The Puppy Episode" was in Birmingham, Alabama. A local gay organization, Birmingham Pride, arranged for a satellite feed and rented a concert hall with a five-thousand-seat capacity, which was sold out.

The station, managed by Jerry Heilman, contended the episode was "not suitable for family viewing." Barbara Spivey, a mother of two teenage daughters, said she was upset at Heilman's decision because it "cheated me out of a terrific chance to talk to my girls about the ways that a person's sexual choices can make their lives easier or harder."

Another viewer voiced the concern that "if the show is going to turn into 'let's explore what lesbian relationships really mean,' I wouldn't want to watch that."

Two occasional advertisers on *Ellen,* JC Penny and Chrysler, announced they wouldn't continue to sponsor the show. The latter said it didn't want to be involved with a "polarized" issue.

Wendy's also announced it was forever jumping ship. Said spokesperson Denny Lynch, "The story content no longer fits our advertising guidelines. Storylines that could be controversial or cutting-edge we would definitely avoid." It should probably be noted that Wendy's founder is a vocal supporter of Pat Robertson, who was quoted as saying, "I find it hard to believe because she's so popular. She's such an attractive actress."

Ellen could only let that comment roll off her back. "God, it's weird that somebody popular and attractive can be gay. See, things like that, I don't even have to address those people. They just speak for themselves."

Jamie Tarses, speaking for ABC, declared, "We're very proud. We think Ellen and the show's staff have executed [the episode] beautifully. Obviously, this is an experiment. We're not sociologists. We don't know how this is going to be received. This is not a date-of-the-week show. It never has been. It will be another aspect of her character. This is not going to be a day in the life of Ellen DeGeneres, lesbian."

Among the creative community, that was going to be the truest test of whether the experiment was successful. Bruce Helford, coexecutive producer for *The Drew Carey Show,* wasn't so sure that the change of sexuality for Ellen Morgan could fix the underlying problem of the show. "I think there will be a big spike in the ratings. But if it's just one big thing and then they go back to the same show and she's a lesbian but the same old things happen to her, the boost won't last."

Regardless of what happened after the show aired, gay organizations across the country used the occasion of "The Puppy Episode" to stage their own awareness events such as a fund-raiser called Coming Out With Ellen, sponsored by the Gay and Lesbian Alliance Against Defamation (GLAAD), which hosted parties in several cities.

"A lot of people are going to come out after they watch the show," suggested gay comic Judy Carter.

In Georgia, the *Atlanta Journal-Constitution* used the occasion to ask readers to share their own experiences with coming out. One who did was a minister who had posed his entire life as straight but decided he couldn't stand living a lie anymore. "My sin is not being gay," he said. "My sin is lying about it."

The media attention to Ellen's dual coming out was overwhelming to the point of overkill in the week preceding the broadcast. But to some, the saturation was actually a good thing. As AmFAR (American Federation for AIDS Research) spokesman Jay Blotcher noted, while the pre-episode hype was exasperating, "that was the way to do it, I think; all of Ellen's Lebanese jokes, the slow, steady prepping of the audience and the media. Yeah, now it's almost 'Who cares?' And isn't that the attitude we want? Who cares? So she's gay. Big deal."

Actually, to Ellen it was a big deal because it meant she was truly her own person. Whatever the consequences, she was finally living an honest, open life. All she could do was wait to see how her fans and the public would react to an episode she had literally put her career on the line to get produced.

17
"New Beginnings"

Few sitcom writers have ever had to walk quite so precarious a tightrope as the team responsible for putting together "The Puppy Episode." Perhaps more than at any other time, the writers and director, Gil Junger, paid close attention to Ellen's comic instincts. No matter what negative things had been said about her, even her critics had to admit the woman "knew from funny." Nor could anyone deny her work ethic. Junger recalls that once Ellen memorized a fifty-page script in just a few hours. "I've never seen anything like it," he said.

He was also duly amazed by how quick she was to spot comic opportunities in a situation presented by the script and improvise. Usually, she would do the scene once as written, but the next time around, her comedy radar would take over.

"She catches *herself* by surprise," said Junger. "She's said to me, 'I don't know where it comes from.' More often than not the second take," the one in which Ellen improvised, "is the one we'll use."

When the cast showed up for work the week "The Puppy

Episode" was scheduled to film, they could almost hear the energy crackling on the set. Joely Fisher remembers the week vividly. "We didn't even know, really, how it was going to play out until that Monday that we had our table reading. We all opened up our scripts, and it was just fresh. It was liberating for everyone. It was like, 'Oh, thank God, we can all talk about this, and we can all be who we are and not worry about, you know, covering things up anymore.' I saw a definite change in Ellen that day."

The reason was simple. Ellen never knew how burdened she had been living in the shadows until she was about to step into the light. "Because I never thought it was anybody's business who I am and who I am with, I thought, 'Why do people need to know?' But then I realized that as long as I had this secret that I worried about all the time, that it made it look like [I thought it was] something wrong."

By all accounts, although she was understandably hyped up on one hand, Ellen was also possibly the most relaxed she had ever been. And as much as it was about her—which she never denied—she was also aware that, like it or not, she was about to become a symbol for many people, both good and bad. All she could do about those people who thought she was a tool of Satan was try to give them the understanding they refused her. But she also knew that there were people whose lives she could touch in a positive way.

It is a well-known statistic borne out by repeated studies that a gay teenager is three times more likely to attempt suicide than one who's straight. In her *20/20* interview, Ellen told Diane Sawyer that whatever happened to her career after her coming-out episode, part of her effort was an attempt to hold on to those kids.

The hour-long episode boasted some heavy-hitting guest stars appearing in cameos including Billy Bob Thornton, Demi Moore, Dwight Yoakam, Gina Gershon, Kathy Najimy, k.d. lang, and Melissa Etheridge. The two most important guest stars would be Laura Dern, who would play Ellen's love interest, and Oprah Winfrey as the therapist who guides Ellen through her journey of self-discovery.

"I suggested Oprah," says Mark Driscoll. "I think Oprah is a terrific actress. She's so well liked by the American people, it was perfect to have someone like her who connects with middle America, where if Oprah said it was okay, then it's okay."

For Oprah, the decision to appear on the show wasn't without repercussions. She received bags of mail, much of it from people who accused her of promoting lesbianism merely by being associated with the show. She also became the target of rumors about her own sexuality. Believing it was important to explain her feelings, Oprah told viewers that "I simply wanted to support [Ellen]. And what I gathered from a lot of the mail is that there's a perception—and I've been fighting this for years on TV—that gay people are just swinging from the chandeliers, having sex all the time. They don't understand that to the greatest extent, gay people want the same thing everybody else does. That's why I thought that part of the show was so interesting."

"The Puppy Episode" was taped on Friday, March 14, before a deliriously enthusiastic crowd of invitation-only guests—who had to pass through a security checkpoint with metal detectors. The studio had received a bomb threat, prompting worried network officials to call the police and have them sweep the sound stage and surrounding areas.

Members of the LAPD bomb squad brought in specially trained dogs capable of sniffing out explosives. To the relief of all concerned, none were found, but the call reminded everyone that what Ellen was doing was not without some personal risk.

The bleachers were filled to capacity. In her usual place, front row center, was Ellen's mom, Betty, who had never been prouder of her daughter. It was hard for Betty not to cry

just watching the audience, who were all so obviously supportive of Ellen.

When Ellen finally made her first appearance, she stood
in front of the bleachers and addressed the audience, who
were screaming and cheering for both Ellen and the song
playing, Diana Ross's "I'm Coming Out."

"What can I say?" Ellen asked, a look of amazement on
her smiling face. "This is the most amazing experience of
my life, and to have these people with me, it's just unbelievable. I thank everyone for their support. Thanks for coming
out!"

The episode opens with Joe, Audrey, Paige, and Spence
waiting for Ellen, who is in the other room. They grumble
among themselves:

"It feels like she's been in there forever."

"Ellen, are you coming out or not?"

"Yeah, Ellen, quit jerking us around and come out already."

That set the tone for the episode, which has Ellen being
forced to confront her sexual preference after she finds herself attracted to an openly gay woman. The most poignant
scene in the one hour show was when she admits to the therapist that she's had an inkling all along that she was gay but
never wanted to admit it to herself. "I thought if I ignored it,
it would just go away and I could have a normal life."

"And what is a normal life?" the therapist asks.

Ellen says, "I just want to be normal. I mean, you never
see a cake that says, 'Good for you. You're gay.'"

"Well, then, I'll say it. Good for you. You're gay."

Interestingly, director Junger had to film several takes of
this scene, because the first few were too intense. It was
clear to everyone present that Ellen had stopped acting and
was speaking from her heart, and the view was a little too
personal and painful. Junger gently coaxed Ellen into hitting
the comic notes in the scene.

The final scene takes place in what is supposed to be Little Frieda's, a real gay coffee shop in West Hollywood where Ellen was a frequent customer. Arranged by Audrey, the get-together is both to show Ellen she and Paige support her newfound lifestyle and to introduce Ellen to others in the community. The episode ends after a pretty young woman comes and sits on the couch opposite Ellen. Everyone thinks this is finally Ellen's big chance—only the woman is interested in Paige, who shrinks back into the couch. "Nice to see some things don't change," Ellen says, then looks wistfully off into space, realizing that just because she now knows who she is, it doesn't mean her love life will automatically change.

When the director finally called it a wrap, the crowd stood and cheered for countless minutes. Joely Fisher remembers that it felt like "the longest time you can imagine." When they wheeled out a huge cake that said, 'Good for you, you're gay,' Ellen broke down, overcome by emotion.

"When they brought out the cake, and it was pretty incredible," recalls Fisher, "I saw this look on Ellen that I have not seen before ever, I don't think. And it was incredible. I mean, everybody cried, *everybody*. It was just an amazing, liberating thing."

So much so that others found themselves getting caught up in the hoopla. *Ellen*'s ABC publicist, Jill Lessard, took the occasion to come out herself. "I just got swept up in the moment," she explained afterward.

When she could compose herself enough to think clearly, Ellen addressed the friends and associates who surrounded her. "I can't even tell you how wonderful this has been. I feel so proud to be part of such a brilliant show. My cast is so amazing, everybody has been so supportive. It's overwhelming, the support I've received. I just don't know what else to say other than thank you so, so much for being a part of it, and reacting the way you did, and being moved by the story the way that we hoped you would, because it's just human emotions. That's all it is. It's just feelings, and it's so amazing that this has become such a big deal. I don't understand it. But thank you so very much. I love you all."

Reflecting on the night later, Ellen said she could sense that everyone was drinking in every moment. "Everyone who was there that night—we all knew something huge had just happened . . . it was a huge party. Little did we now it would turn out to be a huge party for the world."

The day after the taping, Ellen phoned Savel. "She called up, crying, saying, 'Thank you. It was fabulous,'" the producer recalls. "She feels on top of the world. She's so happy the show was done right. It was everything she wanted it to be. So in that sense, she is free." However, to show that indeed some things don't change, Savel recounted that "Monday came around and it was back to 'I can't do this script. I can't stand it.' That's Ellen."

The episode aired on April 30, 1997. Ellen's theatrical agency, CAA, along with her manager, Arthur Imperato, hosted a party in honor of Ellen and screened the episode's broadcast in the agency's private screening room. On hand to toast Ellen were Laura Dern, Shirley MacLaine, Billy Bob Thornton, and Ellen's new love interest, actress Anne Heche.

Despite the unbelievable media attention, "The Puppy Episode" managed to live up to its hype. An estimated forty-two million people tuned in to watch Ellen's historic moment. The vast majority, even those who were uncomfortable with the subject matter, agreed it had been handled in the best possible way: touching without being preachy, funny without being flip.

A *New York Times* editorial stated: "She was right to say that if the self-appointed defenders of 'traditional' values are incensed, they should by all means watch something else. But if last night's show was any indication, the new *Ellen* can hardly be accused of promoting a lifestyle as much as promoting tolerance.

"In the end, the fate of Ellen and *Ellen* will not be decided by the Rev. Jerry Falwell or potentially skittish advertisers or by her own off-screen romances but by the ratings that have always determined success or failure in television. If Ms. DeGeneres can sustain the quality of last night's show, she deserves to succeed."

But sustaining that quality was indeed Ellen's biggest challenge going forward. Now she and the writers had to use this new direction wisely. What she realized with more than a little irony was that coming out, in the end, had been easy; comedy was still hard.

Her new found openness wasn't the only change in Ellen's life. In her interview with *Time* magazine she revealed that she had "just met somebody. This appears to be something I want to last forever."

During her appearance on *20/20*, Diane Sawyer asked if Ellen, thirty-eight, was in a relationship. "Yeah," Ellen nodded. "Very happy. I think it's forever. That's a good feeling. It's the first time I've ever, ever felt like forever."

By the time the mainstream media was starting to turn their attention to Ellen's love life, the tabloids had already made a case as to who the object of her desire was. On April 10, Ellen had attended the VH1 Honors Awards with twenty-seven-year-old actress Anne Heche. To many of those attending the event—especially the photographers, who were practiced at picking up such telltale clues as body language or duos who are *too* careful about the way they interact—Ellen and Anne seemed very much a couple.

While nobody would have given much thought to seeing Ellen out with another woman, what made this twosome so intriguing was that as far as anyone knew, Anne had only ever been linked to men. And when reporters checked with their sources within the Hollywood gay community, they confirmed that Anne was not known to have been involved with a woman.

All of a sudden, this relatively obscure actress became the focus of an intense information-gathering effort by both the legitimate and tabloid media. What they discovered was a family history that was a ready-made blockbuster.

Anne Heche was born in Aurora, Ohio, on May 25, 1969, but her family later moved to Chicago. Like Ellen, she was raised in a strict household, but unlike the DeGeneres clan, the Heches were awash in dark family secrets. Her father, Donald Heche, was known in their community as a solidly religious man and a devout member of the local Baptist church—but according to Anne his life was a lie. At night, when he was away from the church and his family, Donald could be found trolling gay bars for one-night stands.

"My father was one of the choir directors who was gay that no one talked about," Heche freely admits. "He was so much in the closet that nobody ever talked about it."

Nor did Donald own up to the truth of the illness that struck him in the early 1980s. It wasn't until his health started to fail and he was close to death that Anne finally found out about her father's life. "He did not admit he was dying of AIDS to his family until about a month before he died in 1983," she says. "I watched my dad disintegrate from AIDS because he was ashamed to be what he wanted to be."

The trauma of finding out that her father had not only been living a double life in the eyes of their neighbors and friends but had been so dishonest and hypocritical with his own family had a profound effect on Anne, who was only fourteen years old.

"When you watch somebody who lives their life lying and then destroys himself through a disease, you tend to look at that and go, 'Now, how can I do something different?'" Anne would explain later.

Anne and her mother, brother, and two sisters were still

mourning Donald's death and coming to grips with the shock of his homosexuality when another tragedy struck the already shell-shocked family: Her brother was killed in a car crash. Suddenly, the primary responsibility of helping support the family financially fell on Anne's teenage shoulders.

Even prior to her father's death, Anne had already been encouraged to help bring in extra money by getting jobs singing in dinner theaters. With both her father and brother abruptly gone, she felt under even more pressure to make money in order to help take care of her mother and sisters, so she began acting as a means to increase her earning potential. It soon became apparent that she had talent.

For most teenagers, high school is a time both to prepare for the future and to enjoy the last carefree days of youth. But for Anne, the future was now. Because her family relied on her acting income, her after-school time was spent going on auditions and performing.

When she was fifteen, Anne appeared in a production of Thornton Wilder's *Skin of Our Teeth.* After one of the performances, Anne was approached by a talent scout from the daytime drama *As the World Turns* who offered her a role in the long-running serial, but she turned it down because it would have meant relocating from Chicago to New York. In a testament to her appeal, she was offered a similar job, this time by *Another World,* as her senior year drew to a close. So, almost immediately after she graduated from high school in 1988, Anne was on her way to New York to start her professional career. It was baptism by sudsy fire.

"The day I arrived, the producer said, 'Oh, by the way, you're playing twins, and one of them is a real sexpot. In your first scene you'll be naked in a bathtub and you've just lost a million dollars.'" Anne was up to the challenge, and her four-year portrayal of the good-evil twins Marley McKinnon and Vicki Love would catapult her quickly to soap stardom and earn her a daytime Emmy as Outstanding Younger Actress in 1991.

After Anne left *Another World* in 1992, she contemplated dropping out of performing and going to design school. However, even though acting had begun as a necessity, it was now a passion, so she headed to Los Angeles to try breaking into movies. Never one to sit around the apartment and wait for the phone to ring, Anne studied and performed with the Bridge, a Los Angeles–based dance company, while waiting for the opportunities she was sure would come.

It didn't take long. Her first roles were in the 1993 tele-film *O Pioneers!* with Jessica Lange and the movie *Girls in Prison,* which included no recognizable names, then or now. Although neither project brought her much notoriety, she did gain the experience and credits she needed to be offered small supporting roles in the feature films *The Adventures of Huck Finn* and *An Ambush of Ghosts.*

In 1993, Anne was cast in *A Simple Twist of Fate* and began what would be a two-year relationship with Steve Martin, who would later describe their time together as a "torturous love affair." Martin took their breakup so badly that friends of the comic took to calling Anne "the Heartbreak Kid."

In 1995, she had her first breakthrough with the festival hit *Pie in the Sky,* which was made in conjunction with Robert Redford's Sundance Institute. Although the recognition she received for the film was limited to industry audiences, it was enough to bump her up the casting ladder. She was cast in a succession of higher-profile roles in films that performed solidly at the box office, including Nicole Holofcener's *Walking and Talking* and a short but flashy part in *The Juror,* in which she is seduced and murdered by Alec Baldwin. During this time she was linked romantically with a number of men, including John Cusack's older brother, actor Billy, and was also allegedly one of George Clooney's companions.

Her biggest movie role to date was her critically acclaimed performance as Johnny Depp's deeply dissatisfied wife in the hit film *Donnie Brasco,* which also starred Al Pacino. From the buzz generated during *Brasco*'s filming, Anne was cast in her first true leading film role—opposite Tommy Lee Jones in the disaster flick *Volcano.* During the production, she began dating the movie's producer, Neal Moritz; their relationship would last until just before Anne met Ellen.

As fate would have it, just weeks before they met for the first time, Anne Heche's name came up in an *Ellen* casting meeting. "She was actually on the list of actresses to play [Ellen's would-be love interest] Susan," reveals Ellen. "And I said, 'Oh, yeah, she's great.'"

The role ultimately went to Ellen's good friend Laura Dern, which only postponed what both Anne and Ellen believed was their fated meeting. That came on March 24, 1997, a month before "The Puppy Episode" aired, at the annual *Vanity Fair* Oscar bash, one of the most popular of the post-Oscar festivities. Ellen was attending the party alone; her relationship with Teresa Boyd, which had always been rocky, was over, and Boyd had recently moved out of Ellen's house.

With characteristic flair, Anne describes their initial encounter. "I saw Ellen across a crowded room, not knowing anything at all except how I was just drawn to her. It was very clear from the moment I saw her that this was something more powerful than anything I could have controlled. So I went on the chandelier, swung across to her, and bounced down in front of her and said, 'Come on!'

"I think at certain times in people's lives, you just radiate an energy and a glow of fabulousness. And that was her! I had never seen anybody so lit up. When we started talking I asked her for her number. She said, *What are you doin'? There's a reporter right here. Do you have any idea . . . who I am?*" After Anne approached Ellen, the two spent the evening talking, and for Anne, her destiny had been sealed by the time the party ended. "I don't think it was immediately a sexual attraction. I think it was just, 'Wow. You are the most incredible person I've ever met, and I want to be with you.'"

Ellen laughs, recalling, "She had never seen my show . . . and I hated that. And I'd only seen her in one movie." Nevertheless, the two quickly found they had much in common—even if sexual preference wasn't one of them.

Heche went home with Ellen that night and says she immediately fell in love. In a 2001 interview with Anne Stockwell, Heche says it was the best sex of her life. "Hands down. I think I was allowed to embrace the masculine side of me for the first time and also enjoy the feminine side of me for the first time. To me, a girl who's into pleasing men her whole life . . . it was a great orgasm, it was beautiful, I felt like I was exploring something new, which was awesome. It was not what I always thought it would be, which was touchy-soft love. It was masculine and feminine. It was everything."

Anne repeatedly claimed that until falling in love with Ellen, she had never contemplated being attracted to a woman romantically. "Nobody could have been more confused than me, but I was not gay before I met her. I don't feel there was ever an inkling."

That, as it turned out, worried Ellen a lot more than it apparently did Anne. "I said, 'Get away from me. You're straight. I don't want to have anything to do with you.' I thought, 'You don't know what you're doing.'"

But Anne says she knew exactly what she was doing. "There are times when souls come together and they're just meant to be. That's all that mattered. I looked beyond the sex. I think in love there's no sex, there's no segregation, there's no anything. There's just love. I didn't all of a sudden feel like I'm gay. I just all of a sudden felt, 'Ooh. I love.' "

Anne says that from the time her father died, "I think my life became about truth. No matter what, no matter how, no matter when, tell the truth. Live, love, and enjoy yourself. And little did I know how much that would be appropriate for my life once I met Ellen."

Over the next month, Anne and Ellen were inseparable. Not only did they attend the VH1 Honors together, but Ellen was Anne's escort to the premiere of *Volcano*. Even so, Anne's publicist, Simon Halls, vehemently denied there was any romantic relationship between the two. That would later make him look not only dishonest but silly, especially after Anne and Ellen appeared together at the annual White House Correspondents Dinner in Washington, D.C., where they met President Clinton.

The couple created more than just a little stir because of their continuous public displays of affection and apparent scorn for protocol. They mingled hand in hand and posed together for photographers.

In her online column for *Salon* magazine, Camille Paglia expressed her feelings in her typical no-holds-barred way: "Nor was the gay cause helped by the grotesque way both women reportedly behaved at the black-tie White House Correspondents Dinner in Washington, D.C., on April 26. Who among the heterosexual guests were ostentatiously nuzzling and necking like that?—Always the sign, by the way, of people insecure in their own mutual feelings.

"In a photograph that will live in infamy, the two women are standing with the tuxedo-clad president of the United States, a formal situation that demands dignity and respect. But Heche has her arm obnoxiously thrown around Ellen's shoulders, as if it were the annual softball picnic of a small-town gay bar."

Later, acknowledging that they felt a backlash stemming from the evening, the couple reacted defensively. "People have to find something wrong with love, that is what this all boils down to—people are crazy," Ellen said defiantly.

Once again deciding that public silence was tantamount to an admission of wrongdoing somehow, Anne and Ellen decided to go mainstream with their relationship. They used *Oprah* as their vehicle to do so. Ellen would later explain that she went public simply because there had been so much scrutiny about them in the media. "We hide from the press. Literally, we can't go anywhere. Getting off the plane in airports is just a nightmare," Ellen recounted. So she just wanted to go on the air and say, "See, here we are. We're together. Now leave us alone."

The segment was aired on April 30, which, not coincidentally, was the air date for Ellen's coming-out episode. The first half of the show was a one-on-one interview with Oprah. Then Winfrey introduced Anne, who unfortunately came across strident and grating—not so much what she said, but her in-your-face presentation of it.

"We laugh a lot and thank God every day we found each other. We are very much in a relationship together, and we are looking forward to a long future together. We're happy. We fight a lot. We talk a lot," Anne asserted.

"And we shop a lot," Ellen interjected, mindful that humor was her best ally in front of a studio audience that had decidedly mixed feelings about her sexuality in general and her relationship with Anne in particular.

It was Anne's response to questions about her prior sexuality that sparked the most controversy. Ironically, though, it was the gay community that was up in arms, because of Heche's claims that prior to meeting Ellen she wasn't gay and hadn't ever considered the possibility.

"I don't feel like I'm coming out, because I've never been in a closet," Anne explained. "I don't have any fear about this. This was the easiest thing in my life I've ever done . . . This is heaven to me."

But not necessarily to her movie producers. Shortly before Anne and Ellen became a couple, she was cast opposite Harrison Ford in *Six Days Seven Nights,* but her representatives were still working out contract details as word of her relationship with Ellen began to leak out. The speculation led the movie's casting director, Michael Chinich, to arrange a meeting with Anne's agents concerning her relationship with Ellen and the filmmakers' worry that it might have a negative impact on the film.

Appreciating Chinich's anxiety, Anne's agent, Doug Robinson, and managers suggested she keep things hidden until the contract was signed. "Her career is ascending to the sky, and her managers felt a responsibility to advise her about the potential ramifications so she could make a smart analysis of her options," explained a source familiar with the conversation. "Though they were supportive of her choice, she regarded the advice as less supportive than she had hoped."

The day after the deal was closed, she fired her agency, Endeavor, and her managers, Keith Addis and Nick Wechsler, claiming they had been opposed to her announcing her relationship with Ellen.

She wasn't without representation for very long, signing with Creative Artists Agency, which also represents Ellen, and with Ellen's longtime manager, Arthur Imperato. But the controversy didn't abate. There were persistent rumors that Ivan Reitman, who was to direct *Six Days Seven Nights,* was uncomfortable with the casting of Heche.

On April 23, he was quoted as saying "It's a question of whether this will blow over after weeks of public fame and then everybody will go on with their lives. I think it will do the movie some harm, and that makes me nervous."

However, according to Caravan Pictures chairman Roger

Birnbaum, he, Reitman, and Ford knew about Anne's romance with Ellen prior to hiring her. "Harrison had veto power over casting and was immediately supportive," Birnbaum said. "If Anne did something heinous, that might interfere with the public's ability to accept her in the role. The only thing she did was love another human being. I can't imagine why it's an issue."

But all of Hollywood would carefully monitor how the audience would respond to Anne Heche as Harrison Ford's love interest, although not everyone thought it was fair to place too much of the burden on Anne; at least one film critic posed the possibility that people were tired of watching fiftysomething men trying to keep up with their twentysomething costars. Still, regardless of Hollywood's continued tendency to give actors love interests young enough to be their granddaughters, Anne was going to be the focus. As Jeffrey Friedman, one of the creators of the documentary *The Celluloid Closet,* noted, "It seems especially courageous of her because there's so much at stake for her now. She's not an established movie star and not a nobody."

Mark Johnson, *Donny Brasco*'s producer, concurred. "Anne is an extremely attractive, sexy woman. It's how she plays on screen, not off. I believe Hollywood will take the high road."

If anything, the suggestion that Anne would suddenly lack for roles simply because of her off-screen relationship seemed to make her more appealing to many directors and producers, who saw a way to put their film-finance money where their political mouths had long been. Therein lies the foundation for the suspicion many harbored that Anne was little more than an opportunist who saw a very public relationship with Ellen as a way of thrusting herself into the national spotlight.

Leading the anti-Anne charge was Camille Paglia. "It's already irritating that whatever career damage Heche may suffer will be solemnly attributed to her lesbo affair with DeGeneres, when in fact Heche has herself to blame for flibbertigibbet exhibitionism of asinine proportions.

"Heche zeroed in on the then very stressed Ellen like a heat-seeking missile. 'I saw Ellen across a crowded room,' Heche proclaimed on *Oprah.* 'I was just DRAWN to her.' Can lasting romance be instantly born at a glitzy *Vanity Fair* party? It smacks of the high-tabloid *Confidential* era of Jayne Mansfield and Mickey Hargitay, when scotch-soaked show-biz types would meet, mate, and marry on sleepless, three-day junkets to Las Vegas.

"Heche confided to Oprah, 'It was very clear from the second I saw her that this was something more powerful than anything I could have controlled!' Dare one suggest that Ellen's media-fueled, center-of-everything, charismatic, super-celebrity status at that heady Hollywood moment might explain her sudden irresistible appeal to the roving Heche?

"The women's joint *Oprah* appearance gave me the willies because it reminded me of the way that that boring Big Issue Priestess, Yoko Ono, got her claws into John Lennon and sucked all the surrealist comedy out of him. I loathed the way Heche treated Ellen and their relationship as a vehicle for Moral Abstractions and Salvation through Self-Discovery."

Howard Stern was briefer but just as much to the point. "Would somebody just shoot that woman!" he begged on the air.

Gossip columnist Liz Smith felt compelled to address the issue in her column: "Everybody seems to adore Ellen, but people are taking a wait-and-see attitude about Anne. (The other night on *Saturday Night Live,* there was an Anne-Ellen-Oprah skit in which Anne said: 'I used to date men for years, but nobody noticed.')

"What Heche needs to do is calm down—she seems edgy, anxious, and over-the-top."

Six Days Seven Nights, which had Heche and Ford stranded

à la *The African Queen,* wasn't a blockbuster but it wasn't an unmitigated disaster, either. The chemistry between Ford and Heche seemed no better or worse than that between him and, say, Carrie Fisher in *Star Wars.* And it was hard not to wonder whether Reitman's own expressed reservations contributed to some hesitant directing.

By the time *Six Days Seven Nights* was released, it seemed as if the issue had become moot, partly because Anne continued to work without any noticeable gap of unemployment. Her next film was *Wag the Dog;* then, in *Return to Paradise,* she starred opposite Vince Vaughn. He would also be her costar in Gus Van Sant's remake of Alfred Hitchcock's masterpiece, *Psycho,* in which she took the Janet Leigh role. In November 1998, Heche would film *The Third Miracle* opposite Ed Harris.

If there was a backlash against Anne among moviegoers, it was so slight as to be unnoticed. And while some filmmakers may have passed over her name when reviewing a list of actresses to consider for a role, her career seemed to be initially unaffected by her relationship with Ellen. It remained to be seen whether the DeGeneres' television audience would be equally as accepting and whether the show's writers were up to the task of making Ellen Morgan a three-dimensional character with universal, human issues as opposed to a one-trick queer pony. The latter would prove to be a harder task than Ellen, or ABC, ever anticipated.

18
Life After "Puppy"

Ellen devoted most of her 1997 hiatus sequestered with Anne inside DeGeneres's $3 million home on three acres near Beverly Hills. Ellen also accompanied Anne to Hawaii, where much of *Six Days Seven Nights* was filmed. So out of touch was Ellen with her castmates that Patrick Bristow noted, "I haven't actually seen her much since we wrapped because she's been kind of busy. She's with Anne right now, making sandwiches."

Whatever fears Ellen had that she would become a social pariah after coming completely out of the closet were mostly allayed in the months following the broadcast of "The Puppy Episode." She reported, "I cannot tell you the amount of support I have received—flowers, cards, letters—from everyone. I come home to stacks of this every day."

However, as much as Ellen deeply appreciated the support she was receiving from both her friends and total strangers, she was ready to move on. "I want to get beyond this. I understand the curiosity and the not understanding of it, because I didn't understand for a long time. I have the same problems a lot of people do. But let's get beyond this and let me get back to what I do," she said earnestly, then smiled. "Maybe I'll find something even bigger to do later. Maybe I'll become black."

One thing she wouldn't be doing was writing her autobiography any time soon. In the months following her coming out, Ellen was offered as much as $4 million by two publishing houses to write her life story. After considering it, Ellen told her manager, Arthur Imperato, to say thanks, but no thanks. "I know I want to write another book," she told him. "And I know I could make a lot of money right now, but I don't want to exploit being hot because I'm gay."

However, if Ellen thought that the tabloid press's fascination with her and Anne would die down, she was in for a disappointment. The photographers were as relentless as ever, so much so that earlier in 1997 Ellen had abruptly decided to move out of her Laurel Canyon home to the more secure place in Beverly Hills. She and Anne were also spending time house-hunting in the San Francisco area for a weekend pied-à-terre.

But new digs wouldn't stop the paparazzi from hassling her in public. "When Anne and I travel, these guys are in the airports with video cameras. They'll say anything to get you mad—they'd bring up stuff about my sexuality. I never thought about getting violent, but we did think about putting shaving cream on their lenses."

Nor could moving prevent papers from running articles about them. The next flurry of features dealt with Ellen and Anne's alleged desire to become parents. In the past, Ellen *had* stated on the record, "I would love to have children. I just don't want to *have* them."

Using that as a jumping-off point, the tabloids concentrated on the scenario that Heche would be the one to go through the pregnancy. When asked to comment on the persistent reports, Anne laughed and derided the articles as fantasy.

"That's such a lie," she told *People* magazine. "It's hilarious what people are making up about us. No, it's shocking. Some silly things that are written about us are painful. This supposed fact isn't painful, it's just wrong."

Ellen added that "for a long time, I wanted a baby. But right now, I'm too selfish. I just can't."

Ellen and Anne also endured constant reports that their relationship was "on the rocks," as the tabloids love to phrase it. Arthur Imperato officially dismissed such reports as rumors propagated by people who were opposed to his clients' relationship. "I've known Ellen five years," he said in a 1997 *Variety* interview. "And she's the most wholesome and moral person who's always wanted the kind of relationship where you meet someone and know it's the real thing. And I think this is it. They're in love and very happy."

Ellen expanded on Imperato's comments by saying that with Anne she had finally "learned the difference between love and being in love. I always used to be so envious of married people. Now this is it for me, for both of us, forever. No one knows what we have together. No one."

Nor could Ellen escape from those who wanted to enlist her as a spokesperson for various political issues, such as gay marriage. In fact, Ellen was wearing two rings on her left ring finger. "She surprised me four days after we met," Ellen says. "She wanted to make the point she wasn't joking around."

Even so, Ellen didn't want to enter the political fray. "I'm not going to say no to anything. But I don't see myself campaigning for anything, either. My opinion is yes, it should be legal, but I'm not going to become some political activist. I never wanted to be the poster child for gays."

Ironically, her mother was far more willing to become involved with the political aspect of the issue. Betty agreed to become the first heterosexual spokesperson for the Human Rights Campaign (HRC), America's largest national gay and lesbian political organization.

"I still don't think my mother understands it," Ellen maintained, "but she loves me and she sees how happy I am. To have a mom like this, not only to accept me and love me but to come out and be a spokesperson and travel, I'm so proud of her. When you think about the teen suicide and the gaybashing, people who are beaten up and kicked out of their families. . . . Someone told me that between the work my mom and I are doing, we're saving about five lives a day."

To Betty, speaking out for the legalization of same-sex marriages was simply another way to show support for her daughter, as well as the children of others. "Why feel so threatened by it? People who are in loving relationships that go on for twenty-five [or] thirty years have no legal recourse if one of them is deathly ill in the hospital. You know, if the world doesn't want to call it marriage, then let them call it a legal commitment. But it should happen." Betty reminded other parents that "we're not all alike" and urged them to just "accept there are differences."

Betty readily admitted that she had had her reservations about Ellen's sexuality since learning about it so many years before, but she also said that many of her concerns had been tempered over the years. "It's been a real joy to see how eminently capable Ellen has been. She's buying houses and doing whatever needs to be done, and being really happy with her life."

As far as Betty was concerned, hatred was the real sin. She was horrified to learn of the radio talk show host in California who urged his listeners to demand that legislators punish homosexuals according to his personal interpretation of biblical law. Rick Agozino, host of *Crosstalk* on KBRT-AM, had declared, "Lesbian love, sodomy, is viewed as being detestable and abominable, so serious a civil offense that if you're discovered and two witnesses are able to bring a charge, civil magistrates are to put people to death who practice these things."

Betty was determined to fight this sort of intolerance, and it made her realize that her daughter's coming out had ramifications far beyond what it meant to a network and a studio—or even to Ellen herself.

Most people assumed that Ellen would be looking forward to implementing all the new comic possibilities inherent in Ellen Morgan's coming out. In truth, Ellen would have been happy to end her sitcom on the high note of the fourth season. This was partly because of her lingering unhappiness with how she felt ABC had emotionally manhandled her while wavering over whether to let her character discover she was gay. Other persistent rumors centered around Ellen's alleged upset over what she perceived as ABC's lack of promotion for the post-"Puppy" episodes, in which she comes out to her parents and boss.

The first printed hint of Ellen's ambivalence about the upcoming season appeared in a May 1997 *TV Guide* article, which quoted a source close to her as saying, "She hates ABC. She's done with them. If they pick her show up, there's nothing she can do. She's under contract [for two more years]. But she doesn't want them to pick it up."

One friend recalled, "While all the publicity was building, Ellen was telling everyone she didn't want to come back. She felt like this was as big as the show was going to get."

Another source offered a different possibility. "A lot of this is fear. It's one thing to come out and have your show be so well accepted, but then comes the fear of what do you do next year. Why not go out on top?"

If Ellen had been hoping ABC would take her series off

the air, she would have been disappointed on May 13. That day, ABC announced its 1997–98 schedule; *Ellen* was officially renewed for another season, the show's fifth. Once again there would be changes behind the scenes. The two co-executive producers, Jonathan Stark and Tracy Newman, left the show, as did Mark Driscoll and Dava Savel. Savel explained her decision by saying, "I like writing best. When I was running *Ellen* [with Mark Driscoll] I only got to write on three episodes."

Once it was clear that she would be doing the show for at least another year, Ellen wanted to make sure that the series built on the momentum established in the final three episodes of the previous season. She instructed the writers to make Ellen Morgan "more of an adult, to make the stories more real."

Back when Ellen first revealed her desire to have her character be gay, she had made a point of saying that she had no interest in having Ellen Morgan kiss another woman on screen. In the months since making that statement, Ellen had undergone a change of heart.

Now she wanted her character to get a girlfriend and have a relationship, a prospect that made many in the executive offices at ABC very nervous. When asked how the network planned to proceed with such a storyline in general, and specifically with a kiss between Ellen and a girlfriend, Jamie Tarses said the network was "taking baby steps" with *Ellen*'s new direction. "Ellen pushed really hard for a relationship this fall. And we're behind it, but it's premature to say where it's all going." Talking about an on-screen kiss, Tarses added that "if it's handled effectively, we should be able to do it."

Ellen had put the network on notice that she wasn't going to sidestep any issues and would push the envelope as far as she could. In her mind, it was the best thing for the show, and anything less than full support from her network and studio would be construed as a personal affront.

By the time the season was underway, she had also changed her mind about being there. "Now I'm glad we're back. But I didn't want to do it," she admitted. "I was hoping I could just move on because I didn't want to have happen what sort of has happened. Ellen Morgan and I are in very different places in our lives. She has just discovered she was gay, but I've known this for a long time, and believe me, I can go a whole day without having a single gay reference. I can't just be the gay girl all the time. It's only part of who I am."

New executive producer Tim Doyle referred to Ellen's fear of becoming a "Joan of Arc" when "all she really wants to be is a performer." He wholeheartedly agreed with Ellen's desire to pursue her character's new life honestly. "The audience that hates Ellen for being gay is never coming back," says Doyle. "So the only thing to do is pursue the story, and this year Ellen is looking for love and that's universal. It's not about her sex life. I want this to be a show my parents can watch."

In the spring of 1997, Ellen was nominated for two Emmys, one for Outstanding Actress in a Comedy Series and the other as part of the writing team responsible for "The Puppy Episode." Ellen lost out to Helen Hunt in the acting category but was surprised to be saluted by the *Mad About You* star during her acceptance speech. "I was so blown away by Ellen DeGeneres in her coming-out episode, I'm thrilled to be on the same list," said Hunt, whose character, Jamie Buchman, had spent the previous season pregnant.

Ellen got her moment in the sun when "The Puppy Episode" was honored in the writing category. When her name was announced, Anne, who seemed more excited than Ellen, leaped to her feet and applauded wildly.

Clutching her Emmy tightly, Ellen looked out at the audience of her peers but spoke to a group of people she couldn't see, although she knew were there. "I accept this on behalf of all the people, and the teenagers especially, out there who think there's something wrong with them because they're gay. Don't ever let anybody make you feel ashamed of who you are."

Later, Ellen would explain that winning the award made her finally feel accepted within Hollywood's entertainment community. She said, "the Emmy meant so much to me because I never felt like I belonged to the club."

Her moment of bliss was short-lived. Ever since production on the fifth season had started, Ellen had felt as if she were waging a never-ending battle with ABC over the show's direction. Now she was also miffed that Disney CEO Michael Eisner hadn't acknowledged her Emmy win. "I know he's a busy guy," she would later say. "And as soon as he gets done calling Gillian Anderson and offering her a deal, he'll probably send me a box of crackers or some bath oils." Eisner did note, however, when responding to the Baptist boycott of Disney (which started because of the Disney theme parks' "gay nights" and the company's decision to grant partner's benefits), that he thought the show had been "very well done." But for Ellen, the praise was like an afterthought.

By October 1997, the tension between Ellen, now listed as one of the series' executive producers, and ABC boiled over into reports that Ellen had walked off the set. The dispute concerned two separate but related incidents. First was the network's decision to tag an episode that included a kiss between Ellen and Paige, who was posing as her girlfriend, with a TV-14 rating. Ellen decried it as "blatant discrimination" in the press, particularly because the kiss was a playful one, not a sexual embrace with a paramour.

Disney CEO Michael Eisner had this to say about the flap: "It [the kiss] didn't offend me. Does it make some people uncomfortable? Probably. Did we put an advisory on it? Yes. Would we in the future? I don't know." He said the advisory was used because "the same-sex kiss makes people uncomfortable or we feel there is something in the program that we should warn parents about that may be against what they believe in."

On October 10, *Variety* reported that "despite a rift with ABC and veiled threats to quit the show, Ellen DeGeneres and the producers of her sitcom *Ellen* were at work as usual Thursday preparing for tonight's taping.

"So far, DeGeneres has made threats to the press, but has not asked ABC to let her out of her contract.

"Tensions have been simmering for months between Disney-ABC, DeGeneres, and the show's producers over creative direction of the show following the famous coming-out episode last season."

The episode being filmed that particular week would be the other source of friction. In the episode, Ellen and her girlfriend walk toward the bedroom door, the implication being they would be making love. ABC Entertainment president Jamie Tarses had reportedly warned Ellen that the scene might be cut from the final version.

Liz Smith reported that it was something else that worried the network: "Wasn't ABC's specific objection *not* to the two women entering the bedroom but to the line spoken by [Lisa Darr], 'I just want to jump your bones'? Fastidious folk at ABC felt the utterance too raunchy and explicit. (I guess network execs thought a recent episode of *Spin City*, about men getting erections and how to hide this public embarrassment, was just nifty and suitable for children of all ages.)"

Whether ABC objected to the inference or the dialogue, Ellen's discontent stemmed from what she saw as a double standard, with the network being more concerned about gay references on her show than about violence, nudity, or heterosexual sex on other shows. Again, because she was so invested in the character's gay identity, some thought she might be taking the network's position personally rather than viewing ABC's objections strictly from a business point of view.

Daily News columnist Eric Mink had this to say: "DeGeneres has every right to make a show she hopes will help gay kids feel comfortable with their sexual identity and to feel proud about it. ABC has every right to air it and, within reason, to keep an eye on its content. And parents have every right to decide if they want their kids to see it. Unless DeGeneres is really just tired of doing the show, it seems to me she'd be better off concentrating on keeping *Ellen* as funny and honest as it has been so far this season—for the first time in its TV life."

A column in *Time* disagreed. "Instead of being integrated into the show, Ellen's homosexuality has become the show. *Ellen* is now as one-dimensional as *Bewitched,* where every storyline, every moment, every gag relies on the same device. Those flaws aside, the real problem may be mediocre writing. The problem with *Ellen* has always been that DeGeneres is better than the show, and that's still true. If it were only more clever and less narrow."

That opinion, though, was in the minority. The reality was that *Ellen* was still winning its time slot. That made it important to ABC, which was struggling to reverse its failing prime-time fortunes. The network could ill afford to lose a solid performer, whatever headaches she brought with her. By the end of October 1997, *Ellen* averaged a 10.6 rating, placing it twenty-third out of more than one hundred prime-time shows, according to the Nielsen ratings.

Ellen, when all was said and done, was still a professional. She certainly didn't want to be labeled the new Brett Butler, so she got a grip on her emotions and tried to make the best of the situation. The two sides realized it was to their mutual benefit to find some kind of middle ground.

Evidence that Ellen was trying to take the high road could be discerned the next time ABC slapped a parental advisory on an episode. She barely reacted. Instead, she chose to concentrate on the positives.

"I'm really excited that we're doing something nobody is doing," she told the *Los Angeles Times*. "But it is a fight. It's advertisers who seem to control a lot of what goes on, and it scares the people who are in charge of making these decisions. I can see why everyone wants to go slow. ABC is a big corporation, and now with all the standards-and-practices labeling, I'm up against a lot. But it does seem like once you start the relationship, you want to see where it goes."

As the season wore on, ABC apparently decided to back off and accept the show's direction, for better or worse, abandoning, according to a source, "the idea that they're going to be able to put the genie back in the bottle. Ellen engages in constant conversations with ABC president Robert Iger and ABC entertainment executives Jamie Tarses and Stu Bloomberg about content. It's a case-by-case basis, and they're all trying to be reasonable."

In an effort to show the star that they were solidly behind her, *Ellen* was given promotional spots during a highly ranked *Monday Night Football* game. An ABC spokesman said, "It also speaks to the relationship we have with the star of the show. Ellen did the promo. I think that answers some of the questions as to how DeGeneres and ABC are getting along."

In the spot, Ellen joked about the plot of the upcoming episode, in which Ellen Morgan begins dating her mortgage broker: "I can't tell you the plot of this week's show, but it's titled 'Ellen Kisses a Girl and Upsets the Network.'"

Although the fifth season was uneven, with some episodes too one-note, overall *Ellen* was a better show than ever before, a fact not lost on many television critics. The *New York Times* published a lengthy, thoughtful review of the show that attempted to put the new direction in perspective. "Ellen is not immersed in a gay world; she's trying to discover a comfortable place that includes her straight family as well as her newfound sexuality.

"That accepting attitude, tolerant yet sill tentative, plays well to the mainstream audience it most likely reflects. This season's hype has turned into something better: genuine comedy and social commentary."

Entertainment Weekly was equally positive in its assessment. *"Ellen,* now in its fifth season, keeps getting funnier, even as its star conducts the most relentless gay-empowerment campaign prime time has ever seen. ABC is allowing DeGeneres to do this"—but, as *EW* noted, "with nervous reluctance."

The review was sensitive to the personal investment Ellen had in the current storylines but urged her to take a step back and try to view the situation dispassionately. In one of the episodes, the article pointed out, Ellen says, "I wish you would stop assuming everything is tied to my sexuality." If DeGeneres can acknowledge such feelings in the context of her show, why can't she also see that this is the exact discomfort ABC believes its viewers may be experiencing?

"But her protests seem a little beside the point," the review went on. "By upping both the quality and ratings of her show while never backing away from the subject she's had the guts to raise, DeGeneres has already won the battle."

While Ellen waged her personal battle with the network, her costars watched their roles subtly but necessarily diminish. Joely Fisher probably spoke for the others when she commented, "We all really feel like this is our last year on the show. The coming-out episode was bittersweet because the regular cast wasn't really a part of it." Not wanting to sound petulant, she added that the upside was that "this year we get to have more weeks off to pursue our own projects."

What's curious about *Ellen's* fifth season is the perception that the sitcom was underachieving. At the winter Television Critics Press Tour, Jamie Tarses fielded questions about why *Ellen* was still on the air, as if the series were suddenly scraping the bottom of the ratings barrel.

It wasn't so much that the series was failing as that it was a victim of frayed emotions. Whether Ellen was creatively burned out, or was no longer willing to sacrifice her personal life to the demands of a weekly series, or felt she had outgrown the Ellen Morgan character, or had been depleted emotionally and physically by the constant struggle with the network, Ellen seemed ready to let the series go. ABC—which, it could be argued, made a conscious decision to stop promoting the show and let it slip through the cracks—seemed to take the stance that it was cleaner and easier just to let the series die of neglect.

On April 23, 1997, the network officially notified the producers that *Ellen* wouldn't be renewed for a sixth season, pointing to deteriorating ratings. Ellen had anticipated the cancellation as early as February, despite ABC's insistence that no decision would be made until May, when the fall schedule would be set. Her prediction was based on the network's decision to shelve what would have been the season's final two episodes.

Looking on the bright side, Ellen told friends, it only took the network about half as long to confirm the show's demise as it had to approve the coming-out episode. The official series finale was an hour-long, star-studded episode that aired on May 13. Linda Ellerbee hosted a faux look back at Ellen DeGeneres's fifty years as an entertainer, from her early years as a vaudeville and radio star to her decades-long TV show. Among the guest stars were Bea Arthur, Richard Benjamin, Glenn Close, Cindy Crawford, Helen Hunt, Christine Lahti, Jennifer Aniston, Ted Danson, and Mary Steenburgen.

It was obvious why so many well-known faces agreed to appear on the show. More than for her comic talent, for her success, for having produced over one hundred episodes of her series, what Ellen would be remembered for was being the first television star willing to risk it all on principle as opposed to ego. In spite of her proven talent, in spite of her ability to make us laugh out loud, in spite of her appeal and genuineness, Ellen was forced to endure undeserved personal taunts as painful as the chants of "Ellen Degenerate" were in grade school. Yet she found it within herself to remain an unwavering example of true grace under pressure. She was able to maintain her sense of humor because she realized the ultimate punch line was her ability to keep laughing.

19
You Gotta Pass the Crocodiles

Ellen finished the 1995–96 season ranked forty-third out of 101 primetime network series. It was finally shelved for good when *Two Guys, a Girl, and a Pizza Place* premiered in its time slot on March 10, 1998.

Once it was official that the sitcom was canceled, DeGeneres told *Variety,* "I loved doing the show every week. This was an important chapter of my life, and although I'm disappointed the show was canceled, I look forward to moving beyond the stereotype. Look for me in my new sitcom, *Two Girls, a Horse, and Some Wine Coolers.*"

At first, Ellen seemed to be making the transition from sitcom star to unemployed TV actress with little problem. With no place to be anytime soon, Ellen took a trip to London in April 1998 with her mother and Anne. She enjoyed the city so much, she mused in some interviews that she might buy an apartment there.

In October 1998, she was back on television hosting the *VH1 Fashion Awards*, once again exuding her easy comic wit and prowess as an emcee. She also finished two feature films scheduled to be released in spring 1999: *The Love Letter*, a DreamWorks production starring Kate Capshaw and Blythe Danner, and Ron Howard's *Ed TV* with Jenna Elfman and Woody Harrelson. In the latter movie Ellen costars as a TV-studio executive who convinces a video clerk, played by Matthew McConaughey, to let her film his life for twenty-four hours.

Even though she still harbored anger toward ABC for its perceived reluctance to publicize the program, Ellen initially appeared to have adopted an overall more philosophical perspective about the experience. "I may not have gotten support and I may not have got the ratings because they did not promote the program, but I did get to do my art . . . and change the world.

"Right now, the jury is still out on my career. Let's see if I can accomplish what I want to accomplish, which is getting over stereotypes. I still think in thirty years we'll be dealing with homophobia and it would be nice to have Ellen on *Nick at Night* along with Mary Tyler Moore, someone that gay kids could identify with.

"I have a tendency to diminish what I do for a living, but I also know I'm going to leave here and I won't be somebody who just had a sitcom but someone who helped change people's minds."

However, in late November 1998, Ellen's perspective underwent a dramatic reversal. In an interview published in the *Los Angeles Times*, DeGeneres lashed out at Hollywood. She claimed coming out had damaged her career, the inference being that because ABC had felt justified treating her—via her show—like a professional pariah, then the rest of the entertainment community felt validated to follow suit. "Everything that I ever feared happened to me," DeGeneres said. "I lost my show. I've been attacked like hell. I went from making a lot of money on a sitcom to making no money." DeGeneres added that after the series was cancelled, "I just went into this deep, deep depression."

She told *Newsday*, "And it's not like any other networks have called. *Okay, we don't want you to play another openly gay person, but we think you're talented, come talk to us.* No one called. I used to get a lot of commercial offers. Now, do you think one company has called?

"My show wasn't appreciated, and my talent isn't appreciated and I wish people could get beyond the fact that I'm gay. I'm sure even talking like this brings it up again. *If she would just shut up for two years then we'd hire her*—that's what people say. Has it been enough time, has it died down?"

Later Ellen would admit her comments sounded like whiney complaints from "poor little rich girls who have all this money and are celebrities and yet are complaining about not getting more work." But she stresses the crux wasn't about money; "It was about the shift in people's attitudes and the loss of work. It hurts any person if you want to do something and you don't get the opportunity to do it anymore.

"It was hard to watch the numbers drop every single week. The slow and painful death of the show was a rejection of me as an artist and a human being. I felt like the popular kid who was not only not popular anymore, but had everybody telling her how unpopular she was.

"I really was sitting at home thinking: I've worked for 15 years to build up to this, and it's all been wiped away by the very thing I tried to hide for so long. Whether it's a sexuality thing or anything, most people hide these little secrets because they think nobody is going to like them anymore. Sure enough, that was the case."

Heche was upset enough to accuse one studio of blacklisting her. "I learned that Fox won't hire me because they still have this bitterness about the timing of my falling in love with Ellen and the opening of *Volcano*. I have my own opinions about why the movie didn't do well, as anybody with half a brain would, but they want to blame it on somebody."

More surprising was their claim that it wasn't necessarily the homophobic element putting the squeeze on them. "The people who are going to hurt you the most are going to be gays," claimed Ellen. "They're the biggest hypocrites, the gays at the studios and networks."

At the same time, DeGeneres admitted that film work wasn't necessarily her heart's desire, either. "Sometimes I think, *Do I really want to read scripts and go fight for something that shoots in three months and sit in a trailer for hours*? That's not appealing to me, and since I'm not the kind of performer who needs to be hired in a film or TV series to make money—I made a good living doing stand-up and I turned down a huge amount of money to write a book about what's happened—I can go back to that."

Obviously, DeGeneres felt the lack of work was a personal affront and attack, based solely on preference. But many outside observers felt that it wasn't so much Ellen's lifestyle revelations that made some producers and networks skittish as it was her sudden mantle as poster girl for same-sex couples and gay rights. DeGeneres and Heche seemed to be constantly in the news—photographed with President Clinton on several occasions; appearing at rallies ("When I came out I really did it for personal reasons," she said. "I don't care if people don't like me anymore" because coming out was giving up "the shame that I had been living with"); speaking at colleges ("We don't have a lifestyle. We have a life"); railing in interviews ("There're so many people who are closeted today because it isn't safe, and because you have people like Dr. Laura Schlessinger who calls us biological deviants and biological freaks"), and in general being seen as more activist than performer. While overt politics and comedy might work in stand-up, for a medium like television it was a potential minefield that nobody was anxious to detonate.

Two days after the interview appeared in the paper, Ellen and Anne dropped yet another bombshell in the *Los Angeles Times*, announcing that they were "taking at least a year off" and "leaving town. We've quit our agents, let go of our publicist, and we're selling our house and leaving town," DeGeneres was quoted as saying. She also revealed she had cancelled plans to develop a TV series and an HBO comedy special. "I know everyone is going to say that our leaving is just another bid for attention, but what we've found is that this is a very hard town to be truthful in." *Newsweek* reported the decision to leave Hancock Park was prompted in part by a neighbor who had lectured them about "keeping our private lives private around here."

While they indeed did drop their agency, Creative Artists, their publicist, Simon Halls, told the trade paper *Variety* that he believed Ellen's comments were taken somewhat out of context. "They are not quitting the business," he said, and went on to add that Anne had recently been hired to direct a project for Showtime, the same cable network that had named Ellen the Funniest Person in America. Also, Ellen was planning a return to stand-up and was busy preparing for an upcoming tour.

While they never truly turned their backs on Hollywood, the couple did make good on their desire to move away from the media spotlight. Their 5,000 square foot, three-bedroom Spanish-style house, located in L.A.'s Hancock Park, went on the market for $3.5 million.

Built in the mid-1920s, the home was designed by the same creative team responsible for Hollywood's famed Graumann's Chinese Theatre. Inside it had three baths, three fireplaces and three walk-in closets in the master suite. Outside, there was a pool and walled gardens. They had lived there for less than a year.

Gossip columnist Liz Smith reported that Ellen and Anne had bought a home in rural Ojai, located ninety miles north of L.A. inland of the seaside community of Santa Barbara, where Ellen said she and Anne "would simplify their lives." However, their self-imposed exile would prove short-lived. After *Six Days Seven Nights* proved to be a modest box office success, earning over $70 million in domestic receipts, Heche started getting scripts sent to her again and by late summer of 1999, the couple returned to L.A., still feeling slighted but ready to move on.

As for how Ellen came to view Hollywood, a story she told on a talk show seemed particularly telling. "I was watching this fascinating show about the migration of the wildebeests to the Serengeti—this is how I spend my time. The poor little babies, how sad. The baby is born and within two hours it has to learn to stand on its feet and start moving with the pack or else it gets left behind. There are all kinds of wild dogs and hyenas waiting to eat it, and some of the babies get eaten, and even if they do survive that long, they can get separated and get eaten or they drown in lakes or if the mother dies then they die. Then they are almost where they need to get to and they have a drink of water and crocodiles are getting 'em out of the water. Some of them finally made it but a lot didn't.

"And I started thinking, *This is very much like show business*. There are so many ways to get you. They want to stop you. People say, *You're no good. You're not pretty enough. You're not small enough.* But you just gotta keep walking. You gotta pass the crocodiles. You got to keep up and say, *I can make it.* You gotta bat those hyenas away and just keep going."

Rather than dwelling on what she felt had been taken from her, Ellen was making a conscious effort to focus on the positives the experience of coming out had brought her, including her ability to overcome her own upbringing. "To go as far as I have is just amazing coming from my family," she observed to writer Judy Wieder. "I don't want to be scared of anything. And this last year and a half I got the beautiful blessing of facing just about every one of my fears," including almost losing her home in a brush fire. "We had to evacuate the house. It's the weirdest feeling to all of a sudden decide what you're grabbing. We grabbed our animals and we grabbed pictures and we left. It was Christmas time; we left the presents there, we left everything, we just got out with the animals.

"All I would have had left was my mother and my girlfriend and my animals—and that was enough for me. I realized when we were grabbing things that nothing else was important. As long as I'm happy and I have friends and have family and I have animals; that's all I need.

"I was raised to believe that celebrity is important. Money is important. I was taught that if somebody has money, then they're very important. And if they're a celebrity—wow! That's really important. And so of course I became a celebrity. And of course I wanted to make a lot of money. All those things seemed to be what would make me happy. Then I learned after having money and becoming a celebrity that it's not what makes you happy. It doesn't matter if you have the whole world loving you or hating you. And knowing this has enriched my relationship with Anne."

Looking back on her depression, Ellen says, "When I met Anne I was in this beautiful place of just knowing that whatever we create in our minds, we create in reality. Yet I slipped into the darkest, darkest place. But I had to go that far down. I had to slip into that place to confront all of these fears because I was still trying to hold on to approval and all the things that I'm trying to let go of—pride, ego. But now I'm there, and, hopefully, I won't slip so far down again."

It also enabled DeGeneres to get past her bitterness and start her post-*Ellen* life. In July 1999, *Variety* announced she had signed a deal with CBS to develop a sitcom that was described as "a cross between *The Larry Sanders Show* and *The Carol Burnett Show* in which DeGeneres would play the host of a TV variety show, à la the Burnett-hosted comedy hour that ran on CBS from 1967–78, but the show would delve into the character's life off-camera as well. Project is targeted for the 2000–01 season."

Ironically, being back in the Hollywood fold brought its own issues. Although Anne was working, Ellen wasn't always thrilled about the projects she accepted. DeGeneres admitted she had deep reservations about Heche being cast as Marion Crane in Gus Van Sant's remake of *Psycho*, in which she took on the role originally played by Janet Leigh. "I was very upset by it; I just hated seeing that," she said about the infamous shower scene in which the character is stabbed by the deranged Norman Bates, played in this incarnation by Vince Vaughn.

Equally bothersome to Ellen was her girlfriend doing love scenes. "It's her job, but it makes me physically ill," she admitted to *Newsday*. But making DeGeneres sicker were stories circulating that Heche and Vaughn were having an affair. "It's hard enough for me to deal with watching somebody I love," on screen being intimate with someone else, "but because it's so sexy and so real and because Vince is a friend and they have great chemistry together, it's like, *Of course there must be something going on*."

Ellen claimed that even when they had put the gossip behind them, it was still an issue. "Now, we argue about who [the rumor] offends more. I say me because it makes me look like an idiot who wouldn't know," she said in a case of ironic foreshadowing.

Although DeGeneres seemed to be ratcheting down her off-camera activist activities, her mom was just gearing up. While Ellen claimed she didn't want to be defined by her sexuality, her mom was making it the family business. In March 1999, Betty DeGeneres appeared on *Good Morning*

America to promote her new book, *Love, Ellen*, which was a personal memoir about coming to terms with having a gay child. Betty noted that the fact that she was able to accept her daughter's life choices proved "we can do all kinds of things if we just open ourselves up to the possibilities in life. It is all about love."

Betty also made it clear she supported Ellen's relationship with Heche, who increasingly came under fire as an opportunist—and not just from the gay community. Heche was said to be ex-boyfriend Steve Martin's inspiration for the role he wrote in his movie *Bowfinger* of a blond actress who sleeps with every man she thinks can help her career, then jilts them all for a Hollywood power lesbian. "I think I loved her almost as much as Ellen did from the start," Betty DeGeneres told Diane Sawyer. "She's brilliant and wonderful and a joy. And the three of us have a relationship that I just treasure." So much so that in her bio, Betty included Anne as one of her own.

> She has three children, Vance, an actor on Comedy Central's The Daily Show; Ellen, most recently featured in The Love Letter and Ron Howard's film, Ed TV; and Anne Heche, last seen in Gus Van Sant's remake of Psycho.

Then in June it was announced Betty had joined PlanetOut, a leading gay online portal, as an advice columnist. According to the press the "best-selling author and tireless civil rights spokesperson, will host a new online advice channel entitled, 'Ask Betty.'

"I guess you could say I'm already a cybermom," she said. "So it seemed perfectly natural for me to extend my civil rights work to the digital domain via PlanetOut. I want to help lesbian, gay, bi, trans and questioning youth (of all ages) make peace with their parents, just as I supported

Ellen over 20 years ago. I hope to convey to parents the message that your gay children are still your children, who need your unconditional love now more than ever."

Tom Rielly, founder and chairman of PlanetOut was effusive. "She is an icon for millions . . . who see in her the parent they had (or wish they had) when they came out. She's the perfect person to help our members with their parental and family issues. The only difference between Betty and the rest of our parents is that she happens to have 3 movie and TV stars as children."

In the fall of 1999, *Goodbye Lover* and *Ed TV* were released. Although the films themselves received mixed reviews, Ellen was generally given positive notices. Even so, *The Advocate*'s Kevin Maynard wrote, "The verdict is still out on DeGeneres's post-*Ellen* movie career, although wry supporting turns are more of a step in the right direction than *Mr. Wrong*—and that might be just the way she likes it. In a particularly bittersweet moment in *Ed TV*, DeGeneres wistfully watches some kids jump up and down excitedly in front of a mini-mart security camera Sure, it's tantalizing to capture the media's eye, she seems to be saying, but at what cost?"

By the time the movies came out, Ellen's well-documented worries to many seemed much ado about nothing. Fenton Bailey, co-director with Randy Barbato of *The Real Ellen*, a one-hour documentary that explored DeGeneres's struggle to out her television character, told *The Boston Herald*, "People at large are less prejudiced than those in Hollywood. The audience is far cooler and more wired in than the executives, the gatekeepers. The executives are always underestimating the compassion, the humanity and the sophistication of the audience."

He for one was not worried about any backlash or blacklisting. "They've still got their best work to do, and they will do it. The good news is they haven't lost their careers over this. They may have felt the cold shoulder of homophobia and wisely decided to move out of Hollywood, but their careers haven't suffered at all."

Scott Seomin, entertainment media director for GLAAD in Los Angeles, added, "Career longevity, gay or straight, in this town is a tough thing, and I think Ellen's making some smart choices."

One of which was agreeing to executive produce and star in HBO's *If These Walls Could Talk 2*, a three segment movie detailing three stories of gay women in different decades. The film was a sequel to the 1996 original which had tackled the equally hot-button issue of abortion. DeGeneres would appear in the final segment, which would be directed by Heche, who had also written the piece. Ellen told the press, she wanted to make the movie "an honest portrayal of people in three very different times, all searching for the same things we all want—love and acceptance."

In September, Anne and Ellen quietly moved back to L.A., buying a $1.7 million, four bedroom, four bath home in the hills above the Sunset Strip. According to *Entertainment Weekly*, "The 2,800-square-foot stucco-covered abode, built in 1966, has an outdoor pool and is surrounded by bamboo, lavender, Mexican sage, and fountain grass. A modern flair is carried throughout by sandblasted glass windows, stained concrete floors, and a stainless-steel-accented kitchen."

But the time away had allowed Ellen a chance to gain some perspective and regain her sense of humor. "I think I was very naïve," she admitted in an ABCnews.com interview. "I thought that I was doing something for myself, and it certainly would be an interesting way to do it on television. I did not realize that I was going to be the so-called *leader* of the gay community. I mean, so far I've received no banner, no crown, nothing. There's no payment for this job, and the hours suck because I've got to be gay 24 hours a day, every single day. And that's exhausting.

"So it kind of hit me pretty hard to take on this responsibility of carrying the torch. You know, people talk about dog years being seven years to every human year. I think that gay years even surpass that. I feel like the last three years of my life have been like 30 years. When you're fired from any job, it's hard, but when you're publicly fired and humiliated it's really hard. So I went through a pretty deep depression for a while, and didn't know if I was going to be able to make it back out. And I did, so I feel like I survived something. I feel like I know what compassion is now because I know what that feels like to be in that place I had never been before.

"I got to experience *Who am I when no one likes me? Who am I when I don't have a show? Who am I when nobody's laughing at me*? And I found out that I'm still okay.

"I've learned a whole lot and so that's a blessing. I would not change one thing that I've done. It's not about the career; it's what's good for me and for my soul."

Through her experiences, Ellen came to understand what legacy she really wanted to leave. "I just want to get refocused back on what got me here in the first place, which is the fact that I'm a stand-up comedian and that I love doing comedy and I love making people laugh. And that's really what I want to be known for."

As the new millennium approached, it was clear that there had been a subtle shift in the television universe in two and a half years since the hoopla surrounding her personal and professional outing. The fact was, primetime broadcasters had not shied away from gay themes. In 1999 a main character on *Dawson's Creek*, played by Kerr Smith, revealed his homosexuality around the same time the drama's creator, Kevin Williamson, came out in real life. The most striking thing about the two events was how little press it received, as if audiences had already adopted a *been-there, done-that* attitude about such things. "It's a very good sign, and I'm thrilled about the lack of controversy," Williamson, the show's creator commented in the *Seattle Post-*

Intelligencer. "I was kind of expecting this. I was hoping, at least, that the climate was better."

When asked why the Parents Television Council, a conservative media watchdog group, didn't feel the need to trumpet concern over the small screen outing, executive director Mark Honig noted, "To bring up the fact that there are homosexuals in society is not something to rant and rave about at this point."

That same year, NBC premiered *Will & Grace*, a sitcom about a gay man and his best friend, a straight woman, which would go on to be an Emmy-winning, Top Ten show. On *Buffy the Vampire Slayer*, Alyson Hannigan's Willow discovers she is gay with little if any personal angst attached to the revelation.

A thoughtful *Time* magazine piece in October 1999 observed, "There are nearly 30 gay or lesbian characters in prime time . . . and they are no longer limited to bit roles and punch lines. TV has come out, within fuzzily defined but undeniable limits.

"The first strange rule: gay men are more lovable than gay women. But girl kisses are better than boy kisses—and it's best if at least one girl is straight. Straight actors playing gay (Eric McCormack) go over better than openly gay actors (DeGeneres), and so on."

But by 2000, Ellen was turning that last conventional wisdom on its ear and her career was enjoying a cathartic resurgence. She had announced a national stand-up tour that would end in New York and be taped for an HBO special scheduled to air in July; she was working with CBS on honing the premise for her new sitcom and she was gearing up to start a publicity blitz for *If These Walls Could Talk 2*. While she was now fully emotionally prepared for the possible slings and arrows of professional fortune, she would soon find herself blindsided by a completely unexpected turn of events.

20
An Unexpected
Heartbreak

Early in 2000, Ellen described her new sitcom to newsman Sam Donaldson. "I'm going to do something totally different. It's me and a bunch of 20-year olds living in a very nice apartment in New York. It's called *Pals*."

The confused reporter asked, "Haven't I seen this show before? Isn't it called *Friends*?"

"Well, that was *Pals* . . . and then I changed my mind."

It seemed to fans that the Ellen they had first fallen in love with was back, ready to make the world safe for laughter once again. It also seemed DeGeneres was eager to spread the word and make peace with the same media she had felt so abused by three years earlier. She also endeavored to reconnect with fans of all preferences and persuasions.

In March, Ellen did an extended interview with *The Advocate* in which she offered a calm analysis of what had gone so wrong three years earlier. "People kept saying how sick of all the media about me they were," regarding the lead up to "The Puppy Episode." "But what people got so sick of was all the press on press on press. It was never me talking. It was everyone else going at it."

DeGeneres also revealed that she had actually wanted *Ellen* to end at the end of the 1996–97 season. "I didn't want to come back on the air because I didn't really know where to go with it. I was 40 years old, and I deserved to be a sexual being. Suddenly it wasn't about Ellen getting her toe stuck in the blinds. They had to deal with a grown-up. And that's a different kind of funny. So I was fighting them, saying, *Let me go, let's end on a high note, let me out of this. I don't know where to go with this. I can't go back in the closet. We're going to have to deal with this.* But Michael Eisner wouldn't let me.

"So now I'm coming back, and they're not behind [the show]. I heard stories that affiliates were threatening ABC if they aired it." Ellen says the network's solution was to not promote the show at all so they could tell the offended affiliates, "Look, we're not trying to help it! We're not doing anything. We have to air it because we already paid for it."

But DeGeneres also admitted she contributed to the freefall. "Maybe I did a lot of things wrong, maybe I didn't go slow enough . . . and I should've just trusted that the path that I was on was the path that I was meant to be on. I was going through a birth." She would also tell ABCnews.com that "in retrospect I look and I see that any network would have probably done the same thing. There should have been a digestion process that I didn't take into consideration. I really expected everybody to open up their arms and say, *We love you no matter what.* And that was naive of me." Although she did add pointedly, "I would have liked a little more support and a little more help and just a gentler way of saying goodbye rather than reading it in the trades."

But even that slight was water under the bridge. "Today I am in a place of total forgiveness and compassion for how everyone feels but at the time, when I was going through such major grieving over losing my show . . ." Ellen says she appreciates that she was looked at as a trailblazer but she re-iterates it wasn't on purpose. "I just accidentally did something that people look at as a very courageous, brave thing. And it wasn't. It was just something that I did, and it accidentally helped a lot of people. But I'm not a brave person. I'm learning to be."

She took the opportunity to speak directly to her fans. "I will be the first to admit I have to take responsibility for the bad things, the negative things, the mistakes I've made. I can't change them, but I take responsibility for them. And I just want to apologize to anyone I've rubbed the wrong way. Sorry for making my mistakes in public." She thanked those who had continued to support her and her career. "And for the people who haven't, please come back and give me a chance to be funny again, which is what I want to do. Not avoid who I am as a gay person but really just get back to doing what I do and what brought me here in the first place."

While the public at large seemed willing to embrace Ellen, there was still hesitancy when it came to Anne Heche. DeGeneres remained steadfastly loyal and rationalized the distrust so many seemed to harbor against her girlfriend. "It was a new picture in people's minds, and they didn't know how to process it," she concluded to Judy Wieder. "People had never seen me with somebody before." Interestingly, she took the criticism of her relationship with Anne as a personal attack. "I went ahead and showed you exactly who I am. It was like, *Oh, God. They're seeing who I am, and they don't like who I am!* And that's what hurt."

Ellen admitted their relationship had gone through troubled times in response to the media attention. "We went to couples therapy and dealt with a lot of stuff that we were going through. And our therapist said, *I'm amazed that y'all have made it this long and that you're still together. You should be proud of yourselves.*"

But for the first time, DeGeneres acknowledged that she understood why there was such deep suspicion of Anne's motives. "Honestly, I was doubting her too when I met her because I thought, *You can't possibly be for real; you don't know what you're getting into*." That Anne was using Ellen for some headline inducing bi-curious fling "certainly could've been [the case]. And I would think that if you're a betting person, you're going to bet that this is not going to last."

Ellen claims that she initially rebuffed Heche's advances by telling Anne she was flattered but wasn't into flings or affairs. "And she kept saying, *I'm not playing games*." So DeGeneres ignored and dismissed her initial gut reaction and ended up falling truly in love for the first time in her life.

Such admissions simply humanized Ellen because the vulnerability and doubts she exposed were universally understood. Heche, however, still tended to sound like she was performing in her own badly written one-woman *It's-all-about-me* romance novel. In a first-person article that appeared in *The Advocate* Anne rhapsodized that when she was asked by the magazine's editor to write about "coming out as a gay woman while simultaneously coming into the DeGeneres family, I immediately wanted to correct her. I didn't come out. I came in. I came in to love. I came in to family. I came in to myself."

Lest anyone forget, she reminded the readers that Ellen's struggle had become her struggle. "As some of you may know, my birth family did not embrace my coming in. This was my first horror . . . Next came Hollywood."

She went on to say that thanks to the support she received from Betty and Vance, "I came to understand that I was here to show love . . . and set an example of the joy that comes when one can be herself, without lies, without shame . . . Hate is a powerful emotion. The only thing that is stronger than hate is love . . . I know this because of the love I received from this sublime family called the DeGeneres family."

While the sentiments expressed were noble and inspiring on their face, many fans still got a hinky feeling and worried Ellen was being set up for a heartbreak. For her part, Ellen was content to let time prove all the doubters wrong. So strong was her commitment to Heche that she told Sam Donaldson were it legal for a same-sex couple to marry, she'd be one of the first in line. It wasn't so much to validate the relationship—"I mean, in my mind we're married"—as it was for financial and personal rights. "So if something would happen to Anne or to myself in the hospital, [we'd want] to be able to make decisions [for each other] or if something would happen to either of us we'd be able to take care of the house and things wouldn't be taken away. Maybe that will happen in our lifetime, but we're committed as we can possibly be and we've taken all the separate legal steps to make sure we have the same rights in hospital situations."

While promoting the upcoming *If These Walls Could Talk 2*, DeGeneres also admitted she and Heche were struggling over whether or not to become parents. In the HBO movie, DeGeneres and Sharon Stone star in the third story as a committed couple trying to get pregnant. The piece was written by Heche and was admittedly biographical in spirit. Ellen says during the time Anne was working on the script, "It was a daily conversation between us. We did a lot of research on the sperm bank, the donors, and what you have to go through. So we were really trying to have a baby at the time she was writing it. Right afterward we decided not to have a baby so we've gone back and forth, and at this point we're at the stage of not. But that changes every day. Tomorrow you may find out that we're pregnant."

DeGeneres admitted they had differing views on the best way to become parents. "Anne wants to have the baby because she wants to have that experience. I really want to adopt a baby because there are so many children in this world and we're overpopulated. Anne was just offered a documentary project in China that was about panda bears, which would have been fun. But she would have been in China, and she said, *You know, if I go to China, I'm going to come home with a baby*. I would've come home with a panda bear." But it seemed clear that if they did become parents, Heche would be the biological mother. "If we could get pregnant, we'd get pregnant now."

Ellen though was openly conflicted about whether she truly wanted to take on such a responsibility and genuinely wanted to be a parent. "Well, that's the question. We love our lives so much. This is so nice now to have our time and be able to be spontaneous, to stay in bed all day. A child, of course, would change that and is a responsibility for the rest of my life. It's not just a cute little baby that I could put in Gap clothes. It's also going to be a teenager that's going to want to pierce its nose. And as much as I think I'm liberal, I think I'd be very conservative as a parent. And the whole potty training thing scares me! I like the fact that with a cat you have a litter box. And I don't know if that's appropriate for a child to just have a litter box."

Heche and DeGeneres's involvement in *If These Walls Could Talk 2* happened after executive producers Suzanne and Jennifer Todd, the sister team who produced the original movie, asked her to pitch them ideas for their planned sequel which focused on gay story lines. Anne came up with several ideas, including a look at two longtime partners' attempt to get pregnant via artificial insemination that the producers approved.

In addition to Heche's *2000*, there were two other episodes. The first, *1961*, was directed by Jane Anderson and starred Vanessa Redgrave as a woman facing an uncertain future after her longtime companion dies unexpectedly of a stroke and her relatives come to claim all her belongings, including the house they have shared for fifty years. Anderson says she was drawn to the story because it was about "two ladies who are innocents. The episode is about a lifelong relationship that isn't recognized." Redgrave won an Emmy, a Golden Globe and a Screen Actors' Guild award for her performance.

In *1972*, the women's movement provides the backdrop of a story about an openly gay college student, played by *Dawson's Creek* star Michelle Williams, who becomes involved with Chloë Sevigny's cross-dressing butch dyke, much to the consternation and disapproval of her other gay friends. Director Martha Coolidge joked, "It's exactly like [my earlier film] *Valley Girl*, except with Chloë in the Nick Cage role. To me, it's a classic story about first love, set amid all the anger and arguments of the feminist and lesbian movements of the early '70s."

Heche's segment, which she would also direct, was the most lighthearted of the three. "I wanted to write Ellen a role that was more expansive and fuller than anything audiences have seen her do," Anne explained to writer Greg Kilday. "It kind of started off as a love letter about our relationship, all the struggles that we went through, how we were able to keep together and blossom in a relationship that is so joyous for us. One of the things that confused everyone about me was that it was so easy for me to 'become' a lesbian, I just wanted to explain the joy that I felt.

"Individually, each story is great, but all together, they have a real emotional impact. I get the blessing of having two stories before mine that build a consciousness and awareness and emotion that I get to take to the next level. I wanted to end on a feeling of the future, of what lesbian and gay couples should have the right to feel all the time, just a normal, happy couple."

One of the two lovers was to be played by Ellen; it was Anne's idea to offer the role of the other woman to Sharon

Stone. After she read the screenplay for *2000*, the *Basic Instinct* star was on board. "How often do I get to play a happy woman who isn't punished at the end?" Stone asked. "If I lend a familiar face that can have the middle-American parents of an adolescent gay person say, *Okay, I don't have to be freaked out by this*, then I've done my job. I want their hearts to be touched. And even if the only way someone can justify watching it is to say to their friends, *I just tuned in to see two naked chicks*, that's also fine by me."

The script's love scene wasn't so easily digested by DeGeneres. "This was my first love scene," DeGeneres explained to *Newsday*'s Frank Lovece. "So we're starting to talk about what we're gonna do. Now, it took me a long time to even get to *Okay, I'm gonna be comfortable with this, we're gonna do this, it's important for the story* . . . Then Sharon and Anne, both at the same time said, *You know what? Let's just go for it.* And they just got up and walked away! And I'm following them saying, *What do you mean, go for it? What does that mean?*"

The scene called for DeGeneres and Stone to be in bed nude, their conversation leading to love making. Although both actresses are topless, the scene is shot discretely. "The thing is, Ellen had never done a love scene before," Anne explained, "and she was giving the audience a lot more of her than we'd ever seen before—not just the gay girl next door. I wanted to show her adult side. I wanted her to be a full woman. She hadn't presented that to the world.

"She didn't want to push too much or go too far, but her sensuality is so much a part of her, and I wanted to portray the most loving relationship between two women. I think there's a misunderstanding that lesbians are just really good friends. But passion is a big part of our relationship, and I felt that I would be cheating the story without that."

In the end, with some nudging by Stone, DeGeneres

agreed, although she says, "I had to have a sip of alcohol before I did it. It was just Sharon and I and the cameraman."

In an interview, Stone dismissed DeGeneres's reticence as unwarranted. "Ellen has no idea how beautiful she is— how beautiful her body is, how sexy she is. I don't know why. You don't have mirrors in your house? You don't see yourself on TV?"

Ellen waved off the compliments. "I'm happy with how I look. But it certainly isn't what most people find attractive."

While promoting the movie, Stone went out of her way to be provocative, teasing that "I learned that I'm exactly like a gay woman except I don't have sex with women." But her real intent was to instill enough curiosity for people to want to watch what in reality was an affecting, tastefully done piece of television. "I'm the expert on salacious material," she commented. "I think that if it draws someone to the project . . . then we have accomplished something with that; that has value.

"You never walk into any environment that people don't decide as you walk through the door what they like and don't like about you. That's about life. This isn't that much different than any other thing. It's just today's prejudice."

While certainly there were those who would forever be turned off by DeGeneres because of her personal revelations, it was becoming evident they were in the minority. On the heels of the well-received *If These Walls Could Talk 2*, Ellen took her stand-up act back on the road for an eight week, 35-city tour that would culminate in New York with the taping of an HBO special. Ellen freely admitted she was nervous going back to live performance after a more than six year layoff.

"I was really scared of getting back on stage again," she told the *Cincinnati Post*. "When you don't do something for a long time, whatever it is, even if it comes naturally, it's hard. But it's how I got started. The name of the tour and the HBO special is *The Beginning*. And I do feel like this is a new beginning for me. This is how I began my career. I think people forgot for awhile that I'm a comedian."

To that end, DeGeneres admitted to *Newsday* that her fear was "I'll walk on stage and there'll be 2,000 militant gays expecting me to spew *How dare they* . . . I think that will be like a tenth of what I talk about. When you stand up for something, you're going to narrow an audience down, and that seems to become political, whether it's your political party or religion or whatever. So I didn't want this to be a big show about me being gay; I wanted to blend everything." That said, she acknowledged, "It would be a big gaping hole if I didn't address at all my life for the last three years. So I do talk about it in the beginning, just to get it out of the way."

The media attention she had gotten in the months before and after "The Puppy Episode" reinforced Ellen's belief in the need for gentle humor. "There was a period of time I couldn't turn on TV without being a sketch on *Saturday Night Live* or the butt of a joke in a monologue," she recalled in a *Seattle Post-Intelligencer* interview. "That was my first glimpse of, *Wow, this is such a negative world*, and it's every arena: it's television, it's press, it's just people talking, it's sitcoms . . . You don't notice it until you are the recipient of it.

"I started seeing that everybody is making fun of somebody else. There's a joke at someone else's expense. Or it's a cynical sense of humor or critical and I thought, *That's not what I've ever done. My comedy has been nice, and it's always been gentle and lots of silence and pauses, and I need to bring that out to the world. That's missing right now*."

Ellen said the tour gave her the opportunity "to refocus everyone on what I do. First of all, I'm a comedian. Yes, I'm gay, and everybody knows that. Now let's get beyond that and remember how I got here in the first place. I was a comedian; people did like me; and if I left some audience members along the way, that's more about them than it is about me.

"I just wanted to remind people about who I am as an artist, that I'm funny and love giving people joy. I became a representation of someone who's gay and kind of became a symbol instead of an artist, and now I hope I'm a representation of survival."

If Ellen's worst fears had come to pass when she publicly came out in 1997, her hopeful expectations were exceeded during her 2000 stand-up tour; in every city she performed it was impossible not to feel the love.

And there to capture it on film was Anne Heche, who was shooting footage for a planned documentary that was both a behind the scenes look at Ellen's return to stand-up as well as a window into their own relationship.

When the tour ended with a triumphant finale on Broadway, it seemed as if Ellen had finally chased away any lingering demons. But just a month after HBO aired her comedy special, fans were stunned when DeGeneres announced in late August she and Heche had broken up. Their August 19 official statement tried to paint a picture of mutual agreement. "Unfortunately, we have decided to end our relationship. It is an amicable parting, and we greatly value the three years we have spent together. We hope everyone will respect our privacy through this difficult time."

But the breakup was anything but amicable or mutual; Anne had walked out on Ellen, leaving her blindsided and emotionally devastated. When she was finally ready to talk about it a year later, she told Judy Wieder it was the first time she had her heart broken. "I hadn't experienced it before. I had never been left by anybody—I was always the one to leave. It feels like your insides are cracking open. It feels like you cannot go on. And I would sit and literally not know where the day went. The sun would come up and the sun would go down, and I didn't notice because I was just staring at the wall. I didn't leave my house. I would go through days of crying. I didn't turn on a TV. I didn't listen to music. I just would sit. It felt like I would never live again. But you do.

"No matter how painful it is, no matter what the source of the pain is, you just put one foot in front of the other and live. I finally decided, I can't continue to wallow in this and feel sorry for myself, even though I have every reason to feel sorry for myself. I mean, this is bad!"

Ellen recalled it was a case of two steps forward, one step back every time there was a new hurt to reopen the wound. "In the beginning it was because she'd just walked out the door. And then it was because she was with Coley, and then supposedly she was pregnant, and then it was marriage. But that initial thing, when she left, well, I could've just sat and felt sorry for myself for a long, long time."

DeGeneres pulled herself out of her miasma by taking the best-revenge-is-living-well approach. "I decided, *I'm going to get up and I'm going to start working out every single day*. No, I didn't feel like getting up and going to the gym and working out, but I just had to do something to take care of myself, and I couldn't make myself feel better in any other way, other than physically. So I worked out with a trainer every single day. And it started making me feel better. I started reading *The Four Agreements* again. I read *The Power of Now*, which I recommend to everybody. I just forced myself, even though I really didn't feel like it. If you don't push yourself, that's when you just give up. And it doesn't do any good to give up."

Out of her hurt, Ellen found an upside to her break-up with Anne—the fact she survived it. "When the next bad thing that happens, you realize you can get through it. I'd been in relationships before—and I love being in relationships. I'm a relationship person. I am not good at being single. I don't even know how to date. I don't know what that is.

I've always loved love! I love companionship. But what the breakup did for me is that it made me treasure love. When I had my heart broken, instead of just thinking, *There'll be somebody else*—because there's always been somebody else right there—I had to really suffer the loss.

"The women that I've been in relationships with are still very special to me and are all friends. But this time, after having my heart broken, it made me treasure love more. It made me understand how precious it is and how much work it is and how you fight for it and try to keep it no matter what. Because I really, truly believed we were going to be together the rest of our lives."

Ironically, DeGeneres admits she initially was the one who resisted the relationship. "I was constantly questioning," she said in a 2001 *Advocate* interview. "And when she finally convinced me that she was not going anywhere and this was forever and ever—she left. At that point, every part of me believed I was going to be with her. So when I suddenly wasn't going to be with her—well, then, who was I?"

Ellen says that the only issue they fought over was love scenes. "I don't think I could be with an actress who does love scenes again. I didn't like that. It was really hard for me. There are certain actresses that take their clothes off in a movie and certain actresses that won't. I wondered, *Why can't you be one of those people that doesn't?* It was threatening to me. Especially since she was straight before I met her and she was doing love scenes with men. I worried, *Is this something you would enjoy?* I've gotta tell you, this is something I'm so happy never to have to deal with again."

Somewhat ironically, a month after Anne and Ellen split, Melissa Etheridge revealed her longtime partner Julie Cypher, had ended the twelve-year relationship. Etheridge's label issued a release that stated: "With the utmost of love and respect for one another, we have decided to separate. As committed parents, our top priority continues to be what is in the best interest of our children. Though elements of our lives will change, our family will always remain intact."

Etheridge told *USA Today* she and Cypher, who had divorced actor Lou Diamond Phillips to be with Melissa, were doing "very well with parenting the children—better than ever," adding, "but I have a lot of healing to do." Cypher's announcement that she "wasn't gay anymore" left the singer confused. "I didn't understand it then, I don't understand it now."

When asked if she would ever date a straight woman again, Ellen stopped short of issuing a flat disavowal. "To negate somebody's feelings? That's wrong. I think it is possible to fall in love with a person and not necessarily think you're gay. I mean, that was Anne's whole argument before. She wasn't gay. She was in love with me. Yes, and I remember that she said that right from the beginning. So I could care less if it's a choice or if it's biological. People should be allowed to love who they want to love.

"Who's to say that there's something wrong with somebody saying, *I'm open to everything, and I just fall in love with the soul and with the spirit* because ultimately that's what the love is . . . I really try not to have concrete opinions about other people's lives. It's different for everybody. I just know what's good for me and what's right for me. I know who I am. I really want to be with somebody who knows clearly who she is and has known for some time who she is. I know who I am. I have a really strong sense of self. And I want to be with somebody who has a really strong sense of self and is proud and likes themselves. You have to work on knowing who you are. It's a daily thing to be in touch with your spirituality and be in touch with something bigger. I want to be with somebody who is on the same journey. I'm very picky. And I like that I'm picky and that I'm not going to settle."

For her part, Anne told writer Anne Stockwell that sexual preference of any kind had nothing to do with her leaving. "I broke up with Ellen because our relationship didn't work. God, do not diminish this to *I left her because I was not gay.* That makes me so angry because it makes my commitment not truthful! Part of what happened [with Ellen] is that I stopped being many parts of me. This is a pattern in all of my relationships—to gain the trust and love of somebody, I would become what they wanted me to become. [With Ellen] I stopped doing acting roles because I thought, *Well, this will prove that I'm worthy of love!*"

Specifically, she says she was trying to avoid Ellen's discomfort with love scenes. "I was very fearful of getting a role because I thought I might not be loved by the woman I was with. And so in order to not even be put in that position, I put out the energy of I can't work." But she says it wasn't so much the love scenes that she feels disturbed Ellen. "I think she was threatened by me meeting men. I felt like I was not trusted, which was offensive to me. I never, *ever* gave her reason to believe that she could not trust my love. I brought her to the premiere of *Volcano*; I went on Oprah; I stood by her side. I am a monogamous person. And I think the fear that consumed her was not about me. The fear was about a big ghost gay women abide by: Do not sleep with straight women."

But when it was revealed that Heche was dating Coley Laffoon, whom she had hired to work on the documentary she was filming of Ellen's stand-up tour, that axiom seemed more wise than paranoid. Anne would claim their romance didn't begin until a month after leaving Ellen. "I wanted to get back into the world, go to the theater, go to concerts. I thought, *Coley was cool. I'm gonna call Coley.*" She says he was upset when he answered the phone and told her he had just broken up with his girlfriend. "I said, *I know what that's like—why don't I take you out for a drink*? That's how we began." The couple married a year later in September 2001 and six months after that Anne gave birth to a 7-pound boy they named Homer Heche Laffoon on March 2.

In November 2001, Heche did an extensive interview with *The Advocate*, to both promote her new autobiography, *Call Me Crazy*, and to answer questions regarding the break-up.

When told that many in the community resented her apparent preference flip-flop, Anne seemed unperturbed. "Anything you do in your life, people are going to be angry at you. People were angry at me when I was in love with Ellen, when I broke up with Steve Martin, when I left the soap opera . . . when you make choices and you're a public figure, people have reactions."

She also evaded labeling her sexual preference, saying unlike those who were born gay, she chose to be in a gay relationship with DeGeneres. "I don't call me anything. The labeling is about what makes *you* feel comfortable. I have been very clear to everybody that just because I'm getting married does not mean I call myself a straight."

Heche says she has "recovered memories" of her father, who she says was a closet homosexual who eventually died of AIDS, raping her as a child—a scenario that if true would be statistically rare.

Anne repeated the allegations in a *20/20* interview with Barbara Walters. After which her sister Abigail had this to say: "It is my opinion that my sister Anne truly believes, at this moment, what she has asserted about our father's past behavior . . . [but] based on my experience and her own expressed doubts, I believe that her memories regarding our father are untrue."

But to Anne, they were far too real and she says her reaction to the incest was to retreat into her mind by creating an alter ego, named Celestia, "that was from heaven. Celestia is the reason I believe I survived. She was the consistent love that allowed me to know that I could get to the other side of my abuse." Even as an adult, rather than talk to anyone about her abuse, Heche "escaped into my fantasy world; I became an actress."

Anne reported that she confided in Ellen about Celestia the first week they were together and showed her a video excerpt of a movie she had filmed called *Stripping for Jesus* which dealt with her abuse. In one of the scenes, Heche's character is handcuffed to her mother's bed. Anne says that DeGeneres called her crazy, threw the tape out and said, "*Don't ever show the tape to anybody.* And I agreed! That's part of why I wrote this book. Every single choice I made in every relationship was because I was not ready to be out about who I was. Here I was, in love with a woman who was telling me I'm out of my mind . . . *Yes, you're right, I am; I'll be quiet. Sure, I'll hide that I was abused—look what I get to do! I get to merge with a woman who is talking about love,* which is my only message. It was a perfect union." She notes that coming out of one closet forced her into another because "I could not be Celestia around Ellen unless I was hiding."

Anne says it was the sudden freedom of being able to embrace Celestia that led to the bizarre incident that occurred the day after Heche and DeGeneres announced they had broken up when Anne showed up at a house in a remote rural area of Fresno County, California, acting erratic. Heche, who her reps claimed was supposedly driving to a music festival, told the home's occupant, Araceli Campiz, that her SUV had run out of gas a mile and a half away. Campiz recognized the actress and was more than willing to lend the use of her phone so Anne could call for help. But to her surprise, she told *People* that Heche "took off her Nikes and said she needed to take a shower." After Campiz complied, Anne then requested "to watch a movie," Campiz said, "but the VCR was broken."

When Heche showed no signs of planning to leave, Campiz became uncomfortable and called the Fresno County sheriff's department. According to the subsequent police report, when the officers arrived, Anne explained to them that she was "God, and was going to take everyone back to heaven . . . in a spaceship." An ambulance was called and Heche was transported to Fresno's University Medical Center but was released a few hours later. The next day, Heche—now accompanied by her business manager—retrieved her car and later flew together to Toronto, where she was filming *John Q* with Denzel Washington.

Heche now admits she had taken the drug ecstasy that day "to go on a spiritual journey. I was coming to the culmination of a fantasy world that I'd been living in for five, six years." When she woke up that morning she said she heard a voice telling her "Today's your day to leave."

Stockwell questioned the rapidity with which Heche recovered from self-described insanity. "It's not snapping out of anything. I had created a fantasy world where I was safe. I realized that the earthly life I created at the same time was now giving me the safety I'd always wanted. So I could integrate both lives."

When asked about the revelations made in *Call Me Crazy* DeGeneres was circumspect. "Nothing surprises me anymore. It just doesn't matter what she says. It's her truth, and she has different truths than I do and different experiences. It's just weird, since there's been no interaction between us. I just wanted to forgive and move on. Mainly, I don't want our breakup to become the same circus that our relationship was."

To that end, DeGeneres ended up scrapping the more than 200 hours of footage Heche shot of the planned documentary, which Ellen pulled the plug on at significant financial cost after realizing there was no way to salvage the project to her satisfaction.

"I just kept trying to put funny stuff together for a special, and no matter what I did, she was in it, and he [Laffoon] was in it. And let's be honest here, nobody would be looking at this project for any other reason than to be looking at them together or to be looking back at our relationship. I decided that there's no need to rehash that time in my life. Trying to go through all of that was torture for me. You're watching yourself and you're watching yourself interact with your girlfriend, looking at what your relationship was together. It was also very hard to watch my life, but I have to tell you, it was also very healthy. It was purging."

When asked what she learned from watching the footage, DeGeneres said, "I guess what I learned was, yes, she did love me. . . . I guess when Anne does something, she does something one hundred percent." But for all she learned, "I'll probably never have closure," she admitted to *USA Today*. "We haven't spoken since she walked out the door. I'll probably never know anything."

But as the song says, every new beginning comes from some other beginning's end. The breakup with Anne freed Ellen to move forward with a clean personal and professional slate and she would make the most of the opportunity by staging one of the most uplifting comebacks in Hollywood history.

21
A New Beautiful Place

It would turn out that one of Ellen's most shining professional moments was borne out of our country's greatest tragedy. The attacks on the World Trade Center and Pentagon on September 11, 2001, had forced two postponements of the annual Emmy Awards and for a while there was the possibility they would be canceled outright. But eventually the decision was made to go on with the show, but in a much scaled down incarnation. As host, it was up to DeGeneres to find and set the tone. "I'm the most sensitive person in the world about being inappropriate or hurting people's feelings," she says. "I didn't want it to be a light moment when what had happened was so devastating."

Prior to the start of the show DeGeneres recalls, "I'm sitting there, I have my eyes closed and I'm taking deep breaths and I'm preparing to walk out there. I hear the stagehands next to me, they're watching a monitor, and one of them says *Oh, wow*. And I look to see what they're looking at, and there's a guy singing the national anthem on stage, and there's a shot of Kelsey Grammer bawling. Not just a little bit, but crying, sobbing. I'm like, *I've got to go out now? While the audience is crying?* At that point, I thought this was a no-win situation, and not to expect anything from it."

But within minutes, Ellen showed she was the right person in the right place at the right time. She opened the show by saying, "Welcome to the 53rd . . . 54th . . . and 55th Emmy Awards." In her monologue she noted, "They can't take away our creativity, our striving for excellence, our joy. Only network executives can do that." Then she explained the real reason it was important for her to be on stage. "I'm in a unique position as host because, think about it: What would bug the Taliban more than seeing a gay woman in a suit surrounded by Jews?" From that moment on, she had the audience, and the American public, in her hands.

Later, she would comment, "People underestimate how healing a thing it is to laugh. I'm aware of that when I'm on-stage and I hear 2,000 or 3,000 people laughing, and that energy is coming toward me, and I'm kind of conducting it almost. To be around that energy is really important. The audience becomes like one organism, one entity. Sometimes you'll hear individual people laughing harder or giggling a little bit longer, but it's normally like this solid kind of movement, like a school of fish in the ocean that turns at the same time and goes back and forth. It's why I do it. That's my contribution. That's what I can do. I'm best when I'm just being myself, thinking on my toes."

And it was never clearer than at the Emmys. When the show ended, the audience gave her a spontaneous standing ovation, which caught the surprised comic completely off-guard. Typically, Ellen thought the cheering was for the show's surprise guest. "I thought Barbra Streisand had just walked out on stage [early]," DeGeneres told *Entertainment Weekly*. "I couldn't believe people were doing that. It didn't compute."

Once it sunk in, she was visibly humbled. "That's unbelievably kind," she said, motioning for the audience to stop clapping. "She pulled it off with flying colors," said *West Wing* creator Aaron Sorkin. "The tone of the whole thing was just right."

"She had the hardest job in show business tonight," said Best Supporting dramatic actor Bradley Whitford. "She was funny and appropriate."

Sopranos star Edie Falco, who had won the Best Actress in a Drama Emmy, agreed. "That Ellen, she's really something. Serious and funny; it was a very tasteful evening."

The Emmys would be a turning point for Ellen because it reminded people both in and out of the industry just how talented and funny she was. So it was with a renewed sense of professional optimism that DeGeneres began working on her new sitcom for CBS. Originally, she had wanted to do a half hour variety series in the vein of the old *Carol Burnett Show* and had shot a pilot and been given the go-ahead for the series. But in the end, Ellen pulled the plug on herself.

"I think everybody thinks that the network changed their minds about the variety show. It wasn't them. It was me." After she had proved to the network she could do a show "that was just funny for the sake of being funny," Ellen realized how difficult it would be to maintain the level of humor week in and week out. "We started realizing that when Carol Burnett was on, there weren't all these other shows to compete with and all these other channels. And I didn't know how to make it different. I just started looking at it and thinking, *A weekly variety show is going to be really hard.*

"It's not like I do characters and dialects. Carol did great characters. I think I would be a good host, which is why I like hosting things, but as far as being in different sketches, being something different all the time—no. I can be myself all the time in different sketches—but that's a sitcom."

So Ellen says she had to go back to the CBS executives

and say, "I've changed my mind. I convinced them that in the long run it really is best that we shelve it and do a sitcom. We had to burn the money we spent."

Instead, Ellen agreed to do what the network had actually wanted all along—for her to do another series. DeGeneres says the reason she was initially resistant was "because I'd just come out of one. It was like, *Okay, what do I do now, where do I go*? That's why I thought a variety show would be good, because it was hard for me to do anything other than be Ellen DeGeneres. It was hard for me to figure out who the sitcom character would be. It was just too soon, too close to the last show."

But along with co-creator Mitch Hurwitz and Carol Leifer, who had worked on *Seinfeld* for three years, she was able to come up with a concept she felt comfortable with. In it, Ellen would play a dot.com executive who loses everything when the bubble burst and is forced to move back home with her small town family. Although her character would be a gay woman, it would be as much of a central issue as the fact she had blue eyes.

"People don't want to see someone struggle," says DeGeneres. "They want to see everybody having fun. . . . So we've created this wonderful fantasy town where nobody has a problem with it. It's like those ridiculous shows I grew up watching, like *Petticoat Junction*—a classic TV show that makes you feel good."

To Ellen's relief, she found putting her toe back in sitcom waters to be painless. She told *The Advocate* the new show "has that old-fashioned feel, that's just funny, that's not mean-spirited. Somehow we captured it. There's this chemistry between everybody in the cast. And it feels like an old *Mary Tyler Moore Show*. It feels like we're in our third season or something." After spending years believing she would never have the opportunity to have a show, "suddenly I was on a stage doing a pilot that just felt so good to me. I felt calm and natural and funny and all the things that I had really missed."

DeGeneres also revealed that she had tried to make peace with ABC. "I have reached out to someone at ABC just because I don't like bad blood, and I apologized for any behavior on my part. And we both were passionate about our sides, and I was passionate that I was doing the right thing. I felt misunderstood." But Ellen says she was rebuffed. After she apologized, "there was just silence on the other end of the phone. It really is a shame when you have a relationship of any sort for five years and it ends badly."

But Ellen was ready to focus on the future. During the summer of 2001, she tirelessly promoted her new series, which co-starred Cloris Leachman as her mom and Martin Mull as her old high school principal. Her mantra from the outset was this time around she wasn't about issues; she was all about being funny.

"I think what happened with the last show is it got to be too issue-oriented, and I take responsibility for that," she told TV critics in an interview session. "That was something that I felt I needed to do. I did a show for four years, and then suddenly I did something that kind of overshadowed everything else. So now I just want to be funny again. I think people want to sit at home and turn on their TV and just laugh. That's all they want to do. And I understand that now."

Nothing, not even the terrible 8:00 p.m. Friday time slot the show had been given, could deter her from her mission. When asked about where the show had ended up in the schedule, Ellen deadpanned, "I'm thrilled. I'm hoping we can move to Sunday morning at 7:00 a.m. eventually, but for now this is great."

And no, her character would not be dating. "We're getting away with it by saying I just got out of a relationship, so I don't really have any interest in dating. And it's pretty easy when it's just you and the P.E. teacher in town."

Although *The Ellen Show* was well-received by critics, it failed to find an audience or live up to its potential. When CBS pulled it after 13 episodes, the writing was clearly on the wall that the show would not be back for a second season. This time, however, Ellen was philosophical. "Cloris Leachman was great to work with. I think we had potential, but we hadn't found what it was yet. Shows really don't get a chance to find themselves and grow anymore. Everyone's in too much of a hurry. But it was what it was, and I'm grateful to have had the experience. I have no hard feelings about anything with CBS. I understand now it's not personal. I'm a slow learner in some parts of my life. I'm getting the hang of this game now. You roll with the punches. It's a matter of riding it out and waiting for the thing that works for you."

DeGeneres would also admit the show might have suffered because she was trying a little *too* hard to please. "I think, when that show was launching, I was coming from a place of *Oh my God, I hope they like me again*. And that's never a good place to come from. It was important for me to get back to the place I was, but I don't think you should ever come from a place of needing someone's approval."

The lesson was well learned. Suddenly, it seemed as if Ellen was everywhere exuding the confidence of a seasoned performer who knows she is at the top of her game. In May 2002, she hosted VH1's fifth *Divas* special, which combined her prowess as a host with her love of music to create a perfect comic synergy. The Divas featured in this installment were Cher, Celine Dion, Whitney Houston, Mary J. Blige, Shakira, Anastacia, Stevie Nicks and the Dixie Chicks. DeGeneres said she was ready for the onslaught of egos, "as long as I don't have to please them and stock their dressing rooms. You're not supposed to feed them or get too close to them."

When asked if she had the heart of a diva, Ellen demurred. "No, unfortunately. I'm going to look like a little sheep next to these women. I don't have any weird demands or anything. Maybe I should. But I feel if you don't like brown M&Ms, you should pick out your own brown M&Ms. I'm pretty easy to get along with." Then she added, "But I am starting to demand that glasses be filled a certain way when I drink my water. And I'm bathing in Pepsi . . . very tingly, wakes you up."

But the biggest news for Ellen was that she had been signed to host a daily talk show that would start in 2003. In April 2002, Dick Robertson, president, Warner Bros. Domestic Television Distribution, and Jim Paratore, who serves as both executive vice president, Warner Bros. Domestic Television Distribution and president, Telepictures Productions made the announcement.

"This is advertiser-friendly, quality content with a big star that stations are looking for and viewers love," said Robertson. "We have the production experience, the distribution expertise and a superstar host in Ellen. While there are very few sure things in television, I'd place a big bet on this one."

"Ellen has the intelligence, comedic skills and mainstream sensibilities to create a unique daytime television franchise," added Paratore. "There are not many people who can do this kind of show. To get someone of Ellen's talent as well as her stature is a real coup for us and for the stations that buy the show."

In reality, the idea for the talk show first came up back in 1997. "It was a conversation that we had had a long time ago about Ellen, internally, when she was doing the 'coming out' episode and it looked like it was going to be the end of the run." But then ABC picked up *Ellen* for another season. "So it was something that we had had in the back of our mind for years. And we kept pursuing it, you know, through her agency and finally, after the CBS show ended, there was an opening to sit down and do it. And I sent Ellen an expensive bottle of wine. It turned out to be her favorite wine. And it was all kismet after that."

It was as if the planets were finally aligning once again in her favor. "I was really excited about it," says DeGeneres, who had frequently over the course of her career commented on how one day she'd like to try her hand at a talk show. "It was something that I really have thought about. But I always thought I would do it much, much later." But once *The Ellen Show* didn't pan out, the future was now. "It gave me an opportunity to do it earlier than I probably thought I would in my career."

What a difference five years can make. By the summer of 2002, DeGeneres was once again a sought after talent. She was receiving rave reviews for her new *Here and Now* stand-up act, she was finishing up voice-over work on Pixar's *Finding Nemo* and had been signed by Simon & Schuster to write a new book of comic essays, *The Funny Thing Is . . . ,* which would be published to coincide with the debut of her talk show. "Why write a second book, you ask?" DeGeneres said. "Because there are some words I didn't use in the first one."

DeGeneres describes the book as "just a bunch of chapters about weird things. Sometimes they end up a cohesive story and sometimes they're just random thoughts. I write differently for a book than I do for stand-up, but it's a way of expressing myself that I enjoy. I mean it is a tortuous process—it's like childbirth. Every time I do this I think, *I'm never going to do it again*."

In *Finding Nemo* Ellen explained she plays a fish "trying to help Albert Brooks find his son. I have short-term memory loss, so I'm really no help, but I do lighten things up. They videotaped me while I recorded the dialogue, and the fish will end up looking and moving as much like me as possible. I think that's everyone's dream—to find out what you'd be like as a fish."

Her love-hate relationship with stand-up continued. Although she hated the travel and the work entailed in creating new material, she acknowledged, "It's the most freeing thing for me as a creative outlet. I'm feeling like I want to get back onstage and connect with people again. I'm the director, the writer, the producer and the performer. I can go in other directions," as long as those directions veered away from anything mean-spirited.

I've been having thoughts and feelings. I thought about going to a therapist. And then I thought, Why would I pay money to have someone listen to me talk when I can get other people to pay money to listen to me talk?

We've got all-you-can-eat places. We don't need to be eating all we can eat! We're not bears; we're not hibernating! . . . And only in the darkness of a movie theater do we not feel guilty about eating a three-pound box of Sno-Caps. We stock up on popcorn and candy like we're crossing the Sierras. . . . "Is that the largest popcorn, that bucket? You don't have a barrel or anything like that?"

"I'm never tempted to go that way," she said in a *Star Tribune* interview while on tour. "I'm amazed it's the norm. People are so conditioned by it on television; it's become a part of our consciousness. If you really pay attention, you're usually laughing at someone else's expense," she said. "I'm laughing at my own expense, and everyone else is relating to it, how absurd we all are, trying to be cool and okay with ourselves. But when the slightest thing happens, that judge inside keeps saying, *You're stupid.*"

The important thing for any comic, Ellen explained to *The Post-Standard*, was to "pay attention to what the public responds to. There are a lot of comedians who don't want to *sell out* that way—or they feel like they're selling out if they go mainstream. In a way, my style hurt me in the beginning because I wasn't the typical female comedian. I didn't do the kind of stuff people got. A lot of my humor is very subtle and very dry. And most people are used to being spoon-fed jokes or hit over the head. Put a curse word in front of anything and it will make people laugh. But I like a challenge. I think the audience is fed a constant diet of generic, easy humor, and I don't like to spoon-feed the audience."

In June 2002, POWERUP, the national organization for gay women in entertainment announced its second annual list of the "Top 10 Most Powerful Gay Women in Show Business." Rosie O'Donnell, who had just come out was ranked first, bumping Ellen, the previous year's champ down to #2. DeGeneres couldn't resist poking fun at the "honor."

"I've just found out I've been named the number two most powerful lesbian in show business. Does this mean I'm runner-up? If so, I am prepared to step in and take care of any Most Powerful Lesbian in Show Business duties should photos surface of Rosie in compromising positions with a man."

Much of Ellen's good humor could also be traced to a tranquil and fulfilling private life. Although it was no secret she was living with girlfriend Alexandra Hedison, a photographer and sometime actress she had met through friends not long after her break-up with Heche, Ellen had been much more closedmouthed about her relationship when dealing with the press. "I got off course for a little while," she says, tacitly referring to the highly public days with Anne Heche. "Everybody makes mistakes. I'm back to being who I am and having a quiet relationship.

"This is a really calm period of my life," she told *Philadelphia Inquirer* reporter Gail Shister. "I'm happy. I'm excited about what's to come. Laughter is such a healing thing. It's what we need now." Ironically, Hedison, who is the daughter of *Voyage to the Bottom of the Sea*'s David Hedison, was accompanying Ellen on her 24-city tour. This time around, however, there would be no trauma. "Things are great with us."

DeGeneres had also finally found a house—which she shared with Hedison, her two cats Harlow and Subtle and their new mixed-breed puppy Lucy—that felt like a true home, reported *Entertainment Weekly*. "Everybody who's lived in the house has been a writer. I'm inspired when I'm there. I've moved a lot, and I hope I don't ever move again. Everybody keeps saying that they're going to write that down and remind me when I say that I want to move in a year."

Ellen began working on the talk show in earnest as soon as she finished her stand-up tour, which she says would be her last, at least for a long while. "I just didn't announce it, like Cher. She keeps coming back. I felt this was due for a long, long time. A show takes eight months to write, and another four to tour. I never say never, but right now I'm looking forward to the talk show."

Ellen joked that the talk show better work because she was running out of names to title a show. "First there was *Ellen*, then *The Ellen Show* . . . This will probably be the *Ellen DeGeneres Show* or something like that. And if this one doesn't work I'll have to change my name before I do another show."

One luxury the talk show provided Ellen was time. "I've never had so much time to prepare for something," she told Gene Stout. "And I need the time because I really want to do this right. I want to look at a lot of different talk shows and see what I like about them and what I don't like about them. I just want it to be fun. But I'm not reinventing the wheel. But I feel really, really good about this. I feel confident and happy. It's something I've always wanted to do. It's the closest thing to doing stand-up because I get to think on my feet and have conversations with people."

She also had a backup plan she shared with *USA Today* if a guest proves reticent. "If it's not going well, I'll have some lions chained up next to my desk, like *Gladiator*. They'll pop out. I'll make it a kind of combination *The Chair, Fear Factor* and a talk show. A log swings down. An alligator comes down. I'll get 'em to talk!"

For all her lightheartedness, the talk show was serious business to the syndicators and producers because of its financial potential. According to *Broadcasting & Cable*, an entertainment trade publication, "*Oprah* is a *billion*-dollar-a-year franchise . . . In its last issued annual report as a public company (1998), King World said about 42 percent of its $684 million in revenue that year (almost $290 million) was attributable to *Oprah*. In addition, the show generates many millions more in local ad sales for stations."

That's why it was so important to try and develop talk shows. "We're going after that audience with Ellen," Paratore said in 2003. "We think she'll be a major player there."

It was a confident and relaxed DeGeneres who appeared before TV writers in July 2003 to promote her new show and explain why this was such a good fit for her. "I'm genuinely curious about people. Even boring people fascinate me. I get to meet anybody that I want now. I get to talk to interesting people. And I really do listen. Not all comedians listen. But I think in order to be the kind of comedian that I am—I observe people and I observe life and so I have to pay attention. I have to listen. And I think that's where I will be best."

DeGeneres said she had the added advantage of having been on so many talk shows as a guest. "Carson to me was the best because you always knew his point of view. He expressed it without expressing it. And I think you have to have a host with a point of view. Because if you become too much of a blank canvas, you really don't know if someone is being genuine or not. Carson was great at letting the guest shine, being funny when it was necessary, being funny just by responding to the guest's comment. And I was really lucky that I got to be on that show before he retired."

While Ellen and her producers didn't want to reveal too much about the planned format of the show, she stressed that it would be unique because it would reflect her as opposed to trying to copy another successful show.

"People keep asking if it's going to be like *Rosie O'Donnell*. And I keep saying, *No . . . it's going to be like Ellen DeGeneres*. I think what makes a show work is that you're staying true to who you are. Johnny Carson was brilliant because he was Johnny Carson. The format for Leno and Letterman and Carson are all basically the same, a desk and chairs. And yet, they are all completely different. I think it's the host who kind of drives the type of show.

"I have no preconceived idea of what it's going to be. I just want it to be real and funny and spontaneous. And you don't know what you're going to see every day. And I don't know what I'm going to do every day."

Ellen was aware that the timing for her new show couldn't be better. First, she was receiving unprecedented rave reviews for her voice-over work in *Finding Nemo*. "I was asked to do that when I was touring three years ago for my HBO special when nothing was going on in my life. Pixar approached me and asked me to do this, that they had created this character for me." She says she worked on the picture for over three years. "You're by yourself in front of a microphone and it's not like you're watching the character. They create it after they film you and create the character for your facial expressions. And it was great because they would give me the lines, but then they would also say, *Do whatever you want to do now*. So I could just go anywhere I wanted to go without worrying about upsetting another actor and throwing off somebody else or ruining their setup. And it's unbelievable what it's done. It's really exciting, and the timing . . . I couldn't have planned it better."

She also admitted, "I don't think this would have worked a few years ago. I'm in a different place. I think people are in a different place with me. I just don't ever approach anything looking at the odds. I never would have gotten into this business. I never would have been a stand-up because most stand-ups never make it and you're on the road forever and that's your life. I never would have gotten a sitcom. I never would have tried another sitcom. I mean, everything that I've done, I've done because I just either haven't learned and I just never will learn. And I hope I don't ever get hard that way. I'm optimistic. I'm confident. I love what I do. I love making people laugh. I can only go into it knowing that I'm going to love doing this. And I think people will feel that I love doing it. I want to make people happy. I think there's a very big need for that in the world today; that people just need to be entertained and laugh really hard."

In addition to the requisite celebrities, DeGeneres says she looked forward to having a cross section of people on her show talking about an infinite number of topics. "I'll have animals. I'll have kids. I'll have plants. I plan to talk about soup. Everyone has an opinion, and everybody's had it."

Ellen seemed good-naturedly wry when asked if her mother would be involved. "If she has anything to say about it, she will be. Yes. She's pitched something called Betty's Corner already, which is where we're going to keep her."

Looking back at her now classic post-9/11 Emmy hosting performance, DeGeneres was thoughtful. "That show was not about me showing everybody that I could be funny and get everybody ready for the CBS show that was going to bring me back, which is what I really had intended it to do before 9/11. But once that happened, the show became a way of me making the audience feel better and the audience at home feel better and the celebrities who were scared to even show up or didn't know if it was appropriate to celebrate themselves when so many people had suffered.

"So I think that it was a beautiful, humbling lesson for me to realize that when you don't think about yourself and you put it all out there to make other people feel good, which is what comedy is about anyway, that something much bigger happens. And it really was a beautiful night for me, a beautiful experience that I got to thank the world for grieving with us. I got to make people feel better and walk that line. So it was very satisfying, but in a very bittersweet way."

Jim Paratore believes, "That was the turning point. Ellen came out there and made people proud. People began to step back and remember how talented she was. And talent, over time, wins out in this business."

As the debut of her show neared, Ellen's confidence soared. "I think it will be the thing that will overshadow everything else I do in my career," she said. "I want this to be the last thing I do. I can only be myself and be real and make it entertaining and fun and something I would like to sit down and watch every day." Besides, she added, "I've been doing stand-up for 25 years so I'm really looking forward to sitting down."

She admitted in *Broadcasting & Cable* that the process of launching the show had been exhausting. "I've done a lot of stuff that prepared me for this kind of schedule. I've been training myself for this for the last two years as if I'm training for a marathon—that's what I want this show to be. I don't want this show to run forever. I want it to run for 15 years . . . Forever is too long."

Executive producer Mary Connelly said DeGeneres reminded her of David Letterman in that "the two of them share an incredible work ethic. She's not only on time; she's there ahead of time. They both work hard and expect people around them to do the same."

The Ellen DeGeneres Show premiered on September 8,

2003 to positive reviews and warm audience response. From the outset it was clear that Ellen had taken the genre and molded it to fit her comic sensibilities. If there is one word that comes to mind when tuning in, it's *fun*. Connelly told *People* that "You can walk into her dressing room, and there can be any number of people in there dancing. You feel foolish if you're not."

Ironically, DeGeneres, who does admit to being a poker freak, claims she's much less entertaining at home with Hedison. "We're not walking around with big shoes and red noses by any means. When I go home, I just want to sit and look at my animals. I'm no fun at all. I'm boring as hell. I never go out. It's terrible. I'd rather stay home and go to bed at ten every single night. I love my house. I like silence . . . When I hit 60, I'll go out again. I'm hibernating for a little while."

All that silence gives Ellen a chance to reflect. "Now it seems like everything is so flattering and positive," *The New York Times* reported. "I'm savoring this. It's interesting: you try to plan every step when you have a career but there's no controlling it. To think that we're ever controlling anything is just ridiculous."

DeGeneres told Gail Shister she is thankful every day. "I get to do stand-up every single day. I talk to the audience, getting that energy exchange. If there was a downside to the life of a talk show host, it was the daily sessions in the hair and make-up chairs. "It's torture. It feels like it's smothering my face. I like my pores to breathe. During breaks in the show, it's nonstop powdering my face or putting on lip gloss. I kind of want my space."

But once in front of her audience, Ellen is obviously in her element. Among the regular features that have evolved is "Fat Cats," where DeGeneres shows photos sent in by readers of obese felines. The gag started after Ellen talked about being scolded by her vet for having a fat cat. "So then we started getting all these pictures people sent in of their own fat cats," she explained to the *Washington Post*. "[Viewers] love it and can relate but there are some huge cats out there. Some of them we don't even show because I feel like, *Oh, my God, this animal's going to blow up in a second*."

But it's the dancing that has become the show's most notable trademark. It started after Ellen once danced her way over to her chair and now is an anticipated part of every show. "Everyone's dancing," she said in *Newsweek*, "and no one's drunk. As much as I'd like to stop, I just can't. I can feel how much the audience loves it. But I know I am a parody waiting to happen on *Saturday Night Live*. It's become a thing of its own. It's almost sort of what I'm known for now more than being a comedian."

Ellen says she once "was going through security at the airport and the women at the security point asked me to dance. Of course, I had to because it was easier than taking my shoes off. I get requests to dance all the time, even if there is no music." The set was actually redesigned so there'd be more room for Ellen and her guests to dance.

And soon, there'd be something to sing about as well when it was announced *The Ellen DeGeneres Show* had been nominated for 12 Daytime Emmys. "I didn't really understand what a big deal it was," DeGeneres said in a *Newsday* interview. "They told me, *you got nominations for every single category except the song*, and I instantly said, *What's wrong with our song?* But we're up against the soaps, and they have original songs every week. It's really just nice that I am surrounded by such good people. The show is a well-oiled machine and I could not have done this alone. I'm just so happy everyone is being acknowledged."

She was even happier when her show won three Emmys for technical achievement as well as for Best Talk Show. When she accepted the award, Ellen told the Radio City Music Hall audience, "It's the best job I've ever had." Ellen

would later reveal she keeps her Daytime Emmy on a book-
shelf in the hallway. "It means that when Telepictures was
trying to sell the show, and many people didn't want to buy
it because they didn't think I would succeed in daytime, and
that people didn't really want to watch me, that we were
right.

"Oh, I knew a lot of people thought it was crazy, but I was
pretty confident. If I had been truly skeptical about my
chances, I don't think I would have done it. I just didn't
worry about what I was 'supposed' to do as the host of this
kind of show; I talk about whatever is on my mind, and I
don't underestimate the intelligence of the audience."

Jim Paratore echoes those sentiments. "I knew if we
could get her on the air, viewers would see what her humor
is all about. This is a great American comeback story. And it
is someone who has a huge heart and is a terrific person and
really deserves it. It shows she's succeeding because she's a
talent. Viewers know she's gay, but that doesn't matter. She's
good. Now it's a sweet victory for us all."

Knowing what she had to endure before getting back to
this place made the success of the show more personal. "I've
actually had the fortune and misfortune of falling and getting back up, and being knocked down and getting back up
again," she told *Broadcasting & Cable*. "So I probably have
a take on this career that somebody else in the same career
doesn't have.

"Right now I'm in such a good place, and I'm so grateful
for every step of the way because it makes me appreciate
this time even more. I feel like the success is even sweeter.
I'm so grateful I have another chance. I can relax, and not
have any secrets."

Prior to the start of the second season, the *Palm Beach
Post* reported DeGeneres was asked if she was worried about
a sophomore jinx. "Is there such a thing? There's also probably a first-year jinx from the track record of most talk shows.

I'm actually not worried about anything or any kind of jinx. We were doing something right, and people are responding, and it keeps growing. I think people are responding because the show is very honest, and it's very real."

DeGeneres is quick to point out that despite the show's success, she will never take it for granted. "Not at all. I would never be that cocky. To say, *I showed you* is just a dangerous place, because I don't know how long this will last. I worked really hard to get to the place of success I reached on my sitcom. Then I lost it all. I had to work really hard to get it back. I know what it feels like to achieve something and I know how quickly it can go away. If anything, I feel really grateful but I'm just excited more than anything."

With good reason—early results for the second season reported a 37 percent increase in viewers. Of all the talk shows, only Ellen and Oprah Winfrey increased their viewership. When asked if she has any secrets to success she could share with other potential hosts, Ellen quipped, "Stay out. Leave me alone, all of you," then added, "The reason a show works is because of the individual. I don't think there's a formula. The talk-show format is what it is. I don't think I'm doing anything on paper that's different from anybody else. I don't think anyone can give anyone advice. Just be yourself."

DeGeneres also points out that you have to love it because it is hard work. "Just when you want to just stop, there's another show to do. I have compared it to what it's like to be a new mother. It has to be the most exhausting thing when the baby cries. This show is a crying baby that I don't mind holding and rocking."

It seems that professionally, Ellen is coming full circle. Thanks to the success of her talk show, movie studios are coming to call on her again. In the summer of 2004 it was announced Ellen would star in a remake of the 1977 comedy, *Oh, God!*, playing the title character. DeGeneres gave *Time* her vision of God's house. "There's a coffee table with two magazines—*Teen People* and *Guns & Ammo*. And there are pictures of Jesus everywhere: a picture of Jesus on a pony; a picture of Jesus with a T-shirt that says, MY PARENTS CREATED THE UNIVERSE, AND ALL I GOT WAS THIS LOUSY T-SHIRT."

The movie happened after Ellen pitched the idea to Jerry Weintraub, who produced the original film that starred George Burns. "I wasn't really looking to do another movie, but my manager thought it would be a good idea to have a lot of things going on. We wanted the right role. I didn't want to play somebody's best friend," explained DeGeneres, who will co-write the screenplay. "We were trying to figure out what we could create, and the idea of God kind of evolved. I liked the original a lot. I'll have my own take on it. I know the things I want to say."

Just as she learned lessons from watching the documentary on the wildebeests, Ellen told writer Terry Morrow she has also gleaned wisdom from her goldfish. "I was moving to this new house with this huge pond," she says. "I was excited about bringing them to this fantastic pond. I was trying to take them from this small place to this big, beautiful place. I was trying to catch the fish, and they wouldn't let me. I thought, 'You have no idea where I am taking you. Just get in the bucket. I am taking you to paradise, and you are resisting me . . . I think sometimes that's who we are. We have no idea we are being led to some better place. We keep resisting because we are scared."

Looking back, DeGeneres says she can now see that everything that she experienced was in fact leading her to this new beautiful place. "I am more appreciative now. I am grateful for what I have, because I know how easily it can go away; that's the nature of this business. I know how lucky I am. I know I am so truly blessed," because, Ellen claims, had the show failed, "I would have been finished. It would have been tough to recover, professionally."

While the perfect ending to this story would have Ellen riding off triumphant in both art and love, life is never that clean. In December 2004, it was announced that DeGeneres and Hedison had broken up. The *New York Post* reported that the reason for the split was that Ellen had become romantically involved with *Ally McBeal* and *Arrested Development* actress Portia de Rossi. The paper claimed de Rossi had similarly left her longtime partner Francesca Gregorini, who is Ringo Starr's stepdaughter. According to Page Six, DeGeneres and de Rossi hooked up at VH1's *Big in '04* awards gala in L.A. on December 1, where "events took their natural course. Their respective girlfriends were absent, and this time there was no stopping the lusty ladies. They managed to find a private spot and *things got so hot and heavy between them that they raced to a limo and fooled around for hours*, our source reports."

While her fans can only hope she eventually finds lasting personal happiness, perhaps it is simply Ellen's destiny that she must take the long road before finding her way. As she told newsman Stone Phillips, "Nothing has been easy. Not one step of the way has been easy. I'm really proud that I'm strong, because I didn't think I was strong. There's a moment in *Finding Nemo* when Dory starts crying and says, *I feel like I'm home*. That's what I feel like. I feel like I am finally home with everything."

Episode Guide

SEASON ONE

1. Pilot
(March 29, 1994)

PLOT In the series premiere, Ellen keeps taking awful driver's
license photos; Ellen and her friends are worried the man
Holly is dating is a weirdo, because he likes to bark while
making love.

SEASON REGULARS Ellen DeGeneres (Ellen Morgan); Holly
Fulger (Holly); Maggie Wheeler (Anita); Arye Gross
(Adam)

GUEST CAST William Bumiller (Roger); Matt Landers (Photographer); Giovanni Ribisi (Cashier); Duke Moosekian
(Man in Line); Lois Morgan Viscoli (Depressed Woman)

2. "The Anchor"
(March 30, 1994)

PLOT Ellen feels bad after giving the brush-off to an annoying friend.

OF SPECIAL NOTE The character of Audrey is introduced.

RECURRING CAST Gregg Germann (Rick); Clea Lewis (Audrey)
GUEST CAST Lane Davies (Nate)

3. "A Kiss Is Still a Kiss"
   (April 6, 1994)

PLOT Ellen doesn't like the way a new boyfriend kisses.

RECURRING CAST David Higgins (Joe); Daniel Edward Mora
   (Delivery Man)
GUEST CAST Tony Carreiro (Jackson); Ann Talman (Beth);
   Tracy Tweed (Tara); Todd Waring (William); Jeff Weather-
   ford (Teddy)

4. "The Class Reunion"
   (April 13, 1994)

PLOT Adam poses as Ellen's husband and Ellen pretends to
   be a doctor at her high school reunion.

GUEST CAST Michael Chieffo (Bank VP); Steven Flynn (Joe);
   Greg Germann (Rick); Don Lake (Bob); John Mueller
   (Brad); Jerry Sroka (Engineer); Patty Toy (Engineer's
   Wife); Brenda Varda (Lawyer)

5. "The Promotion"
   (April 20, 1994)

PLOT Ellen is overheard making disparaging remarks about
   Susan.

RECURRING CAST Alice Hirson (Lois Morgan); Cristine Rose
   (Susan)
GUEST CAST Sully Diaz (Maria); Patrick Mickler (Officer);
   Rosie Taravella (Clerk); Gene Weygandt (Gallery Owner)

6.   "The Hand That Robs the Cradle"
      (April 27, 1994)

PLOT When she starts dating a younger man, Ellen tries to re-
   capture her youth.

RECURRING CAST David Higgins (Joe); Daniel Edward Mora
   (Delivery Guy)
GUEST CAST Wendle Josepher (Saleswoman); Peter Krause
   (Tim); Brian Leckner (Karl the Doorman)

7.   "The Go-between"
      (May 4, 1994)

PLOT Ellen sets up Susan and Adam for romance.

RECURRING CAST David Higgins (Joe); Cristine Rose (Susan)
GUEST CAST Jordan Bond (Student No. 1); Sweeney McVeigh
   (Waiter); Ryan Olson (Student No. 2); Scott Sites (De-
   livery Man)

8.   "The Houseguest"
      (May 24, 1994)

PLOT Ellen's cousin who is visiting from out of town is having a terrible vacation and blames Ellen.

RECURRING CAST Steven Gilborn (Harold); David Higgins
   (Joe)
GUEST CAST Dennis Burkley (Nestor); Christopher Darga
   (Officer); Dave Driver (Customer); Joanna Daniels (Tracy);
   Jan Eddy (Big Ed); Charles Mavich (Roy); Molly Shan-
   non (Woman); Jill Taley (Infomercial Woman); Michael
   Shamus Wiles (Bartender); Harland Williams (Ticket
   Taker); Jim Cody Williams (Biker No. 1)

9. "The Refrigerator"
   (August 9, 1994)

PLOT Adam and Ellen buy a refrigerator, which she has to
   keep moving from place to place after he fakes a back injury.

GUEST CAST Kurt Fuller (Dr. Collins); Steve Kehela (Jeff);
   John Riggi (Manager); Lisa Stahl (Delila); Don Stark
   (Repairman); Barry Wiggins (Herbert)

10. "The Soft Touch"
   (August 23, 1994)

PLOT Ellen thinks she cost a car salesman his job, so she
   hires him.

RECURRING CAST Steve Gilborn (Harold); David Higgins
   (Joe); Alison Hirson (Lois Morgan)
GUEST CAST John Bowman (Glenn); Steve Marcus (Agitated
   Man); Dorian Spencer (Young Man); Richard Hicks
   (Coffee Drinker); David Brisbin (Manager)

11. "The Boyfriend Stealer"
   (August 30, 1994)

PLOT Ellen is worried that Holly's boyfriend Steve is coming
   on to her. Ellen and Coffee Joe Farrell butt heads.
OF SPECIAL NOTE This was the last of the *These Friends of
   Mine* episodes to air; although thirteen were filmed, two
   were permanently scrapped.
   The character of Joe is introduced.
   The poem Ellen reads, "A Poem," would later appear in
   her book, *My Point . . . and I Do Have One.*

RECURRING CAST David Higgins (Joe); Cristine Rose (Susan)
GUEST CAST Tommy Hinkley (Steve); Jimmy Danelli (Cus-

tomer); John Mulrooney (Fight Fan No. 1); Don Yesso (Fight Fan No. 2); Amy Weinstein (Woman No. 1); Jo Brewer (Woman No. 2); Steve Albert (Fight Announcer)

SEASON TWO

12. "The Dentist"
(September 21, 1994)

PLOT Ellen cracks a tooth opening a bottle of beer and goes to see a dentist recommended by Paige. Things get silly when Ellen starts breathing in laughing gas.

SEASON REGULARS Ellen DeGeneres (Ellen Morgan); Joely Fisher (Paige Clark); Arye Gross (Adam); David Higgins (Joe Farrell)

GUEST CAST Andrea Parker (Joanna); Harley Venton (Dave); Blaire Baron (Waitress); Christine Romeo (Woman); Martha Thompson (Sarah); Brian McGovern (Romantic Guy); Alicia Anne (Pretty Girl); Robert Gant (Dr. Garber)

13. "Saint Ellen"
(September 28, 1994)

PLOT Ellen wants to become a volunteer but finds it's not really her calling.

GUEST CAST Jane Carr (Glynnis); Patrick Bristow (Peter); Murray Rubinstein (Volunteer); Kathleen McMartin (Volunteer); Leonard Kelly-Young (Volunteer); Kymberly Newberry (Volunteer); Lisa Inodye (Volunteer); Steven Houska (Volunteer); Darla Haun (Volunteer); John McCafferty (Volunteer)

14. "The Thirty-Minute Man"
(October 5, 1994)

PLOT Ellen agrees to go out on a date with one of her bookstore customers only to learn he's a pizza deliveryman—and very content with his job.

GUEST CAST William Ragsdale (Dan); Jerry Penacoli (Richard)

15. "The Note"
(October 12, 1994)

PLOT It looks as if Ellen has an enemy in her reading group, so Paige agrees to infiltrate the group to find out the truth.

GUEST CAST Kenneth Kimmins (Phil); Andrea Leithe (Marion); Helen Siff (Sharon)

16. "The Fix-Up"
(October 19, 1994)

PLOT Ellen is attracted to a guy she thought was weird as a child; now he thinks she's the odd duck. Adam wins a photograph contest for women and asks Paige to pretend she is the one who sent in the pictures.

GUEST CAST Jim Jackman; Stephen James Carver; Garret Davis

17. "So Funny"
(October 26, 1994)

PLOT Ellen, used to being the funniest in the group, feels threatened by Adam's friend, who everyone thinks is very funny.

GUEST CAST Kathy Najimy (Lorna); Larry Poindexter (Don); Mary Otis (Flight Attendant); Milt Tarver (Passenger)

18. "The Toast"
(November 9, 1994

PLOT Ellen's brother is getting married, and she's not only a bridesmaid but the rehearsal-dinner organizer. However, the wedding is put in jeopardy when Ellen reveals that her brother had been engaged once before.

RECURRING CAST Alison Hirson (Lois Morgan); Steven Gilborn (Harold)

GUEST CAST Rebecca Staab (Cindy); Scott LaRose (Jack); Mark L. Taylor (Charles); Ryan Holihan (Billy); Nicki Vannice (Debbie); Jill Baker (Mrs. Thompson); J. Patrick McCormack (Reverend Engler)

19. "Adam's Birthday"
(November 16, 1994)

PLOT Ellen has to adjust to the idea of living alone after Adam announces he's moving out because he thinks living with Ellen is holding him back.

GUEST CAST Bill Calvert (Patrick); Karen Maruyama (Kate); Brian Cousins (Billy); Patience Cleveland (Maisie); Patrick Cranshaw (Mr. Curran); Chris Douridas (Chad); Billye Ree Wallace (Polly)

20. "The Trainer"
(November 23, 1994)

PLOT Ellen acts as an exercise trainer for Paige's difficult boss. When the boss starts asking Ellen for her opinions of what books would make good movies, Paige gets upset, believing Ellen's budding relationship with her boss is jeopardizing her own career.

GUEST CAST Harry Shearer (Joely's Boss)

21. "Mrs. Koger"
(November 30, 1994)

PLOT Ellen fears her outburst caused an elderly neighbor's death, so she attends the memorial service in hopes of giving Mrs. Koger a fitting farewell.

GUEST CAST Nick Bakay (Lloyd); Crystal Carson (Gwen); Damian London (Funeral Director); Matt McKenzie (Officer); Marianne Muellerleile (Edna); Nita Talbot (Mrs. Koger)

22. "Ellen's New Friend"
(December 7, 1994)

PLOT Ellen wants to pursue a friendship with a woman introduced to her by Audrey, but doesn't know how to do it without hurting Audrey's feelings.

RECURRING CAST Clea Lewis (Audrey Penney)
GUEST CAST Angela Dohrmann (Jessica)

23. "The Christmas Show"
(December 14, 1994)

PLOT Feeling it would go against the holiday spirit, Ellen can never find the right time to break up with her unwanted and very clingy boyfriend. As she does every year, Paige's mother gets drunk and spends Christmas day locked in the closet feeling sorry for herself.

OF SPECIAL NOTE Connie Stevens, Joely Fisher's real-life mom, supplied the voice for Paige's mother.

RECURRING CAST Kate Hodge (Stephanie)

GUEST CAST Jeffrey Alan Chandler (Cookie Man); Molly David (Sweet Old Woman); Zachary Eginton (Bud); Jonathan Emerson (Lucky Customer); David Alan Graf (Applicant No. 4); Laurel Green (Lorraine); Lisa Harrison (Bambi); Christian J. Meoli (Matt); Patricia Lentz (Joanne); Eric Lutes (Greg); Mark McCracken (Richard); Annie O'Donnell (Applicant No. 2); Terry Ray (Applicant No. 1); Eric Saiet (Applicant No. 5); David Sederholm (Patrick); Joyce Sylvester (Cookbook Woman)

24. "Ellen's Improvement"
(January 4, 1995)

PLOT Ellen urges Paige and Adam to expand their cultural horizons. Ellen's own self-improvement impresses an attractive college professor. But the tables are turned when Ellen introduces him to the joys of television. Joe and Stephanie move in together.

RECURRING CAST Kate Hodge (Stephanie)

GUEST CAST Kim Kim (Korean Woman); Peter Kim (Korean Man); Gregory Paul Martin (Roger); Mary-Kate Olsen (Herself); Bob Saget (Himself); Alex Trebek (Himself)

25. "The Apartment Hunt"
(January 11, 1995)

PLOT Ellen helps the annoying Audrey find an apartment—far away from Ellen's home. But after a minor earthquake destroys the building, Ellen feels obliged to let Audrey move in.

RECURRING CAST Kate Hodge (Stephanie); Clea Lewis (Audrey Penney)

GUEST CAST Ralph P. Martin (Tony); Marcia Mitzman Gaven

(Debby); Ken Olandt (Juror No. 16); Joseph Slotnick (Mr. Selman)

26. "The Spa"
(January 25, 1995)

PLOT Paige persuades Ellen to relax at a health spa, but Ellen finds the entire experience incredibly stressful. Starving after being fed minuscule portions of food, Paige and Ellen plan a breakout for a fast-food run.

OF SPECIAL NOTE Patrick Warburton would later become better known as *Seinfeld*'s Puddy.

RECURRING CAST Patrick Warburton (Jack)

GUEST CAST Joel Beeson (Brent); Molly Cheek (Sylvia); Kimberly Russell (Tonya); Felicity Waterman (Lauren)

27. "Ballet Class"
(February 8, 1995)

PLOT Ellen tries to fulfill a childhood dream by taking ballet lessons.

RECURRING CAST Steven Gilborn (Harold Morgan); Alice Hirson (Lois Morgan)

GUEST CAST Patrick Bristow (Peter); Scott Fowler (Sam); Elaine Hendrix (Maya); Spencer Rochfort (Jerry)

28. "Guns N' Ellen"
(February 15, 1995)

PLOT Ellen is obsessed with safety after being robbed.

RECURRING CAST Clea Lewis (Audrey Penney); Steven Gilborn (Harold Morgan)

GUEST CAST David DeLuise (Hat-Robber); Eric Allan Kramer (Detective Ryan); Jamie Marsh (Jacket-Robber)

29. "The Sleep Clinic"
(February 22, 1995)

PLOT Ellen and Audrey have erotic dreams about Adam.

RECURRING CAST Alice Hirson (Lois Morgan); Clea Lewis (Audrey Penney); Paxton Whitehead (Dr. Whitcomb)

30. "Gladiators"
(March 1, 1995)

PLOT Ellen is a contestant on *American Gladiators*.

RECURRING CAST Clea Lewis (Audrey Penney)
GUEST CAST Mike Adamle (Himself); W. Earl Brown (Brian); Daniel B. Clark (Nitro); Lori Fetrick (Ice)

31. "5,000 Dollars"
(March 22, 1995)

PLOT Ellen donates her tax refund to charity, then the government wants it back.

GUEST CAST Patrick Bristow (Peter); Dann Florek (Mr. Woodruff)

32. "Three Strikes"
(March 29, 1995)

PLOT Jailed, animal rights activist Ellen winds up in the custody of her parents.

RECURRING CAST Steven Gilborn (Harold Morgan); Alice Hirson (Lois Morgan)
GUEST CAST Kate Benton (Psychotic Woman); Christine Elise (Rosie); Roger Eschbacher (Officer); Clyde Kusatsu (Judge); Chris Young (Ricky)

33. "The Therapy Episode"
   (May 3, 1995)

PLOT Ellen's therapist urges her to be honest with her family.

RECURRING CAST Steven Gilborn (Harold Morgan); Alice Hirson (Lois Morgan); Paxton Whitehead (Dr. Whitcomb)

GUEST CAST Marceline Hugot (Nurse); Michael White (Instructor)

34. "The Thirty-Kilo Man, Part 1"
   (May 10, 1995)

PLOT Dan, Ellen's pizza-delivery boyfriend, is back from Rome, and the two rekindle their previously aborted romance.

RECURRING CAST Steven Gilborn (Harold Morgan); Alice Hirson (Lois Morgan); Clea Lewis (Audrey Penney); William Ragsdale (Dan); Patrick Warburton (Jack)

GUEST CAST Dean Fortunato (Man)

35. "The Thirty-Kilo Man, Part 2"
   (May 17, 1995)

PLOT Ellen suspects that Dan's new business is an illegal operation.

RECURRING CAST Steven Gilborn (Harold Morgan); Alice Hirson (Lois Morgan); Clea Lewis (Audrey Penney); William Ragsdale (Dan); Patrick Warburton (Jack)

GUEST CAST Scotch Ellis Loring (Waiter)

SEASON THREE

36. "Shake, Rattle, and Rubble"
(September 13, 1995)

PLOT An earthquake hits L.A., and the bookstore is severely damaged. Ellen's cousin Spence comes to town after dropping out of medical school and moves in with her. Spence and Paige develop an immediately antagonistic relationship.

SEASON REGULARS Ellen DeGeneres (Ellen Morgan); Joely Fisher (Paige); David Higgins (Joe); Clea Lewis (Audrey); Jeremy Piven (Spence)
DEPARTING REGULAR Arye Gross (Adam)
GUEST CAST Ruth Manning (Customer); Rick Fitts (Reporter); Maurice Chasse (Neighbor)

37. "These Successful Friends of Mine"
(September 20, 1995)

PLOT Ellen feels as if she's stuck in neutral while both Paige's and Adam's careers seem to be moving in high gear. Needing to figure out what she wants in life, she takes to the road.

GUEST CAST Jim Haynie (Jake); Hal Landon Jr. (Bus Driver); Kevin Light (Contractor); David Wells (Mousey Man); Tommy Bertelsen (Kid); Sherlinda Dix (Lady); Paddi Edwards (Smoking Woman)[fcb]

38. "The Shower Scene"
(September 27, 1995)

PLOT After Ellen accidentally tapes an episode of *thirtysomething* over the video of Heather giving birth, she tries to find a pregnant woman at the hospital willing to be taped, hoping that Heather won't notice the difference. To make up for it, Ellen throws a lavish baby shower for her.

GUEST CAST Connie Britton (Heather); Judy Kain (Nurse); Rachel Davies (Mrs. Lowry); Fiona Hale (Grandmother); Dailyn Matthews (Pregnant Woman); Sandra Kinder (Saleslady); Colleen Wainwright (Woman)

39. "The Bridges of L.A. County"
   (October 4, 1995)

PLOT The bookstore book club has a new member, Karen, who Spence initially thinks is a bimbo but whom he later sleeps with. Ellen gets herself in the middle of it, only to get Karen in hot water when her husband finds out about the one-night stand.

RECURRING CAST Anthony Clark (Will Davies); Christine Taylor (Karen Lewis); Brian George (Ranjit Sudar); Kate Williamson (Mrs. Rodgers); Paul Bates (Kenny Burke)

40. "Hello, I Must Be Going"
   (January 31, 1996)

PLOT Adam accepts a job in England and announces he'll be gone for three years. At his going-away party, Adam drops a bombshell on Ellen, telling her he is in love with her, then finds out his trip is delayed a week. Trying to make him feel better, Ellen says she loves him, too, then is forced to be honest when Adam considers not leaving.

GUEST CAST Jay Johnston (Transition Guy); Jamie Kennedy (Tad); Randy Lowell (Messianic Man); Shaun Toub (Foreign Man); K. T. Vogt (Junker Woman)

41. "Trick or Treat—Who Cares?"
(November 1, 1995)

PLOT It's Halloween, and Spence is in the throes of depression over getting kicked out of medical school. Audrey hires herself to work at Buy the Book, and Ellen can't get rid of her. Spence decides to go to law school. Paige has only twenty-four hours to read a huge pile of scripts.

OPENING Ellen tries to hypnotize the audience while holding a sign with the show's logo on it.

RECURRING CAST Anthony Clark (Will); Kate Williamson (Mrs. Rodgers)

GUEST CAST Rachel Duncan (Little Girl); Ramon Choyce (Little Lawyer); Jimmy Galeotta (Little Doctor)

42. "She Ain't Friendly, She's My Mother"
(November 8, 1995)

PLOT Ellen's mother wants to be friends and hang out with Ellen. Against her better judgment, Ellen agrees to play along. They play pool, and Ellen agrees to be a fourth for bridge. When the girl talk moves to sex, Lois finally realizes they should stay mother and daughter. Paige and Spence fight over Ellen's computer.

OPENING Ellen rolls by on inline skates, holding the Ellen logo, then crashes off screen.

RECURRING CAST Alice Hirson (Lois Morgan); Steven Gilborn (Harold Gilborn)

GUEST CAST Doris Belack (Cora); Beverly Garland (Eva); Bruce Thom (Mike); Mara Holguin (Katie)

43. "Salad Days"
   (November 15, 1995)

PLOT Ellen has a book signing for Martha Stewart and is inspired to throw her own dinner party. Spence brings an actress, who is still in alien costume from her job on *Babylon 5,* and Joe brings a surprise guest—Martha Stewart. After the oven breaks, Ellen's dinner party turns into her worst social nightmare.

RECURRING CAST Patrick Bristow (Peter); Jack Plotnick (Barrett); Stephanie Erb (Denise)
GUEST CAST Martha Stewart (Herself); Pat Millicano (Randy)

44. "The Movie Show"
   (November 22, 1995)

PLOT Ellen is upset that Paige is always so busy, so Paige arranges for a scene in Meg Ryan's next movie to be shot at Ellen's bookstore. Meg isn't in the scene, but Carrie Fisher is—and Ellen manages to ruin the scene. Spence tries to put together some assembly-required furniture for Ellen.

RECURRING CAST Jack Plotnick (Barrett)
GUEST CAST Carrie Fisher (Herself); Michael Des Barres (Nigel); Michael Matnard (Colin); Michael Georgio (Dolly Grip); Matthew Sullivan (Salesman)

45. "What's Up, Ex-Doc?"
   (November 29, 1995)

PLOT A movie theater opens next to the bookstore, and the movies can be heard through the walls. Spence finally tells his father he got kicked out of his residency. When Ellen tries to smooth things between them, she and Spence's father end up arguing over Spence's future.

RECURRING CAST Paul Bates (Kenny)
GUEST CAST Brian Doyle-Murray (Burt Kovak); Robert
  Lance (Man)

46. "Ellen's Choice"
   (December 6, 1995)

PLOT The book club is invited on a TV show, *Book Chat*.
  Because the show can't accomodate them all, the members try to get on Ellen's good side in the hope she'll select them. Audrey tries to help Joe serve coffee after he
  hurts his wrist.

RECURRING CAST Christine Taylor (Karen); Anthony Clark
  (Will Davies); Brian George (Ranjit)
GUEST CAST Lise Simms (Lesly); Kate Williamson (Mrs.
  Rodgers)

47. "Do You Fear What I Fear?"
   (December 20, 1995)

PLOT Ellen's parents go on a Christmas cruise, so they celebrate the holiday with her in the car on the way to the airport. Their present to Ellen, a burial plot, makes her
  melancholy. The gang ends up celebrating Christmas together at the cemetery.

RECURRING CAST Alice Hirson (Lois Morgan); Steven Gilborn (Harold)
GUEST CAST Jamie Kennedy (Tad)

48. "Horshack's Law"
   (January 3, 1996)

PLOT Paige is invited to an exclusive party for John Travolta.
  She invites Ellen, who in turn invites the others. After
  Spence's trousers are ruined, the limousine breaks down,

and Paige insults the driver, they get locked out of the car and miss the party. Audrey finds her dream man as predicted in her horoscope, Ron Palillo, TV's Horshack.

GUEST CAST Elya Baskin (Sergei); Bob McClurg (Transient); Ron Palillo (Himself)

49. "Morgan P.I."
   (January 10, 1996)

PLOT After the bookstore is robbed, Ellen agrees to help the police capture the perpetrator in a sting operation on a security firm they believe is a front for a theft ring. Paige and the policeman assigned to the sting fall for each other.
OPENING Ellen is carried by the Flying Karamazov Brothers.

GUEST CAST Ron Canada (Detective Sutterman); Dan Gauthier (Detective Matt Liston); Eric Menyuk (Jim Hogan)

50. "Oh, Sweet Rapture"
   (January 24, 1996)

PLOT Audrey's car, Rosebud, breaks down, so she starts carpooling with Ellen to work. After Audrey buys a new Rapture, she joins a club of devoted, fanatical new-car owners, which convinces Ellen Audrey needs to be "deprogrammed." Matt introduces Paige to his daughter.
OPENING Ellen swings through on a wire, carrying the logo sign.

GUEST CAST Kathy Griffin (Peggy); Nick Toth (Earl); Wayne Wilderson (Ronnie Williams)

51. "Witness"
   (February 7, 1996)

PLOT Spence asks Ellen to be a witness in a mock trial for a law school course, but her theatrics have him on the verge of failing the class. A game of Mystery Date turns into a marathon.

OPENING Three singers strum and twang the theme song.

RECURRING CAST Anthony Clark (Will Davies); Stephanie Erb (Denise); Bari K. Willerford (Burly Delivery Guy)

GUEST CAST Scott Mosenson (Josh Patterson); Concetta Tomei (Professor Bass)

52. "Ellen: With Child"
(February 14, 1996)

PLOT After they take Matt's daughter Mia to the museum, Ellen agrees to baby-sit Mia so Paige and Matt can go camping. Ellen helps Mia with her science project, then finds herself in the position of having to explain why people have sex if not to have a baby.

RECURRING CAST Dan Gauthier (Matt)

GUEST CAST Don Amendolia (Mr. Koundakian); Ebick Pizzadili (Mia)

53. "Lobster Diary"
(February 21, 1996)

PLOT Ellen decides to save a sixty-five-year-old lobster that is being raffled off; she steals it with Spence's help. She becomes a hero when she tells the press she is going to set it free—then the lobster dies before she can release it into the Atlantic.

OPENING David recites the lyrics to the theme, while Jeremy and Ellen do interpretive dance accompanied by a bongo player.

OF SPECIAL NOTE Tricia Leigh Fisher is Joely Fisher's sister.

GUEST CAST Paul Dooley (Thomas Kelsey); Tricia Leigh Fisher (Joanie); Mary Tyler Moore (Herself); Wesley Thompson (Kevin Brown)

54. "Two-Ring Circus"
(February 28, 1996)

PLOT Ellen helps Matt pick out an engagement ring for Paige. He plans to pop the question using the scoreboard at a hockey game but gets hit in the head by a puck. Paige says yes but is disappointed by the size of the diamond and gets a replacement ring to show off.

OPENING Joe reads the theme song, while Ellen and Spence do performance art in the background accompanied by a bongo.

RECURRING CAST Bari K. Willerford (Burly Delivery Guy); Dan Gauthier (Matt); Patrick Bristow (Peter); Jack Plotnick (Barrett)

GUEST CAST Judith Scarpone (Sydelle); Gregory White (Man)

55. "A Penny Saved . . ."
(March 13, 1996)

PLOT Ellen needs to cut back on expenses and tries to fire Audrey. When Audrey's parents invite her to a surprise birthday party for their daughter, Ellen learns the Pennys are extremely rich. They find out Ellen is in financial straights and give $100,000 to help out—but then start to make changes at the bookstore, including commissioning a TV commercial.

OPENING Ellen plays the theme song with a Dixieland band.

GUEST CAST Barry Corbin (Jack Penney); Carol Kane (Lily Penney); Lawrence Hilton Jacobs (Himself)

56. "Too Hip for the Room"
(March 20, 1996)

PLOT Ellen is disappointed to learn her store did not make the list of the twenty hippest places in L.A., so she de-

cides to offer entertainment. When the band she hires
cancels, she's forced to go with the novelty act Del and
Rochelle. Spence lets two beautiful women think Ellen's
apartment is for rent.

OPENING Ellen gets spiked by professional volleyball player
Gabrielle Reese.

GUEST CAST Charlie Brill (Del Shapiro); Mitzi McCall
(Rochelle Shapiro); Tera Hendrickson (Barb); Cynthia La
Montagne (Lesly); Bodhi Pine Eltman (Surfer Dude);
Paul Crowder (Trendy Man); Elizabeth Keener (Trendy
Woman); Nicky Edenetti (Cabaret Singer); Loretta
Palazzo (Guitar Woman); Abbie Jaye (Piccolo Woman);
Ruth Carlsson (Xylophone Woman); Happy Richard Hall
(Drum Man); Venus Con Carne (The Garage Band)

57. "Two Mammograms and a Wedding"
   (April 3, 1996)

PLOT Paige is too preoccupied with her upcoming wedding
to spend time with Ellen, who ends up going alone for a
mammogram. There she meets Chloe, whom she wants
as her new friend.

GUEST CAST Janeane Garofalo (Chloe); Thea Vidale (Tech-
nician); Mina Kolb (Nurse); Michole White (Alyssa);
Susan Powell (Salon Lady); Nancy Serrano (Art Student)

58. "Go Girlz"
   (May 1, 1996)

PLOT Paige is feeling blue the night of Matt's bachelor party,
so Ellen and Audrey throw her a slumber party. Nobody
shows up except Lorna from work; a psychic reads
Ellen's future. Later, the party moves to Ellen's parents
and a stripper arrives. The psychic's predictions come
true.

RECURRING CAST Kathy Najimy (Lorna); Dan Gauthier (Matt); Alice Hirson (Lois Morgan); Steven Gilborn (Harold Morgan)

GUEST CAST Shae D'lyn (Debbie); Timothy Elwell (Security Guy); Jonathan Stark (Gus)

59. "When the Vow Breaks, Part 1"
(May 8, 1996)

PLOT Ellen is Paige's maid of honor and must handle all the last-minute problems before the wedding. She has to get a ventriloquist convention out of the hall, deal with Paige's mother, who is passed out drunk, and cope with the nonarrival of the wedding cake. But her biggest problem is that she catches Spence and Paige in a passionate embrace.

RECURRING CAST Dan Gauthier (Matt); Patrick Bristow (Peter); Jack Plotnick (Barrett); Ron Palillo (Himself); Ebick Pizzadili (Mia)

GUEST CAST Connie Britton (Heather); Gregory Sierra (General Colon); Jeff Dunham (Starky); Kimmy Robertson (Brandy); Greg Collins (Agent Chamberlain)

60. "When the Vow Breaks, Part 2"
(May 15, 1996)

PLOT Spence and Paige try to deny their attraction but can't keep their hands off each other. Ellen tries to get her to cancel the wedding, but Paige decides to go through with it anyway. Matt calls it off at the altar, saying they don't know each other well enough.

RECURRING CAST Dan Gauthier (Matt); Patrick Bristow (Peter); Jack Plotnick (Barrett); Ron Palillo (Himself); Ebick Pizzadili (Mia)

GUEST CAST Connie Britton (Heather); Kimmy Robertson (Brandy); Perry Anzilotti (Minister)

SEASON FOUR

In the months preceding the beginning of the fourth season, Ellen had started to float the idea both in the press and among the writing staff that her character, Ellen Morgan, should come out of the closet. Although the official go-ahead would be months away, the writers and Ellen started dropping noticeable hints and inside jokes indicating what direction they wanted the character to take. Although some viewers see gay-related themes in nearly every scene of this season, the following episode entries will only list the obvious inside gay jokes.

Also, rather than come up with new opening credits, Ellen uses a comic bit to open her show, which will also be highlighted.

61. "Give Me Equity or Give Me Death"
(September 18, 1996)

PLOT Ellen wants a place to call her own and decides to sell Buy the Book to finance her dream. However, Spence's hardball negotiating tactics nearly lose Ellen a big payoff.

OPENING SEQUENCE Ellen does floor gymnastics, with 1996 Olympic gymnastics commentator John Tesh critiquing her performance.

INSIDE JOKE In the bathroom Ellen starts singing to herself, "I feel pretty, oh so pretty. I feel pretty and witty and . . . hey!!!"

RECURRING CAST Patrick Bristow (Peter); Jack Plotnick (Barrett)

GUEST CAST Curtis Armstrong (Tom); Ray Forchion (Smitty); Larry Hankin (Larry); Nancy Lenehan (Margaret)

62. "A Deer Head for Joe"
(September 25, 1996)

PLOT Ed Billik, Buy the Book's new boss, arrives and decides to fire Joe.

OPENING SEQUENCE Ellen attempts to use the rings.

FORESHADOWING During a dream sequence, we see Ellen's bedroom. Directly over her bed is a photo of gay icon k.d. lang.

RECURRING CAST Bruce Campbell (Ed Billik); Sarah Dampf (Willa)

GUEST CAST Dena Burton (Thirsty Customer); Chris D'Arienzo (Customer); Gregory A. McKinney (Officer)

63. "Splitsville, Man"
(October 2, 1996)

PLOT On the eve of her father's retirement, Ellen is shocked to find out that her parents are splitting up.

OPENING SEQUENCE Ellen dances while the Captain and Tennille sing the theme song.

FORESHADOWING The real estate agent is looking for Ellen, who suddenly appears and says, "Oh, I was just in the closet!" Ellen is sitting in the *O* of the Hollywood sign, upset at learning her parents are separating. She says to them: "This is so out of nowhere. I mean, put yourself in my shoes. What if I said something shocking to you, like my whole life has been a lie and I'm really . . . left-handed?"

RECURRING CAST Bruce Campbell (Ed Billik); Steven Gilborn (Harold Morgan); Alice Hirson (Lois Morgan)

GUEST CAST Pat Crawford Brown (Rose); John David Conti (Tom); Nancy Lenehan (Margaret); John Petlock (Uncle Jim)

64. "The Parent Trap"
   (October 16, 1996)

PLOT Ellen tries to reconcile her parents by recruiting the gang to recreate their Cuban honeymoon. Barrett quits his job with Paige after Spence is rude to him. Paige refuses to get romantic with Spence unless he gets Barrett hired back.

OPENING SEQUENCE Ellen faces off with the Tap Dogs.

FORESHADOWING After Ellen's attempt to reconcile her parents fails, she's left to sit and mope in her Cuban skirt. Joe tries to cheer her up by saying they should all go out to a bar where they'll all fit in. Ellen says, "I don't know; I'm in a skirt."

RECURRING CAST Steven Gilborn (Harold Morgan); Alice Hirson (Lois Morgan); Jack Plotnick (Barrett); Paxton Whitehead (Dr. Whitcomb)

GUEST CAST Todd Anderson (of the Tap Dogs); Eddie Fisher (Himself)

65. "Looking Out for Number One"
   (October 23, 1996)

PLOT Ellen is shocked when she accidentally finds her therapist in a compromising situation in a parking lot.

OPENING SEQUENCE Ellen reaches new heights on her trampoline thanks to the encouragement of Joe.

FORESHADOWING After Ellen upsets her therapist by telling the truth about catching her in the parking lot, Ellen says, "When you tell the truth, you run the risk that someone's not going to like you. But you know, I feel better. I feel . . . free."

GUEST CAST Harriet Sansom Harris (Claire); Richard Roat (Mortgage Broker)

66. "The Bubble Gum Incident"
(October 30, 1996)

PLOT Anne Rice makes a special Halloween appearance at Buy the Book. Ellen and Paige go to their twenty-fifth anniversary at camp, where Paige plots revenge on the girl she thinks put gum in her hair. Ellen never told her she was the one who put the gum in her hair.

OPENING SEQUENCE Chef Wolfgang Puck creates a pizza that Ellen finds too hot to handle.

RECURRING CAST Bruce Campbell (Ed); Patrick Bristow (Peter)

GUEST CAST Carol Barbee (Megan); Brittany Paige Bouck (Head Dolphin); Kaley Cuoco (Little Ellen); Juanita Jennings (Therapist); Cynthia Madvig (Admirer); Fred Ornstein (Camp Director); Ashley Peldon (Little Paige); Anne Rice (Herself); Romy Rosemont (Woman)

67. "Harold and Ellen"
(November 6, 1996)

PLOT Joe agrees to drive Spence to his ex-girlfriend's wedding on his way to look for aliens in New Mexico. Ellen's dad moves—to the second floor of his house. Ellen falls off a ladder and ends up in a neck brace.

OPENING SEQUENCE Ellen goes one on one with Oscar de la Hoya.

FORESHADOWING Ellen is talking to her therapist: "I'm not in a relationship. And it's not really because I'm not interested. It's just lately I've begun to question . . ." Just at that moment, the therapist begins to snore, causing Ellen to stop.

RECURRING CAST Patrick Bristow (Peter); Steven Gilborn (Harold Morgan)

GUEST CAST Harvey Korman (Therapist); Anne De Salvo (Waitress)

68. "Not-So-Great Expectations"
(November 13, 1996)

PLOT Ellen is horrified when her mother joins a dating service and starts dating a man named Vic. In order to find out more about him, Ellen pretends to join the dating service so she can see his videotape. Ellen and the gang wind up following her mother on her date to a country-dancing bar.

OPENING SEQUENCE By Devo.

RECURRING CAST Alice Hirson (Lois Morgan)

GUEST CAST Steven Cragg (Greg); Lori Heuring (Cowgirl); Julie Janney (Receptionist); Debra Mooney (Barbara); Lyle Waggoner (Vic); Trisha Yearwood (Herself)

69. "The Pregnancy Test"
(November 20, 1996)

PLOT Paige is worried she might be pregnant, so Audrey and Ellen take a pregnancy test with her for moral support. Ellen is upset that nobody thinks she'd be a good mother and that her friends seem to be moving on in life and leaving her behind.

OPENING SEQUENCE Ellen meets ZZ Top.

FORESHADOWING ELLEN: *So if my little circle turns blue, it means I'm pregnant. That's amazing.*

AUDREY: *Ellen, if your little circle turns blue, amazing is not the word.*

GUEST CAST Dana Gould (Mike); Marilyn Kagan (Therapist); James Kevin Ward (Emcee)

70. "Kiss My Bum"
(November 27, 1996)

PLOT It's an unforgettable Thanksgiving as Ellen invites a
homeless man to her dinner, Paige meets Spence's mom,
Ellen's Aunt Ferne, for the first time, and Peter misses
Barrett, who's in California for the holidays.

OPENING SEQUENCE Ellen battles two girls for world jump-
rope domination.

FORESHADOWING Aunt Ferne asks, "So Ellen, tell me, are you
seeing anybody?" Just then the doorbell rings. Ellen says,
"Oh, and I was just about to answer you. Too bad."

OF SPECIAL NOTE Starting with this episode, in anticipation of
the coming-out episode, ABC moved *Ellen* to the 9:30
time slot, to get it out of the "family hour."

RECURRING CAST Bruce Campbell (Ed); Patrick Bristow
(Peter); Jack Plotnick (Barrett)

GUEST CAST Danny Breen (Homeless Guy); Jeff Feringa
(Edna); Joe Flaherty (Perry); Kathleen Noone (Ferne)

71. "Bowl Baby Bowl"
(December 4, 1996)

PLOT Ellen and Ed become competitive after she beats him at
bowling and he beats her at pool. They decide to settle the
question of athletic superiority by bowling in a grudge
match. Meanwhile, Paige and Spence's jobs keep getting
in the way of their plans to spend time alone together.

OPENING SEQUENCE Ellen and Jeremy try to break-dance.

FORESHADOWING In the opening sequence we see Ellen talking: "I was with a man and then I was with a woman for a
little while. And then I was with a man again and then
with another man and then woman, woman, man, woman
and then another man. And you know, lately I'm beginning to think it doesn't really matter if it's a man or a
woman, you know? It's the person that counts. But one

thing's for sure, I can't keep going from therapist to therapist like this."

RECURRING CAST Bruce Campbell (Ed Billik); Sarah Dampf (Willa)
GUEST CAST Mary Page Keller (Sarah)

72. "Fleas Navidad"
(December 18, 1996)

PLOT Ellen and Paige plan a Mexican vacation over Christmas, leaving behind a pouting Spence, who's on ER duty. Ellen finds a stray dog and wants to keep it, and when she can't find a dog-sitter, she decides to stay home and give Joe her ticket to Mexico. Ellen gives up the dog when her father mistakenly thinks it's his Christmas present. In the end, Ellen, Spence, and Audrey join Joe and Paige in Mexico and spend Christmas together.
OPENING SEQUENCE Ellen duets with Jennifer Holliday for a rousing bluesy rendition of the theme song.
INSIDE JOKE Over the closing credits, the gang is opening their Christmas gifts. Ellen Morgan gets the Ellen DeGeneres comedy CD, *Taste This*. Looking at her present, Ellen says, "Oh, Ellen DeGeneres. I love her show. Do you think the rumors are true?"

RECURRING CAST Steven Gilborn (Harold Morgan)
GUEST CAST John Del Regno (Walter Denbo); Beth Gargan (Customer No. 2); Patrick Harrigan (Customer No. 1)

73. "Alone Again ... Naturally"
(January 8, 1997)

PLOT Ellen's New Year's resolution is to go out more, even if by herself. But her attempts to have dinner out and to join a pottery class do not turn out as well as she would have hoped. Spence house-sits for Paige while she's in Canada and burns down her kitchen.

OPENING SEQUENCE Canada's Jann Arden sings the theme song while Ellen accompanies her on the drums.

FORESHADOWING After pointing out that Barbie is not representative of real women, Ellen says, holding a Ken doll, "I know it's Ken. The point is that these clothes would look fine on a Sparkle Beach Barbie or anybody for that matter. I actually have these pants."

As part of her New Year's resolution, Ellen says, "I am going to do things that I've always wanted to do but I've never had the courage to do."

OF SPECIAL NOTE This is Bob Saget's second appearance; he previously appeared in the "Ellen's Improvement" episode.

RECURRING CAST Bruce Campbell (Ed Billik); Sarah Dampf (Willa)

GUEST CAST Philippe Bergeron (Maître d'); David Fenner (Waiter); Jonathan Fuller (Instructor); Michael James (Guy); Bob Saget (Himself); Esther Scott (Ruby)

74. "Joe's Kept Secret" (January 15, 1997)

PLOT Joe's new girlfriend helps Ellen get a building permit. Because she's older, Joe's kept her a secret. With Ellen's blessing, he introduces her to the rest of the gang. But once Ellen sees the lavish gifts Madeline has given Joe, Ellen thinks that he's a kept man. When Joe decides to break up with Madeline, it's Ellen's turn to become the kept woman.

OPENING SEQUENCE Ellen duets with Aaron Neville on the theme song.

FORESHADOWING Ellen says, "Finally, the world will see me for what I am . . . a homeowner."

After Joe admits to Ellen he's been seeing an older woman, she says, "And I only hope that someday if I have a slightly odd relationship, you, too, will not judge me."

GUEST CAST Rick Hall (Contractor); Florence Henderson (Madeline); Nancy Lenehan (Margaret)

75. "Makin' Whoopie"
(January 22, 1997)

PLOT Ellen donates blood, which causes her to get drunk at a wine-tasting party, where she manages to insult Spence's superior, costing her cousin the promotion he desperately wanted. When Ellen apologizes to the doctor, he makes a pass at Ellen. Joe's Canadian humor causes Audrey's boyfriend to bomb.

OPENING SEQUENCE Me'Shell Ndege'Ocello delivers the theme song with her own brand of funk.

FORESHADOWING After Ellen humiliates herself by getting drunk at a party, Audrey tells her, "Ellen, they can dress you up but they can't take you . . . actually, they can't even dress you up."

GUEST CAST Tim Bagley (Wine Maker); Peter Michael Goetz (Dr. Haddassi); Dana Gould (Mike); Michael Hagiwara (Doctor); Marie-Alise Recasner (Kim); Gary Schwartz (Gary); Bridget Sienna (Nurse); Mindy Sterling (June); Terrence Washington (Dale)

76. "Ellen Unplugged"
(February 5, 1997)

PLOT Ellen and the gang go to Rock and Roll Music Camp, where they get to jam with David Crosby, Bonnie Raitt, and Aaron Neville. Ellen gets stage fright because her singing can't compare with the professionals'.

OPENING SEQUENCE Queen Latifah rocks while Ellen displays her talents on the wheels of steel.

FORESHADOWING In talking to Ellen about the camp, Spence says, "This is Rock and Roll Dream Camp. You can be

anyone you want to be—Melissa Etheridge, right,
k.d. lang, Indigo Girls."

OF SPECIAL NOTE While filming a scene in which Ellen sings
a song she's written, "I'm Scared of Being Afraid," she
added an impromptu line: "So here's what I have to say . . .
and by the way, I'm gay! It's okay! I'm gay, I'm gay." Disney and ABC were not amused and cut the line.

GUEST CAST David Crosby (Himself); Sheryl Crow (Herself);
Andy Kindler (Hesh Finkelman); Derek McGrath (Stan-
ley Peck); Aaron Neville (Himself); Bonnie Raitt (Herself)

77. "Ellen's Deaf Comedy Jam"
   (February 12, 1997)

PLOT Mike breaks up with Audrey. She rebounds with one of
Peter's friends, Brian, who acts in a deaf theater company,
and is starring as Romeo. Ellen misinterprets Brian's sign
language and thinks he's making a pass at her, which
sends Audrey into a tailspin.

OPENING SEQUENCE Ellen walks through a team of jugglers.

FORESHADOWING After Ellen and Audrey make up over the misunderstanding about Brian, Audrey says, "Oh, Ellen, let's
promise to never let a man come between us ever again."
Ellen replies, "Oh, I can honestly say that won't happen."

RECURRING CAST Patrick Bristow (Peter); Dan Gauthier
(Matt)

GUEST CAST Anthony Natale (Brian)

78. "Hello, Dalai"
   (February 19, 1997)

PLOT Peter confronts Ellen at a retreat, letting her know he
can see through her and knows she's not the happy-go-

lucky person she pretends to be. The bookstore is robbed, and Spence, Audrey, Paige, and Joe spend twelve hours getting to know each other while tied up.

OPENING SEQUENCE Ellen accompanies Brian Setzer on the bass as he sings the theme song.

FORESHADOWING Peter tells Ellen, "I don't think you're as happy as you pretend to be. In fact, I think you pretend about a lot of things. And in fact, I don't think you're completely honest with yourself."

OF SPECIAL NOTE Don Yesso, who plays the robber, appeared in the first-season episode "Boyfriend Stealer," the last episode aired under the title *These Friends of Mine.*

RECURRING CAST Patrick Bristow (Peter)

GUEST CAST Judy Nasemetz (Alice); Brandon Maggart (Harry); Iqbal Theba (Dalai Rajhavaari); Don Yesso (Robber)

79. "Secrets and Ellen"
(February 26, 1997)

PLOT Paige treats Spence to a Vegas weekend, but he gets hit on the head and develops amnesia, thinking he's one of Caesar's soldiers. After a lifetime of everyone telling white lies to grandmother Rose, Ellen decides to finally be honest.

OPENING SEQUENCE Ellen tries to keep up with a contortionist.

FORESHADOWING AUDREY: *Ellen, why don't you just tell her the truth?*

ELLEN: *She can't handle the truth! I can't handle the truth.*

RECURRING CAST Steven Gilborn (Harold Morgan); Alice Hirson (Lois Morgan)

GUEST CAST Brett Butler (Grace Kelly); Drew Carey (Himself); Eileen Heckart (Grammy); Wayne Newton (Doctor); Read Scot (Caesar)

80. "Reversal of Misfortune"
(March 4, 1997)

PLOT Ellen's parents are dragging their feet signing the divorce papers. When Ellen tries to get them to finalize the divorce so they can get on with their lives, and out of hers, she inadvertently brings her parents closer together.

OPENING SEQUENCE Ellen, decked out in seventies retro gear, dances frantically while the Captain and Tennille sing the theme song. Same opening as in "Splitsville, Man."

FORESHADOWING AUDREY: Poor Ellen, a child of divorce. You know, studies show that she now has a 50 percent chance of winding up divorced herself.

JOE: Well, at least that's a 50 percent better chance than she had before.

OF SPECIAL NOTE Jean Speegle Howard, who plays Bernadette, is Ron Howard's mom.

RECURRING CAST Steven Gilborn (Harold Morgan); Alice Hirson (Lois Morgan)

GUEST CAST Jean Speegle Howard (Bernadette); Clive Rosengren (Mitch)

81. "The Clip-Show Patient"
(April 8, 1997)

PLOT Ellen volunteers at Spence's hospital and is assigned to take care of an English patient, complete with mask. He tries to tell Ellen about what led him to be in his current state but is constantly interrupted by Ellen's recollections of events in her life, which are clips from earlier episodes.

OPENING SEQUENCE The Boogie Knights give the viewers a disco-funk rendition of the theme song, while the cast dresses in retro seventies clothes.

OF SPECIAL NOTE The patient is played by Michael Des Barres, who played Nigel in the "Movie Show" episode.

GUEST CAST Paulette Braxton (Nurse); Michael Des Barres (Patient); Everett Greenbaum (Older Man)

82. "The Puppy Episode"
(April 30, 1997)

SPECIAL ONE-HOUR EPISODE

PLOT With the help of her therapist, Ellen comes to terms with her own sexuality after meeting a gay woman through an old friend.

OPENING SEQUENCE An opening with Melissa Etheridge was planned but didn't happen. Instead, a static shot of the *Ellen* logo sign on a chair was used.

RECURRING CAST Patrick Bristow (Peter); Jack Plotnick (Barrett)

GUEST CASTS Billy Bob Thornton (Grocer); Demi Moore (Sample Lady); Dwight Yoakam (Bag Boy); Gina Gershon (Cashier); Jenny Shimizu (Woman in the Aisle); Kathy Najimy (Lorna); k.d. lang (Singer/Janine); Laura Dern (Susan); Oprah Winfrey (Therapist); Melissa Etheridge (Herself); Steven Eckholdt (Richard); Jorjan Fox (Attractive Woman); Patrick Harrigan (Waiter)

83. "Hello Muddah, Hello Faddah"
(May 7, 1997)

PLOT Ellen's parents are upset, and her father disappointed, after she tells them she's gay. But at a support group for parents of gay children, they defend Ellen after she is verbally attacked by an outraged parent.

RECURRING CAST Steven Gilborn (Harold Morgan); Alice Hirson (Lois Morgan)

GUEST CAST Chastity Bono (Moderator); Dayton Callie (Father of the Gay Son); James Hong (Waiter); Laraine

Newman (Oversupportive Parent); Catherine Paolone (Mother)

84. "Moving On"
(May 14, 1997)

PLOT In honor of Ellen's coming out, Audrey creates a new Sisterhood corner at Buy the Book. Ed arrives and asks Ellen if she would baby-sit for his daughters; when he sees Audrey's display, he orders her to take it down. Ellen questions Ed about his feelings toward gays and eventually comes out to him.

Meanwhile, Paige is obviously having trouble dealing with Ellen's new lifestyle and is now so uncomfortable she won't change clothes in front of Ellen.

Ed stops by Ellen's new house and tells her he doesn't need a baby-sitter after all because one of the kids is sick. But that night at the movies, she sees Ed and his wife.

The next day she confronts Ed, who tells her he doesn't want her around his children anymore. Ellen quits.

Ellen is at home. Paige stops by to apologize. The gang shows up to show their support, and they celebrate with pizza and champagne.

OPENING SEQUENCE The Bee Gees sing the theme song with Ellen.

RECURRING CAST Bruce Campbell (Ed Billik); Sarah Dampf (Willa); Nancy Lenehan (Margaret)
GUEST CAST Liza D'Agostino (Joanne)

SEASON FIVE

85. "Guys or Dolls"
(September 24, 1997)

PLOT Ellen doesn't understand why she isn't interested in any
of the beautiful women Paige is setting her up with but
still feels attracted to her old boyfriend Dan, the pizza deliveryman—who now owns a successful Italian restaurant.

SEASON REGULARS Ellen DeGeneres (Ellen Morgan); Joely
Fisher (Paige Clark); Jeremy Piven (Spence Kovak); Clea
Lewis (Audrey Penney); David Higgins (Joe Farrell)
RECURRING CAST Patrick Bristow (Peter); William Ragsdale
(Dan)
GUEST CAST Suzanne Lanza (Waitress); Gina Mari (Carly)
***original

86. "Social Climber"
(October 1, 1997)

PLOT Ellen is attracted to her gym instructor, so she goes on
a rock-climbing outing because she thinks the instructor
is attracted to outdoor types. In the end, Ellen learns a lesson in just being herself.

GUEST STAR Dedee Pfeiffer (Lisa)

87. "Roommates"
(October 8, 1997)

PLOT Barrett and Audrey make Ellen think her new neighbors are looking to fix her up romantically with a friend
of theirs who is looking for a roommate. Paige continues
to be uncomfortable with Ellen's new lifestyle and gets
annoyed when she sees Ellen flirting with her potential

new roommate. However, Ellen learns that in this case, *roommate* really means just that.

RECURRING CAST Steven Gilborn (Harold Morgan); Alice Hirson (Lois Morgan); Jack Plotnick (Barrett)
GUEST CAST Jennifer Grant (Erin)

88. "Gay Yellow Pages"
(October 15, 1997)

PLOT At the urging of Peter and Audrey, Ellen agrees to support gay-owned businesses, so she hires a gay plumber. Peter invites his friends to Ellen's party as a way to introduce her to "the community."

RECURRING CAST Patrick Bristow (Peter); Jack Plotnick (Barrett)
GUEST CAST John Capodice (Tony); Shawn Christian (Danny); Michele Laurence (Arianna); Georgia Ragsdale (Woman)

89. "Just Coffee"
(October 29, 1997)

PLOT Ellen meets Laurie and is attracted to her, but is confused when Laurie brings a friend along on what Ellen thought was a date.

RECURRING CAST Lisa Darr (Laurie Manning)
GUEST CAST Deborah Theaker (Maura); Martin Charles Warner (Old Man); Constance Zimmer (Riot Girl)

90. "G.I. Ellen"
(November 5, 1997)

PLOT Ellen's dad is General Grant in an annual reenactment of the Civil War. Ellen wants to participate, to the chagrin of the other men.

RECURRING CAST Steven Gilborn (Harold Morgan); Alice Hirson (Lois Morgan)

GUEST CAST Angie Dickinson (Betsy); Louis Gossett Jr. (Sgt. Timko)

91. "Public Display of Affection"
(November 12, 1997)

PLOT Laurie meets Ellen's parents, and Ellen meets Laurie's daughter, Holly. After apparently hitting it off while going to the movies, Holly starts acting coolly toward her. Ellen thinks it's because Holly doesn't like Ellen being affectionate toward her mom, when actually Holly is upset because Ellen is too shy to be affectionate to Laurie in public.

RECURRING CAST Lisa Darr (Laurie Manning); Steven Gilborn (Harold Morgan); Alice Hirson (Lois Morgan); Kayla Murphy (Holly)

92. "Emma"
(November 19, 1997)

PLOT While at a Hollywood party, Ellen sees Emma Thompson kissing another woman. After Ellen convinces Paige to let her be Emma's assistant, Emma admits she's gay. Ellen convinces Emma to come out publicly to prevent the press from finding out her real secret—she's from Ohio.

GUEST CAST Army Archerd (Himself); Helen FitzGerald (Alice); Seth Jaffe (Messenger); Steve Moore (Waiter No. 2); Sean Penn (Himself); Emma Thompson (Herself)

93. "Like a Virgin"
(November 26, 1997)

PLOT Laurie plans a romantic evening with Ellen and wants her to spend the night. But Ellen gets an anxiety attack at the thought of sleeping with a woman for the first time and bolts. Laurie is deeply hurt, leaving Ellen to make amends.

RECURRING CAST Patrick Bristow (Peter); Lisa Darr (Laurie Manning); Steven Gilborn (Harold Morgan); Alice Hirson (Lois Morgan)

94. "All Ellen, All of the Time"

PLOT Ellen gets a job at a radio station and winds up on the air.

GUEST CAST Anne Heche (Woman at Next Table)
RECURRING CAST Alice Hirson (Lois Morgan); Del Hunter-White (Woman); Kevin McDonald (Chuck); Susan Norfleet (Julie)

95. "The Breakup"

PLOT While having dinner with Laurie on their one-month anniversary, Ellen gives Laurie a charm bracelet with her house key, so Laurie can get into Ellen's house when she's not home. Laurie misunderstands and believes Ellen wants her and her daughter to move in. When Ellen sets her straight, Laurie breaks off the relationship, not wanting her daughter to be hurt again. Instead, it's Ellen who is devastated.

RECURRING CAST Lisa Darr (Laurie Manning); Steven Gilborn (Harold Morgan)

96. "Womyn Fest"
(January 7, 1998)

PLOT Ellen goes on a road trip with Paige and Audrey to see Sarah McLachlan and the Indigo Girls on tour.

RECURRING CAST Lisa Darr (Laurie Manning)
GUEST CAST Amy Ray (Herself—The Indigo Girls); Rachel Rosenthal (Tarot Woman); Emily Saliers (Herself—The Indigo Girls); Rena Sofer (Jean)

97. "The Funeral"
(January 14, 1998)

PLOT Laurie's father dies, and Ellen helps her to reconcile with her family, who rejected her when she came out.

RECURRING CAST Lisa Darr (Laurie Manning); Steven Gilborn (Harold Morgan); Alice Hirson (Lois Morgan)
GUEST CAST Tyler Layton (Leah); Justin Jon Ross (Lie Detector Kid)

98. "Escape From L.A."
(February 4, 1998)

PLOT Ellen and Laurie go on a vacation to San Diego, but things become tense when Laurie wants to do everything on a schedule and carefree Ellen wants to do things in a relaxed manner.

RECURRING CAST Lisa Darr (Laurie Manning); Bobby Edner (Can I Touch Your Boobs Kid)

99. "Ellen in Focus"
(February 11, 1998)

PLOT Paige, now a television executive, comes up with the idea for a cop show in which one partner is tall and the other is short. But if a focus group doesn't like the idea, she could lose her job, so Paige convinces Ellen to become part of the focus group to ensure that her show will be a hit. Ellen does a great job convincing everyone in the group to approve the show, but Paige's boss hates the short cop/tall cop idea and instead wants a tall cop/blond bimbo pair.

GUEST CAST Roger Eschbacher (Derek); Steve Fitchpatrick (Kevin); Raymond Hanis (Wesson); Leslie Jordan (Top Studio Executive); Linda Kash (Sue); Priscilla Lee Taylor (Melanie); Brett Miller (Smith); Marcia Wright (Emily); David Youse (Clipboard Guy)

100. "Neighbors"
(February 18, 1998)

PLOT Ellen tries to make friends with her new neighbors, who keep finding her in extremely compromising situations.

RECURRING CAST Jennifer Balgobin (Mrs. Patel); Marcelo Tubert (Mr. Patel)

101. "It's a Gay, Gay, Gay, Gay World"
(February 25, 1998)

PLOT While shopping at the grocery with Ellen, Spence is hit on the head with bug spray and inhales some of the fumes. In his semiconscious state, he imagines a world where gays and lesbians are in the majority.

RECURRING CAST Patrick Bristow (Peter); Lee Everett (Cindy); Jo Farkas (Mom No. 2); Harvey Fierstein (Himself); Jennifer Palmer (Straight Woman); Charles C. Stevenson Jr. (Dad); Bunny Summers (Mom)

102. "Hospital"
   (March 4, 1998)

PLOT After Laurie is injured in a car accident, Ellen rushes to
   the hospital. While waiting, she strikes up a conversation
   with another woman who is also waiting to visit a friend.
   Their chat becomes heated when Ellen realizes the
   woman is Laurie's ex-lover, Karen.

OF SPECIAL NOTE At this point, *Ellen* went on a six-week hiatus and was replaced by the midseason series *Two Guys,
   A Girl, and a Pizza Place.*

RECURRING CAST Alice Hirson (Lois Morgan)

GUEST CAST Anne Heche (Karen); Tyler Layton (Leah);
   Cynthia Martells (Doctor Newman); Andrew Hill Newman (Male Nurse)

103. "Ellen: A Hollywood Celebration"
   (May 13, 1998)
   Series Finale

PLOT Linda Ellerbee hosts this faux look back at Ellen
   DeGeneres's fifty years as an entertainer, from her early
   years as a vaudeville and radio star to her decades-long
   TV show. On hand is half of Hollywood to pay tribute to
   Ellen and to recount favorite memories and anecdotes.

RECURRING CAST Patrick Bristow (Peter); Steven Gilborn
   (Harold Morgan); Alice Hirson (Lois Morgan)

GUEST CAST Bea Arthur (Herself); Orson Bean (Himself);
   Richard Benjamin (Producer); Glenn Close (Herself);
   Tim Conway (Himself); Cindy Crawford (Herself); Jim
   Doughan (Camera Assistant); Linda Ellerbee (Herself);
   Helen Hunt (Herself); Christine Lahti (Herself); Phil
   Leeds (Old Comic); Julianna Margulies (Herself); Alan

Murray (Announcer No. 1); John O'Hurley (Announcer No. 2); Jada Pinkett (Herself); Cindy Ambuehl (Candy); Steven Anderson (Bookish Man); Jennifer Aniston (Herself); Diahann Carroll (Herself); Ted Danson (Himself); Phil Donahue (Himself); Dan Finnerty (Man); Tricia Leigh Fisher (Megan); Woody Harrelson (Henry); Kathy Najimy (Herself); Gene Allan Poe (Man No. 1); Jazz Raycole (Angela); Mary Steenburgen (Herself); Trent Walker (Man No. 2)

NOTE The following two episodes, previously unaired, were "burnt off" during the summer.

104. "Vows"
(July 15, 1998)

PLOT Ellen's parents decide to renew their wedding vows, which inspires Ellen to propose to Laurie.

RECURRING CAST Lisa Darr (Laurie Manning); Brian Doyle-Murray (Burt); Steven Gilborn (Harold Morgan); Alice Hirson (Lois Morgan); Kathleen Noone (Ferne)
GUEST CAST Jack Kehler (Manager); Jon Simmons (Minister); Andrea Bendewald (Sherry, Ellen's potential roommate); Brittany Ashton Holmes (Girl in Preschool Class); Jay Leno (Himself)

105. "When Ellen Talks, People Listen"
(July 22, 1998)

PLOT Ellen and Paige are astonished that nobody will help them jump start their car. Ellen chastises the people of L.A. on her radio show, inspiring random acts of kindness and good deeds all over the city—which ultimately all backfire. Paige meets someone special.

GUEST CAST Ed Begley Jr. (Himself); Jane Brucker (Mimi Samuel); Krissy Carlson (Girl); James Krag (Peace Corps Guy); Kevin McDonald (Chuck); Susan Norfleet (Julie); Ken S. Polk (Man); Shawn Pyfrom (Scout); Judge Reinhold (Trevor); Amzie Strickland (Old Woman); Diana Theodore (Young Woman)

About the Author

An entertainment journalist for over twenty years, Kathleen Tracy has extensive experience writing celebrity bios and series companions, including *The Girl's Got Bite: A Guide to Buffy the Vampire Slayer* (St. Martin's Press), *Don Imus: America's Cowboy* (Carroll & Graf) and the bestseller, *The Boy Who Would Be King* (Dutton). Her writing has also been featured in magazines including *A&E Biography Magazine, KidScreen* and *TV Times*. Her other books include *Jerry Seinfeld: The Entire Domain* (Carol Publishing) and *Diana Rigg: The Biography* (Benbella Books).